MacBook Air 2025 M4 User Guide

The Comprehensive Manual with Tricks, Tips and Secrets, Simple Instructions and for Beginners & Advanced, Troubleshooting and Setup Explained

Table of Contents

Welcome to Your MacBook Air M4

Hello there, and congratulations on your brand-new MacBook Air with the amazing M4 chip! You've made a fantastic choice. That sleek box holds a world of possibility, blending incredible performance with stunning design and efficiency. Let's dive in together and get you started on this exciting journey.

Unboxing and What's Included

There's nothing quite like the feeling of unboxing a new Apple product, is there? Go ahead, carefully open that box – it's designed to be a satisfying experience! Inside, nestled securely (often in eco-friendly packaging), you'll find everything you need to get going:

1. **Your MacBook Air M4:** The star of the show! Take a moment to admire its thin, light design and the beautiful finish.

2. **USB-C Power Adapter:** This plugs into the wall to charge your Mac. The specific adapter might vary slightly depending on the configuration you chose:
   - The base model (with the 8-core GPU M4 chip) typically comes with a **30W USB-C Power Adapter**.
   - Models with the 10-core GPU M4 chip (including the 15-inch models) usually come with the handy **35W Dual USB-C Port Compact Power Adapter**, letting you charge another device simultaneously! (You might have also had the option to choose a faster 70W adapter during purchase).

3. **USB-C to MagSafe 3 Cable (2m):** This cable connects your power adapter to your MacBook Air. Notice the magnetic MagSafe 3 connector? It snaps easily into place for charging and safely detaches if someone trips over the cord. A fantastic touch is that this braided cable is **color-matched** to your MacBook Air!

4. **Basic Documentation:** Usually includes a quick start guide, warranty information, and those iconic Apple stickers.

M4 Specifics: Colors & Cable

One of the fun parts of getting a new MacBook Air M4 is choosing a color that suits your style. For the M4 generation, Apple offered these gorgeous options:

Color	Description
Sky Blue	A beautiful, brand-new light metallic blue.
Midnight	A deep, dark blue (updated to reduce fingerprints compared to previous versions).
Starlight	A warm, pale gold/silver hybrid.
Silver	The classic, timeless Apple silver finish.

Remember, whichever color you chose, your included USB-C to MagSafe 3 cable will match it perfectly!

Initial Power-Up and Setup Assistant Walkthrough

Ready to bring your MacBook Air M4 to life? It's super simple:

1. **Lift the Lid:** In most cases, simply opening the lid of your new MacBook Air will power it on automatically. If not, press the Touch ID button (the blank key in the top-right corner of the keyboard). You'll likely hear the classic Mac startup chime – welcome!

2. **Hello Screen:** You'll be greeted by a "Hello" screen displaying greetings in various languages.

3. **Meet the Setup Assistant:** Your Mac will now launch the Setup Assistant. Think of this as your friendly guide, walking you step-by-step through the essential initial settings. Don't worry, it's very intuitive! Just follow the on-screen prompts. Here's a rundown of what you'll typically configure:

   - **Language:** Select your preferred language.

   - **Region:** Choose your country or region (this helps set the correct time, date, and formats).

   - **Accessibility:** You'll have the option to configure accessibility features right away if needed (like VoiceOver, Zoom, etc.). You can always set these up later in System Settings.

   - **Connect to Wi-Fi:** Select your home Wi-Fi network and enter the password to get online. This is crucial for the next steps.

- **Data & Privacy:** Apple will show you information about their commitment to privacy.

- **Migration Assistant:** The Assistant will ask if you want to transfer information from another Mac, a Windows PC, or a Time Machine backup. This is incredibly useful if you're upgrading, but if this is your first Mac or you want a fresh start, you can choose "Not Now".

- **Apple ID:** You'll be prompted to sign in with your existing Apple ID or create a new one for free. Your Apple ID is your key to iCloud, the App Store, and many other Apple services. (We'll touch on this more in section 1.3).

- **Terms and Conditions:** Agree to the software license agreements.

- **Create Computer Account:** This is your local user account on the Mac itself. You'll create a username (often pre-filled based on your Apple ID) and a secure password. *Choose a password you'll remember but is hard to guess!* You can also add a password hint.

- **Location Services:** Decide whether to enable Location Services (useful for Maps, Find My, weather, etc.).

- **Analytics:** Choose whether you want to share anonymous diagnostic and usage data with Apple and app developers to help improve products.

- **Screen Time:** Set up Screen Time if you want to monitor and manage your Mac usage (optional).

- **Siri:** Decide if you want to enable "Hey Siri" voice commands.

- **Touch ID:** You'll be guided to set up your fingerprint for unlocking your Mac and making secure purchases. Just follow the prompts to rest your finger on the Touch ID sensor multiple times.

- **Choose Your Look:** Select your preferred macOS appearance: Light, Dark, or Auto (which changes based on the time of day).

And that's it! Once you've completed the Setup Assistant, you'll land on the beautiful macOS Sequoia desktop. Take a deep breath – you're ready to start exploring!

During the Setup Assistant, you were prompted to sign in with or create an Apple ID. Let's talk a bit more about why this is so important. Think of your **Apple ID** as your personal passport to the entire Apple ecosystem. It's the single account you use to access almost all of Apple's services, ensuring a seamless experience across your devices – whether it's your new MacBook Air, an iPhone, or an iPad.

What Exactly is an Apple ID?

It's essentially a username (which is always an email address) and a password that you create. This combination unlocks a whole suite of features and services designed to make your digital life easier, more connected, and more secure. It remembers your preferences, keeps your data synced, allows you to make purchases, and much more. If you've ever bought music from iTunes, downloaded an app from the App Store, or used iCloud, you already have an Apple ID!

Signing In (If You Already Have One)

If you already have an Apple ID, signing in during the setup process is the easiest way to get everything configured right from the start. You simply entered the email address associated with your Apple ID and your password when prompted by the Setup Assistant.

- **Two-Factor Authentication (2FA):** If you have 2FA enabled on your account (which is highly recommended and often required!), you likely received a six-digit verification code on one of your other trusted Apple devices (like your iPhone or iPad) or via SMS to your trusted phone number. You just needed to enter that code on your new MacBook Air to confirm your identity. This extra layer of security ensures that only you can access your account, even if someone else knows your password. It's a crucial step in protecting your personal information.

- **What if I Skipped it During Setup?** No problem at all! If you skipped the Apple ID sign-in during the initial setup, you can easily sign in anytime. Just open **System Settings** (we'll look at how to find this in section 1.4), click on **"Sign In with Your Apple ID"** right at the top of the sidebar, and enter your credentials. Your Mac will then connect to your account and start syncing your settings and data.

Creating a New Apple ID

1. If you're new to the Apple world or just want a separate Apple ID for your Mac, creating one is straightforward and free. You would have selected the option to create a new Apple ID during the Setup Assistant, or you can do it later through System Settings. Here's what's involved:

2. **Provide Basic Information:** You'll need to enter your first and last name, your country or region, and your date of birth.

3. **Enter Your Email Address:** This email address will become your actual Apple ID username. You can typically use your current email address (like a Gmail, Outlook, or other address), or you can get a free @icloud.com email address from Apple during the process. Using an existing address is often simpler.

4. **Create a Strong Password:** This is super important! Your password protects access to a lot of personal information. Apple requires passwords to meet certain criteria (usually length, and a mix of upper/lowercase letters, numbers, and symbols). Choose something unique that you don't use elsewhere and that would be difficult for others to guess. Consider using a password manager to help create and store strong, unique passwords.

5. **Set Up Security Questions or Two-Factor Authentication:** Older Apple IDs used security questions as a backup verification method. However, Apple strongly pushes for **Two-Factor Authentication (2FA)** now, and it's the most secure option. You'll need to provide a trusted phone number (it doesn't have to be an iPhone number) where you can receive verification codes via SMS or automated phone call. This phone number, combined with your password, provides that two-layer security.

6. **Agree to Terms & Conditions:** Review and agree to Apple's terms.

7. **Verify Your Email Address:** Apple will likely send a verification email to the address you provided. You'll need to open that email and click a link or enter a code to confirm that you own the email address.

Once created, make sure you keep your Apple ID password secure and remember your trusted phone number for 2FA.

Why Bother with an Apple ID? Meet iCloud!

Signing in with your Apple ID automatically enables **iCloud**, which is the magic that keeps your digital life synchronized and backed up across your Apple devices. It's not just cloud storage; it's a collection of services working seamlessly in the background. When you sign in, you get **5GB of free iCloud storage** to start.

Here are some of the key things your Apple ID and iCloud enable:

iCloud Service	What It Does	Benefit on Your MacBook Air M4
iCloud Drive	Securely stores your files and folders in the cloud.	Access documents saved in your Desktop & Documents folders (if enabled) or the iCloud Drive folder from any device.
iCloud Photos	Stores your entire photo and video library in the cloud, keeping edits synced everywhere.	View, edit, and organize photos taken on your iPhone directly in the Photos app on your Mac. Saves storage space on device.
iCloud Mail	Provides an @icloud.com email address and syncs your emails across devices.	Access your iCloud email seamlessly within the Mail app.
Contacts	Keeps your contact list updated across all your devices.	Add a contact on your Mac, and it appears on your iPhone instantly (and vice versa).
Calendars	Syncs your appointments and events.	Add an event to your Calendar on your Mac, and get reminders on your iPhone.
Reminders	Keeps your to-do lists synchronized.	Create a reminder on your Mac, and check it off on your iPad later.
Notes	Syncs your notes, including text, sketches, checklists, and web links.	Jot down an idea in Notes on your Mac, and pull it up on your iPhone while you're out.
Safari	Syncs bookmarks, Reading List, open tabs (iCloud Tabs), and browsing history.	Start reading an article on your Mac and easily continue on your iPhone right where you left off.
Keychain	Securely stores your website passwords, passkeys, Wi-Fi passwords, and credit card info. Autofills them.	Log in to websites on your Mac without needing to remember or type complex passwords saved via your iPhone.

Find My	Helps you locate your lost or stolen Apple devices (including your Mac!) and share your location with friends.	Locate your misplaced MacBook Air on a map using your iPhone, or make it play a sound.
App Store	Allows you to download and purchase apps. Syncs purchases across devices.	Buy an app on your iPhone, and it might automatically download to your Mac if available and settings allow.
Books, Music, TV	Syncs your purchases, reading progress, playlists, and viewing history.	Start reading a book or watching a show on your Mac and pick it up on another device.
Backups (iOS/iPadOS)	Backs up your iPhone or iPad data to iCloud (distinct from Mac backups via Time Machine).	While not directly backing up your Mac, it ensures your mobile device data is safe.

iCloud+ Storage Plans

That initial 5GB of free storage is great for getting started, but it can fill up quickly, especially if you use iCloud Photos or iCloud Drive heavily. If you need more space, Apple offers paid **iCloud+** plans. These not only give you more storage (typically ranging from 50GB up to several terabytes) but also include extra privacy features like:

- **iCloud Private Relay:** Helps protect your privacy when browsing the web in Safari by masking your IP address and browsing activity.

- **Hide My Email:** Lets you create unique, random email addresses that forward to your real inbox, keeping your actual email address private when signing up for newsletters or services.

- **Custom Email Domain:** Allows you to use your own domain name (like yourname@yourfamily.com) with iCloud Mail.

- **HomeKit Secure Video:** Provides secure storage for footage from compatible home security cameras.

You can manage your iCloud storage and upgrade to iCloud+ directly within System Settings on your Mac (usually under your Apple ID profile).

In short, your Apple ID is fundamental to getting the most out of your MacBook Air M4. It connects you to powerful services like iCloud, keeps your information synchronized, simplifies purchases, and enhances your security. Take the time to set it up correctly and understand its importance – it truly unlocks the seamless Apple experience.

A Quick Tour of Your New Mac Environment

Alright, you've successfully navigated the Setup Assistant, signed in with your Apple ID, and now you're looking at the macOS Sequoia desktop. It might look a little different if you're coming from Windows or an older version of macOS, but don't worry, it's designed to be intuitive and elegant. Let's take a quick stroll around the main areas you'll interact with most often.

1. The Desktop: Your Digital Workspace

Think of the Desktop as your main work surface, just like a physical desk. It's the background area that fills your screen.

- **Purpose:** You can place files, folders, and application shortcuts directly on the Desktop for quick access. Many people use it for items they're currently working on. Be careful, though – letting it get too cluttered can sometimes make things harder to find! macOS has features like "Stacks" (which we'll cover later) to help keep it tidy automatically.

- **Appearance:** By default, it displays a beautiful wallpaper. macOS Sequoia comes with a stunning collection of dynamic wallpapers that change throughout the day, as well as gorgeous nature scenes, abstract graphics, and solid colors. You can easily change your wallpaper anytime in System Settings (under Wallpaper). Right-clicking (or Control-clicking) anywhere on the empty Desktop also brings up a menu with options like creating a new folder or changing the view settings.

2. The Menu Bar: Commands at the Top

Stretching across the very top of your screen is the Menu Bar. This is a core part of the macOS interface and provides access to commands and information. It changes depending on which application is currently active.

- **Apple Menu (□):** Located at the far left, the Apple logo (□) is always there. Clicking it reveals essential system-wide commands like:
  - **About This Mac:** Shows information about your Mac's hardware, software version, and storage.
  - **System Settings...:** Opens the main preferences application (more on this below).
  - **App Store...:** Opens the store for downloading new apps.
  - **Recent Items:** Quickly access recently opened apps and documents.
  - **Force Quit...:** Allows you to close applications that might be unresponsive.
  - **Sleep, Restart..., Shut Down...:** Power control options.
  - **Lock Screen:** Quickly secure your Mac when stepping away.
  - **Log Out [Your Name]...:** Logs out of your current user account.

- **Application Menus:** Next to the Apple Menu, you'll see menus specific to the application you're currently using. For example, if you have Safari open, you'll see menus like "Safari," "File," "Edit," "View," "History," "Bookmarks," "Window," and "Help." These contain all the commands relevant to that specific app. If you click on the Desktop background, the active application becomes "Finder," and you'll see Finder-specific menus.

- **Status Menus:** On the right side of the Menu Bar, you'll find a collection of icons providing quick status information and access to system features. What appears here can be customized, but common icons include:

Icon (Example)	Represents	Typical Function
Wi-Fi Symbol	Wi-Fi Connection Status	View network name, signal strength, join networks
Battery Symbol	Battery Level & Charging Status	Show percentage, time remaining, energy usage
Spotlight (Magnifying Glass)	System-wide Search	Click to open search bar
Control Center (Switches)	Quick Access to Common Settings	Adjust Wi-Fi, Bluetooth, AirDrop, Display, Sound, etc.
Siri Symbol	Siri Voice Assistant	Click to activate Siri
Clock	Current Time & Date	Click to see date, notifications, widgets
User Icon/Name	Fast User Switching (if enabled)	Switch between user accounts
Bluetooth Symbol	Bluetooth Status	Connect/disconnect devices, view battery levels
Sound Volume	Audio Output Volume	Adjust volume, select output device
Focus Symbol (Moon)	Focus Modes (Do Not Disturb, etc.)	Enable/disable focus modes
Time Machine (Clock Arrow)	Backup Status	See last backup time, start a backup

- You can often click these icons for more options or drag some (like Control Center items) directly onto the Menu Bar for permanent access.

3. The Dock: Your App Launcher and Switcher

At the bottom of your screen (by default, though you can move it to the left or right side via System Settings), you'll find the Dock. This is your primary hub for launching frequently used applications and accessing minimized windows or running apps.

- **Application Section:** The main part of the Dock holds icons for your favorite apps. Some common ones you'll see initially are:
  - **Finder:** The smiley-face icon, your gateway to files and folders.
  - **Launchpad:** Shows all your installed applications in a grid (like an iPhone or iPad home screen).
  - **Safari:** Apple's web browser.
  - **Mail:** The built-in email client.
  - **Contacts, Calendar, Notes, Reminders:** Core productivity apps.
  - **Photos, Music, TV:** Media apps.
  - **App Store:** For finding and installing new software.
  - **System Settings:** The gear icon for configuring your Mac.

- **Running Apps:** Apps that are currently open usually have a small dot underneath their icon in the Dock.

- **Adding/Removing Apps:** Want to keep an app in the Dock permanently? Just drag its icon from the Applications folder (or Launchpad) onto the Dock. Want to remove one? Simply drag its icon off the Dock until you see a "Remove" label appear (this doesn't delete the app, just removes the shortcut). Alternatively, right-click (or Control-click) an app icon in the Dock, go to "Options," and select "Keep in Dock" or deselect it.

- **Folders & Files Section:** Typically on the right side of the Dock (separated by a faint line), you can place folders or even individual files for quick access. By default, you'll usually find a "Downloads" folder here. Drag any folder or file onto this section to add it. Clicking a folder icon often fans out its contents for easy viewing.

- **Trash:** At the very end of the Dock is the Trash icon. Drag files here to mark them for deletion. Remember, items stay in the Trash until you explicitly empty it (right-click the Trash icon and choose "Empty Trash"). You can also eject external drives or servers by dragging their icons to the Trash (the icon cleverly changes to an Eject symbol).

- **Customization:** You can customize the Dock's appearance and behavior extensively in System Settings (under "Desktop & Dock"). Change its size, enable magnification (icons get bigger as you mouse over them), hide it automatically when not in use, and change its position on the screen.

4. Key Applications & Utilities (Brief Intro)

- **Finder (Smiley Face):** As mentioned, this is crucial. Clicking its icon in the Dock opens a Finder window, letting you browse all the files, folders, and drives connected to your Mac. We'll explore Finder in detail in Chapter 3.

- **System Settings (Gear Icon):** This is the command center for customizing nearly every aspect of your Mac – from your display and sound to network settings, user accounts, privacy, and much more. Clicking its icon in the Dock opens the System Settings window. We'll be visiting this frequently throughout the guide.

- **Launchpad (Rocket Icon):** Clicking this displays all your applications in an easy-to-navigate, full-screen grid. You can organize apps into folders here, just like on an iPhone or iPad. It's another way to find and open your apps besides the Dock or Finder.

- **Spotlight (Magnifying Glass in Menu Bar):** Don't forget this powerful tool! Click the magnifying glass or press Command (⌘) + Spacebar to bring up the Spotlight search bar. Start typing anything – an app name, a file name, a contact, a calculation, a definition – and Spotlight will find it instantly.

5. Touch ID Sensor

Remember that blank key in the top-right corner of your keyboard? That's not just a power button; it's your **Touch ID** sensor. You likely set up your fingerprint during the initial setup. You can use it to:

- Unlock your Mac instantly when it's asleep or locked.

- Authorize purchases in the App Store, iTunes Store, Apple Books, and on websites using Apple Pay.

- Approve certain system settings changes or app installations instead of typing your password.

It's fast, secure, and convenient!

This quick tour should give you a basic sense of direction within your new MacBook Air M4's environment. Don't feel pressured to memorize everything right away. The best way to learn is by exploring and using your Mac. In the following chapters, we'll delve much deeper into each of these areas, turning you into a confident Mac user in no time!

Mastering the macOS Sequoia Interface

Now that you've successfully set up your MacBook Air M4, it's time to get comfortable with its beautiful and efficient operating system, macOS Sequoia. Think of the macOS interface as the visual environment where you'll interact with all your apps and files. It's designed to be both powerful and easy to navigate. In this chapter, we'll explore the core components you see right after logging in: the Desktop, the Menu Bar, and the Dock. Understanding these elements is key to feeling right at home on your new Mac.

Navigating the Desktop, Menu Bar, and Dynamic Wallpaper

Let's start with the most prominent parts of your screen – the background you see, and that persistent bar running across the top.

The Desktop: More Than Just a Pretty Background

The large area that fills your screen behind any open windows is the **Desktop**. Just like a physical desk, it serves as your primary workspace.

- **Your Digital Canvas:** You can place files, folders, and shortcuts (called aliases on Mac) directly onto the Desktop for easy access. Many people find it convenient to temporarily store files they are actively working on here. For example, if you download a PDF you need to review, you might save it directly to the Desktop. Double-clicking a file or folder on the Desktop opens it right up.

- **Keeping it Tidy:** While convenient, letting your Desktop become overly cluttered with icons can make it hard to find things and can even slightly impact performance if there are thousands of items. macOS offers a fantastic feature called **Stacks** to help with this. If you right-click (or hold the Control key and click) on an empty area of the Desktop, you can choose "Use Stacks." macOS will instantly organize your Desktop files into neat stacks grouped by kind (like Documents, Images, PDFs, etc.), date, or tags. Clicking a stack expands it temporarily so you can grab what you need. It's a brilliant way to maintain order without having to manually file everything away constantly. We'll explore Stacks more later, but feel free to try it out!

- **Making it Your Own (Wallpaper):** The default macOS Sequoia wallpaper is stunning, but you can personalize your Desktop background to reflect your style.

  - Open **System Settings** (click the gear icon ⚙️ in your Dock or choose Apple menu □ > System Settings...).

  - In the sidebar, click on **Wallpaper**.

  - You'll see a fantastic gallery of options provided by Apple. Browse through categories like Dynamic Desktop, Light & Dark Desktop, Landscapes, Abstract, Colors, and your own Photos library.

  - Simply click on a thumbnail to instantly apply that wallpaper to your Desktop.

Dynamic Wallpaper: A Living Background

Within the Wallpaper settings, pay special attention to the **Dynamic Desktop** category. These aren't just static images; they subtly change their lighting and appearance throughout the day, mirroring the time of day in your location. For instance, a landscape might show bright daylight during the afternoon, shift to warm sunset tones in the evening, and display a starry night after dark.

- **How it Works:** When you select a Dynamic Wallpaper, make sure Location Services are enabled for System Services (you can check this in System Settings > Privacy & Security > Location Services > System Services > Setting Time Zone & System Customization) so your Mac knows your local time and can adjust the wallpaper accordingly.

- **Choosing Your Scene:** Apple provides several beautiful dynamic options, often featuring iconic landscapes or abstract gradients. Just click one to select it. You might see a dropdown menu next to it allowing you to choose between "Dynamic," "Light (Still)," or "Dark (Still)" if you prefer it not to change automatically.

- **Why Use It?** Besides looking incredibly cool, Dynamic Wallpaper can provide a gentle visual cue about the time of day without you needing to constantly check the clock. It adds a touch of elegance and life to your workspace.

The Menu Bar: Your Command Center at the Top

Running horizontally across the very top edge of your screen is the **Menu Bar**. This is a fundamental part of macOS, providing access to application commands, system functions, and status information. Its contents change dynamically based on what you're doing.

1. **Apple Menu (☐):** Always situated at the far-left corner, the iconic Apple logo menu provides access to essential system-wide functions, regardless of which application is active. Let's look closer at its options:

   o **About This Mac:** Clicking this gives you a quick overview of your MacBook Air M4 – its model name, the specific M4 chip inside, the amount of memory (RAM), its serial number, and importantly, the version of macOS Sequoia you're running. You can also access displays, storage, and support information from here.

   o **System Settings...:** Your gateway to customizing almost everything on your Mac. We've already used it for Wallpaper, and we'll be back here often.

   o **App Store...:** Launches the App Store, where you can discover, download, and update applications for your Mac.

   o **Recent Items:** A handy submenu showing the applications, documents, and servers you've accessed recently, allowing you to quickly reopen them.

   o **Force Quit...:** If an application becomes unresponsive (stops reacting to clicks or commands, sometimes showing a spinning beach ball cursor), you can use this command to force it to close. Use it sparingly, as you might lose unsaved changes in the forced-quit app.

- o **Sleep:** Puts your MacBook Air into a low-power mode, turning off the display and pausing most operations, but keeping your work ready to resume instantly when you wake it (by lifting the lid, pressing a key, or touching the Touch ID sensor).

- o **Restart...:** Closes all applications and reboots macOS. Sometimes necessary after software updates or for troubleshooting.

- o **Shut Down...:** Closes all applications and completely powers off your MacBook Air.

- o **Lock Screen:** Immediately requires your password or Touch ID to get back to the desktop, keeping your session secure if you step away.

- o **Log Out [Your Name]...:** Closes all your applications and logs you out of your user account, returning you to the login screen. Useful if someone else needs to use the Mac with their own account.

2. **Application Menus:** Immediately to the right of the Apple menu, you'll find menus that belong to the currently *active* application (the one whose name is displayed bold next to the Apple menu). These menus contain all the specific commands for that program. For example:

- o If **Finder** is active (you clicked on the Desktop or a Finder window), you'll see menus like Finder, File, Edit, View, Go, Window, Help. These let you create new folders, get info on files, copy/paste, change how files are displayed, navigate to specific folders, manage Finder windows, etc.

- o If **Safari** is active, the menus change to Safari, File, Edit, View, History, Bookmarks, Window, Help. Here you'll find commands for opening new tabs/windows, managing bookmarks, clearing history, changing the text size, and accessing Safari-specific features.

- o Common menu titles across many apps include:

  - ▪ **File:** Usually contains commands like New, Open, Close, Save, Print.

  - ▪ **Edit:** Often holds Undo, Redo, Cut, Copy, Paste, Select All, Find, Spelling & Grammar.

  - ▪ **View:** Typically controls how content is displayed – Zoom, Enter/Exit Full Screen, Show/Hide Toolbars or Sidebars.

  - ▪ **Window:** Manages the application's windows – Minimize, Zoom, Tile Window, Bring All to Front, and a list of the app's open windows.

  - ▪ **Help:** Provides access to the application's built-in help documentation or search functionality.

3. Always look to the Menu Bar for the commands available in the app you're currently using!

4. **Status Menus (Right Side):** This collection of icons on the right end of the Menu Bar gives you quick access to system status and controls. The exact icons can vary, but here's a breakdown of common ones and their functions:

Icon (Example Appearance)	Name / Represents	Typical Click Action(s)	Notes
(Wi-Fi Arcs)	Wi-Fi	View current network, signal strength, turn Wi-Fi On/Off, select other networks.	Essential for connectivity.
(Battery Shape)	Battery	Show percentage, charging status, time remaining (optional), apps using significant energy.	Click 'Battery Settings...' for more options.
(Magnifying Glass)	Spotlight	Opens the Spotlight search bar for finding anything on your Mac or the web.	Can also be invoked with Command ($\mathcal{H}$) + Spacebar.
(Two Switches Icon)	Control Center	Opens a panel with quick toggles for Wi-Fi, Bluetooth, AirDrop, Focus, Display Brightness, Sound Volume, Screen Mirroring, etc.	Customizable in System Settings > Control Center.
(Microphone Wave Icon)	Siri	Activates Siri; you can type or speak your request.	Can be enabled/disabled in System Settings > Siri & Spotlight.
(Digital/Analog Clock)	Clock / Date & Time	Shows current time; clicking opens Notification Center with date, widgets, notifications.	Clock format customizable in System Settings > Control Center.
(Person Silhouette/Initial)	User / Fast User Switching	Shows current user; allows switching to other user accounts without logging out.	Enable in System Settings > Control Center > Fast User Switching.

(Stylized 'B')	Bluetooth	Turn Bluetooth On/Off, view connected devices, battery levels, connect new devices.	
(Speaker Icon)	Sound Volume	Adjust output volume slider, select audio output device (speakers, headphones).	
(Moon/Person Icon)	Focus	Turn specific Focus modes (Do Not Disturb, Work, Sleep) On/Off.	Configure modes in System Settings > Focus.
(Clock with Arrow)	Time Machine	Shows backup status (if configured), time of last backup, option to 'Back Up Now'.	Requires an external drive configured for Time Machine.

- **Customizing Status Menus:** You have control over many of these! Go to **System Settings > Control Center**. Here, you'll find modules like Wi-Fi, Bluetooth, AirDrop, Focus, etc. For many items, you can choose whether to always "Show in Menu Bar," "Show When Active," or "Don't Show." You can also drag some icons directly *out* of the Control Center panel (when it's open) onto the Menu Bar for permanent, one-click access, or Command (⌘) + drag icons already in the Menu Bar to rearrange them.

The Menu Bar is your constant companion in macOS. Take some time to click through the different application menus and status icons to see what options are available – it's packed with useful commands and information.

Understanding and Customizing the Dock for Quick Access

Positioned at the bottom of your screen by default, the **Dock** is one of the most iconic and useful parts of the macOS interface. It serves as a convenient launchpad for your favorite applications, a place to see which apps are running, and quick access to frequently used folders, files, and the Trash.

The Purpose of the Dock

Think of the Dock as a dynamic shortcut bar. Its main goals are:

- **Quick Application Launching:** Keep your most-used apps just a click away.

- **Easy Application Switching:** See which apps are running and switch between them easily.

- **Access to Minimized Windows:** When you minimize a window, it often tucks into the Dock so you can bring it back later.

- **Quick Access to Folders/Files:** Store shortcuts to important folders (like Downloads) or specific documents.

- **Trash Access:** The designated spot for deleting files and ejecting drives.

Anatomy of the Dock

The Dock isn't just one long strip; it's typically divided into sections by subtle vertical lines:

1. **Application Section (Left/Main Area):** This is where icons for applications reside. By default, Apple includes icons for core macOS apps. You can customize this section heavily by adding your own frequently used applications and removing ones you don't need quick access to.

2. **Recent Applications Section (Optional, Middle):** Depending on your settings (System Settings > Desktop & Dock > Show recent applications in Dock), a section might appear here showing the last few apps you used that aren't permanently kept in the Dock. This can be handy for quickly reopening something you just closed.

3. **Folders and Files Section (Right Area):** This area is designed to hold shortcuts to folders (like Downloads, Documents) or even individual files you access often. Clicking a folder icon here typically displays its contents in a grid or fan for quick access.

4. **Trash (Far Right):** The Trash bin always sits at the very end of the Dock.

Interacting with the Dock

Using the Dock is straightforward:

1. **Launching Apps:** Simply click an application's icon once to open it.

2. **Switching Apps:** If an app is already running (indicated by a small dot below its icon), clicking its icon brings that application's windows to the front.

3. **Identifying Running Apps:** As mentioned, a small indicator dot appears beneath the icon of any application that is currently open and running.

4. **Right-Clicking (Control-Clicking):** Clicking an icon while holding the Control key, or using a two-finger click on a trackpad, brings up a contextual menu with useful options specific to that item. For app icons, this menu often includes:

   o **Options:** Submenu with choices like "Keep in Dock" (to make the icon permanent), "Open at Login" (to launch the app automatically when you start your Mac), and "Show in Finder" (to reveal the actual application file).

   o **Show Recent / Show All Windows:** If the app is running, you can quickly see its open windows.

   o **Hide / Hide Others:** Hide the application's windows or hide all *other* application windows to reduce clutter.

   o **Quit:** Closes the application completely. (This is the standard way to close apps you're done using, rather than just closing their windows).

5. **Minimized Windows:** When you minimize a window (by clicking the yellow button in the top-left corner), it usually shrinks down and tucks itself into the right side of the Dock (near the Trash). Clicking its thumbnail preview there restores the window.

Making the Dock Your Own: Customization Galore

The default Dock is functional, but the real power comes from tailoring it to your specific workflow. Here's how you can customize it:

- **Adding Items:**

   o **Apps:** Find the application you want to add in your **Applications** folder (use Finder) or via **Launchpad**. Simply click and drag the application's icon onto the *application section* of the Dock and release it where you want it positioned. The other icons will slide over to make space.

   o **Folders/Files:** Drag any folder or file from a Finder window onto the *folders and files section* (to the right of the separator line) of the Dock. This creates a shortcut (alias) in the Dock; the original item stays where it was.

- **Removing Items:** Don't need that app icon cluttering your Dock? Just click and drag its icon *off* the Dock towards the middle of your Desktop. Hold it there for a second until you see a small "Remove" label appear (or sometimes a "poof" cloud animation), then release the mouse button. Poof! It's gone from the Dock. Remember, this only removes the shortcut; the actual application, folder, or file is still safe on your Mac. (You can't remove the Finder or the Trash icons this way).

- **Rearranging Items:** Want your favorite apps grouped together? Click and drag any icon within its section of the Dock to a new position. The other icons will shuffle obligingly.

- **Fine-Tuning with System Settings**

For more advanced visual and behavioral customization, head back to **System Settings > Desktop & Dock**. Scroll down to the "Dock" section, and you'll find a wealth of options:

Setting	Description	Why You Might Change It
Size	A slider to make the Dock icons larger or smaller.	Make icons easier to see, or shrink the Dock to save screen space.
Magnification	A checkbox to enable magnification and a slider to control the zoom level. Icons enlarge as you mouse over.	Adds a fun visual effect and makes it easier to target specific icons if the Dock is small.
Position on screen	Radio buttons for Bottom, Left, or Right.	Move the Dock to the side if you prefer more vertical screen space for wide documents or websites.
Minimize windows using	Choose the animation effect: "Genie effect" (swooshing) or "Scale effect" (shrinking).	Genie is the classic default; Scale is faster and simpler. Purely cosmetic preference.
Double-click a window's title bar to	Choose what happens: Zoom (expand to fit content), Minimize, or Do Nothing.	Provides a quick way to maximize or minimize windows without aiming for the small buttons.
Minimize windows into application icon	Checkbox. If enabled, minimized windows tuck into the app's icon instead of appearing separately near the Trash.	Reduces clutter in the Dock, especially if you minimize many windows from the same app. Click & hold app icon to see windows.

Animate opening applications	Checkbox. Makes app icons bounce in the Dock when launching.	Provides visual feedback that an app is opening. Turn off for slightly faster perceived launch (mostly cosmetic).
Automatically hide and show the Dock	Checkbox. The Dock slides out of view when not in use and reappears when you move your cursor to the edge.	Maximizes usable screen real estate, especially on smaller MacBook Air screens.
Show indicators for open applications	Checkbox. Toggles the small dot beneath running app icons.	Keep enabled (default) to easily see which apps are active.
Show recent applications in Dock	Checkbox. Toggles the separate section for recently used apps.	Useful if you frequently reopen apps you just closed; disable if you prefer a cleaner Dock with only pinned items.

Experiment with these settings! You can instantly see the effect on your Dock as you make changes. Find the combination that feels most comfortable and efficient for you.

The Trash: More Than Just Deletion

Finally, let's revisit the **Trash** icon at the end of the Dock.

- **Deleting Files:** Dragging files or folders onto the Trash icon moves them here. They aren't permanently deleted yet; they're just held in the Trash.

- **Emptying the Trash:** To permanently delete the items and reclaim the disk space, right-click (Control-click) the Trash icon and choose "Empty Trash." You'll often get a confirmation warning because this action is generally irreversible. You can also open the Trash (it acts like a folder) and empty it from the Finder menu.

- **Putting Items Back:** If you accidentally trash something, just click the Trash icon to open it, find the item, and drag it back out to your Desktop or another folder.

- **Ejecting Disks/Servers:** When you connect an external hard drive, USB stick, or connect to a network server, its icon often appears on your Desktop or in the Finder sidebar. To safely disconnect it, *drag its icon* to the Trash icon in the Dock. The Trash icon cleverly changes into an **Eject symbol (⏏◻)**. Release the item on the Eject symbol to properly dismount it before physically unplugging it. This prevents data corruption.

The Dock is a central hub for interacting with your Mac. By understanding its parts and customizing it to your liking, you'll significantly speed up your daily workflow and make your MacBook Air M4 feel truly yours.

Using the Control Center For Essential Settings

Remember those Status Menus we talked about on the right side of the Menu Bar? One of the most powerful icons there is the **Control Center**, represented by an icon that looks like two toggle switches (similar to the Control Center on an iPhone or iPad). Think of it as your instant access panel for many commonly used system settings and controls, saving you the time of digging through System Settings for everyday adjustments.

Accessing Control Center

It couldn't be simpler: just move your cursor up to the Menu Bar and click the **Control Center icon** (the two switches). A panel will drop down, neatly organized with various modules. Click anywhere outside the panel or press the Esc key to dismiss it.

What's Inside? A Tour of the Modules

The exact modules you see might vary slightly based on your Mac model and settings, but here are the usual suspects you'll find in the Control Center on your MacBook Air M4:

- **Connectivity Controls (Top Section):**
    - **Wi-Fi:** Shows the network you're currently connected to. Clicking this module expands it, allowing you to quickly turn Wi-Fi on or off, see a list of nearby networks, and select one to join. You can also jump directly to Wi-Fi settings from here.

    - **Bluetooth:** Lets you toggle Bluetooth on or off with a click. Clicking the arrow (>) or the text expands the module to show currently connected Bluetooth devices (like headphones or mice) and their battery levels (if available), and allows you to quickly connect to previously paired devices or open Bluetooth settings.

    - **AirDrop:** Controls your AirDrop discoverability (Off, Contacts Only, Everyone for 10 Minutes). AirDrop is Apple's super-easy way to wirelessly share files between nearby Apple devices.

- **Focus Modes:**
    - **Focus:** This module lets you quickly enable or disable Focus modes like "Do Not Disturb," "Work," "Sleep," or any custom Focus modes you've created. Clicking the main Focus icon toggles the last used mode, while clicking the arrow (>) lets you choose a specific mode or set a duration (e.g., "On for 1 hour"). Focus modes help you minimize distractions by silencing notifications and signaling your status to others.

- **Hardware Controls:**
  - **Keyboard Brightness:** A slider to adjust the brightness of your MacBook Air's backlit keyboard. Essential for typing in dim lighting! (This might only appear if needed based on ambient light or settings).
  - **Display Brightness:** A slider to control the brightness of your main screen. Drag it left or right to adjust the brightness level instantly. Clicking the icon might offer quick access to Display Settings or features like True Tone (which adjusts color based on ambient light).
  - **Sound Volume:** A slider to adjust the system's audio output volume. Clicking the arrow (>) next to the volume icon lets you quickly select the audio output device (e.g., built-in speakers, connected headphones, AirPlay speakers).
  - **Now Playing:** If music or video is playing (e.g., from the Music app or Safari), this module appears, showing track information and providing basic playback controls (play/pause, skip).

- **Screen Controls:**
  - **Screen Mirroring:** Allows you to wirelessly mirror or extend your Mac's display to a compatible Apple TV or AirPlay-enabled smart TV. Click it to see available devices.
  - **Stage Manager:** If you use Stage Manager (Apple's window management feature), you'll likely see a toggle here to quickly turn it on or off.

Interacting with Modules

Using Control Center is designed to be quick and intuitive:

- **Simple Toggles:** Icons like Wi-Fi, Bluetooth, and Focus often act as simple on/off toggles with a single click on the main icon part.
- **Sliders:** Brightness and Volume use sliders for variable adjustment. Just click and drag the slider knob.
- **Expansion:** Many modules have text labels or an arrow (>) next to the icon. Clicking these areas expands the module to reveal more detailed options or lists (like available Wi-Fi networks or sound output devices).
- **Direct to Settings:** Often, within an expanded module, you'll find a link (like "Wi-Fi Settings..." or "Sound Settings...") that takes you directly to the relevant section within the main System Settings application for more advanced configuration.

Customizing Your Control Center Experience

While the main layout of Control Center itself isn't heavily customizable, you *can* control which items appear *permanently* in your Menu Bar for even faster access, and manage some optional Control Center modules.

1. Go to **System Settings > Control Center**.

2. You'll see several sections:

    o **Control Center Modules:** These are the core items like Wi-Fi, Bluetooth, AirDrop, Focus, Display, Sound, Now Playing. You generally can't remove these from the Control Center panel itself, but you *can* choose whether to also show them directly in the Menu Bar using the dropdown menu next to each (options are typically "Show in Menu Bar" or "Don't Show").

    o **Other Modules:** This section includes items like Accessibility Shortcuts, Battery, Fast User Switching. Here, you can decide whether to show them in Control Center *and/or* show them in the Menu Bar. For example, you might want the Battery status always visible in the Menu Bar, but not necessarily taking up space in the Control Center panel.

    o **Menu Bar Only:** Items listed here (like Spotlight, Siri, Time Machine, Clock Options) can *only* be added to or removed from the Menu Bar itself, not the Control Center panel.

3. **Drag and Drop Shortcut:** Remember the trick from section 2.1? You can also customize your Menu Bar *directly* from the Control Center panel. Open Control Center, then simply click and drag an icon (like the Focus moon or the Sound speaker) from the Control Center panel straight up into your Menu Bar where you want it placed. Release the mouse button, and voilà! It's now pinned to your Menu Bar for one-click access without needing to open Control Center first. To remove an icon added this way, hold down the Command (⌘) key, then click and drag the icon off the Menu Bar until you see an 'X' appear, then release.

Why Control Center is Your Friend

Control Center shines when you need to make quick adjustments without interrupting your workflow. Need to dim the screen quickly during a presentation? Connect your Bluetooth headphones before a call? Turn on Do Not Disturb for an hour of focused work? Control Center puts these common actions just a click or two away, saving you from navigating through multiple levels of System Settings. It's a small feature that adds up to a much smoother and more efficient experience on your MacBook Air.

Managing Notifications Effectively with the Notification Center

In today's connected world, notifications are constantly vying for our attention – emails arriving, messages popping up, calendar reminders, app updates, news alerts, and more. macOS Sequoia provides a centralized place to manage and review these alerts: the **Notification Center**. It also serves as a home for handy **Widgets**, giving you glanceable information from your favorite apps.

Accessing Notification Center

Opening Notification Center is simple: just click the **Date and Time** displayed in the top-right corner of your Menu Bar. A panel will slide out from the right edge of your screen, revealing your recent notifications and widgets. Click the Date and Time again, or click anywhere else on the screen, to dismiss it.

Understanding the Layout

The Notification Center panel typically has two main sections:

- **Notifications (Top):** This area displays notifications you've received but haven't yet dismissed or acted upon. They are usually grouped by application.

- **Widgets (Bottom):** Below the notifications, you'll find your configured widgets – small, interactive snippets of information from various apps.

Dealing with Notifications

Notifications first appear on your screen momentarily as either **Banners** (which show up briefly in the top-right corner and then disappear automatically) or **Alerts** (which stay on screen until you manually dismiss them). If you miss them or don't interact with them, they collect neatly in the Notification Center for you to review later.

- **Viewing Notifications:** Scroll through the list in the top section of Notification Center to see your missed alerts. Notifications are usually stacked by app; you might see a label like "3 Notifications" from Mail. Clicking the stack often expands it to show individual alerts.

- **Interacting with Notifications:**
  - **Clearing:** Hover your cursor over a single notification or a group stack, and an 'X' button will often appear. Click the 'X' to dismiss that specific notification or the entire stack. Sometimes a "Clear All" button appears at the top to dismiss everything at once.
  - **Taking Action:** Many notifications offer action buttons directly within the alert (either when it first appears or in Notification Center). For example, a calendar reminder might have "Snooze" or "Close" buttons. A message notification might have a "Reply" button. Clicking the main body of a notification usually opens the corresponding application (e.g., clicking a Mail notification opens that email in the Mail app).

- o **Options:** Sometimes, hovering over a notification reveals a small options button (like ...) which might offer choices like "Deliver Quietly" (send future notifications from this app directly to Notification Center without a banner) or "Turn Off" notifications for that app entirely.

Taming the Notification Flood: Customizing Settings

Getting too many distracting notifications? macOS gives you fine-grained control over how each application can alert you.

1. Go to **System Settings > Notifications**.

2. In the left sidebar, you'll see a list under "Application Notifications." Click on the name of the specific app whose notifications you want to adjust (e.g., Mail, Calendar, Slack).

3. On the right, you'll see several options for that app:

Setting	Options	What it Controls	Recommendation / Use Case
Allow Notifications	On / Off Toggle	The master switch. Turns all notifications for this app completely on or off.	Turn off for apps you never want alerts from.
Alert Style	None / Banners / Alerts	How notifications appear initially: **None** (go straight to Notification Center), **Banners** (appear briefly, then vanish), **Alerts** (stay until dismissed).	Use **Alerts** for critical things (e.g., Calendar events), **Banners** for less urgent info (e.g., new emails), **None** for low priority.
Show previews	Always / When Unlocked / Never	Whether the notification shows a snippet of content (like email subject or message text) or just says "Notification".	"When Unlocked" is a good balance for privacy on a shared Mac. "Always" is convenient. "Never" for maximum privacy.
Allow time sensitive alerts	On / Off Toggle	Allows critical alerts (like severe weather or emergency alerts from specific apps) to break through Focus modes.	Generally keep On for important apps.

Show in Notification Center	On / Off Toggle	Whether missed notifications from this app collect here.	Keep On unless you *only* want the initial banner/alert and never need to review missed ones.
Badge application icon	On / Off Toggle	Toggles the little red circle with a number count that appears on the app's Dock icon.	Useful for seeing unread counts (e.g., Mail, Messages), but can be disabled if you find badges distracting.
Play sound for notification	On / Off Toggle	Whether the notification makes a sound when it arrives.	Turn off for noisy apps if the visual alert is enough.
Notification grouping	Automatic / By App / Off	How notifications are stacked in Notification Center. "By App" is usually the clearest.	Experiment to see which grouping style you prefer.

1. Take a few minutes to go through the settings for your most frequently used apps. Tuning these options can significantly reduce unwanted interruptions and make your notifications much more manageable.

Widgets: Information at a Glance

Below your notifications lives the world of **Widgets**. These are like mini-versions of your apps, providing quick, glanceable information or simple controls without needing to open the full application.

1. **Default Widgets:** Your Mac likely comes with a few default widgets already in place, perhaps showing the weather, upcoming calendar events, or world clocks.

2. **Viewing Widgets:** Simply scroll down in the Notification Center panel to see your active widgets.

3. **Editing Widgets:** Want to add, remove, or rearrange widgets?

   o Open Notification Center.

   o Scroll to the very bottom and click the **"Edit Widgets"** button.

   o This opens the **Widget Gallery**. On the left, you'll see a list of applications that offer widgets. Click an app name.

   o In the main area, you'll see the available widgets from that app, often in different sizes (small square, medium rectangle, large rectangle).

   o To **add** a widget, simply click and drag it from the gallery to the widget area on the right side of the Notification Center panel where you want it placed.

- To **remove** a widget already in your Notification Center, hover over it (while in edit mode) and click the minus (-) button that appears in its corner.

- To **rearrange** widgets, just click and drag them up or down within the Notification Center panel (while in edit mode).

- Some widgets offer customization options (like choosing a specific city for Weather or a specific list for Reminders). If so, you might see options when adding it, or you can sometimes right-click (Control-click) the widget *after* adding it and choose "Edit [Widget Name]".

- Click **"Done"** at the bottom right when you're finished editing.

4. **Interactivity:** Many widgets are not just static displays. You might be able to check off a reminder, pause music, or click an event to open it in the Calendar app directly from the widget itself.

Widgets are fantastic for getting quick updates on things like the weather forecast before you head out, seeing your next meeting at a glance, checking stock prices, or viewing headlines without needing to launch multiple apps. Explore the gallery and add the ones most relevant to your daily routine!

By mastering both the Control Center for quick actions and the Notification Center for managing alerts and viewing widgets, you gain significant control over your MacBook Air's interface, making it a more streamlined and personalized tool for your productivity and enjoyment.

Finder Fundamentals

Welcome to Chapter 3! Now that you're getting familiar with the basic macOS interface elements like the Desktop, Menu Bar, and Dock, it's time to dive into the heart of file management on your Mac: the **Finder**. If you're coming from Windows, think of Finder as the equivalent of File Explorer, but with its own unique Mac flair and powerful features. Mastering Finder is essential for keeping your digital life organized and accessing your documents, photos, applications, and everything else stored on your MacBook Air M4.

Exploring Finder Windows, Tabs, and View Options

The Finder is always running in the background, managing the Desktop and file system, but you'll primarily interact with it through **Finder windows**.

Opening Finder

There are several easy ways to open a new Finder window:

1. **Click the Finder Icon in the Dock:** Look for the iconic blue smiley face icon, usually the first item on the left side of your Dock. Click it once. If no Finder windows are open, a new one will appear. If some are already open, clicking the icon will bring them to the front.

2. **Click the Desktop:** Simply click anywhere on your empty Desktop background. This makes Finder the active application (you'll see "Finder" next to the Apple menu □ in the Menu Bar). Then, go to the **File** menu and choose **New Finder Window** (or use the keyboard shortcut Command (⌘) + N).

Anatomy of a Finder Window

Once you have a Finder window open, take a moment to look at its different parts. Understanding these components will make navigation much easier.

1. **Title Bar (Top):** At the very top, you'll see the name of the folder you're currently viewing (e.g., "Documents," "Downloads," "Applications"). On the left side of the Title Bar are the familiar "traffic light" buttons:

   o **Red (Close):** Closes the current Finder window.

   o **Yellow (Minimize):** Shrinks the window down into the Dock (usually near the Trash). Click its icon in the Dock to restore it.

   o **Green (Full Screen/Window Management):** Clicking this typically makes the window enter full-screen mode, hiding the Menu Bar and Dock for maximum focus. Hovering over the green button reveals options to "Enter Full Screen," "Tile Window to Left of Screen," or "Tile Window to Right of Screen" (for Split View, which we'll cover later).

2. **Toolbar (Below Title Bar):** This customizable strip contains buttons for common actions. By default, you'll usually find:

   o **Back/Forward Arrows:** Navigate through folders you've recently visited within that window, just like in a web browser.

   o **View Buttons:** A group of icons allowing you to instantly switch between different ways of viewing your files (Icon, List, Column, Gallery – more on these soon!).

   o **Action Button (Gear Icon):** Provides a menu with context-sensitive actions for selected items (like New Folder, Get Info, Quick Look).

   o **Share Button:** Allows you to quickly share selected files via Mail, Messages, AirDrop, etc.

   o **Tags Button:** Lets you add or manage color-coded tags for selected files (we'll explore tags in section 3.2).

   o **Search Bar:** Quickly search for files within the current folder or your entire Mac.

3. **Sidebar (Left Side):** This is your main navigation panel. It's divided into sections:

   o **Favorites:** Quick links to commonly used locations like your Applications folder, Desktop, Documents, Downloads, your Home folder (usually represented by a house icon with your username), and AirDrop.

   o **iCloud:** If you're signed into iCloud, you'll see links to iCloud Drive and potentially your synced Desktop & Documents folders here.

   o **Locations:** Shows the storage devices connected to your Mac (like your internal SSD, often named "Macintosh HD" or similar) and any network locations you're connected to.

   o **Tags:** Lists all the color-coded tags you've used, allowing you to quickly find all files marked with a specific tag.

   o *Customizing the Sidebar:* You have full control over what appears here! Go to the **Finder** menu (next to the Apple menu ☐ when Finder is active) and choose **Settings...** (or press Command (⌘) + ,). Click the **Sidebar** tab in the settings window. Here, you can check or uncheck boxes next to items you want to show or hide in the Favorites, iCloud, and Locations sections. You can also drag items directly within the Sidebar to rearrange their order in the Favorites section.

4. **Content Area (Main Part):** This large central area displays the actual files and folders contained within the location selected in the Sidebar or navigated to via the Toolbar/Title Bar. How these items look depends entirely on the View Option you've chosen.

5. **Path Bar (Optional, Bottom):** This helpful bar shows the complete folder hierarchy leading to the currently displayed folder (e.g., Macintosh HD > Users > yourname > Documents > ProjectFolder). It helps you understand exactly where you are in your file structure. To show it, go to the **View** menu in the Menu Bar and choose **Show Path Bar**. You can double-click any folder name in the Path Bar to jump directly to that location.

6. **Status Bar (Optional, Bottom):** Displayed below the Path Bar (if both are enabled), this bar shows the number of items in the current folder and, importantly, the amount of available storage space remaining on your Mac's drive. To enable it, go to the **View** menu and choose **Show Status Bar**.

Working with Finder Tabs

Just like modern web browsers, Finder lets you open multiple folder locations within a single window using **Tabs**. This is incredibly useful for reducing window clutter when you're working with files in different places (e.g., copying files from Downloads to Documents).

- **Opening a New Tab:**

    o Press Command (⌘) + T.

    o Go to the **File** menu and choose **New Tab**.

    o Right-click (or Control-click) a folder in the Sidebar or Content Area and choose **Open in New Tab**.

- **Switching Tabs:** Simply click on the tab you want to view at the top of the Finder window. You can also use keyboard shortcuts: Control + Tab to move to the next tab, and Control + Shift + Tab to move to the previous tab.

- **Closing Tabs:** Click the small 'X' button that appears on the left side of the tab when you hover over it, or press Command (⌘) + W to close the currently active tab.

- **Moving Tabs:** Click and drag a tab to rearrange its order within the window. You can even drag a tab *out* of the window entirely to create a new, separate Finder window for that location.

Using tabs can make tasks like comparing folder contents or moving files between distant locations much more efficient than juggling multiple separate windows.

Choosing Your View: Icon, List, Column, Gallery

Finder offers four distinct ways to view the files and folders in the Content Area. You can switch between these views instantly using the group of four **View Buttons** in the Toolbar, or via the **View** menu in the Menu Bar. Each view has its strengths:

1. **Icon View (⌘ + 1):**

   o **Appearance:** Displays items as icons (folders look like folders, documents often show a preview or application icon) with their names underneath.

   o **Pros:** Very visual, easy to recognize file types (especially images), feels familiar. You can manually arrange icons anywhere within the window.

   o **Cons:** Can become cluttered, doesn't show much information beyond the name and icon, sorting options are limited compared to List view.

   o Customization (View > Show View Options or ⌘ + J): You can adjust icon size, grid spacing, text size, label position (bottom or right), show item info (like file size or image dimensions below the name), and show an icon preview (making document icons show a mini-preview of their content). You can also sort or arrange icons automatically by Name, Kind, Date, Size, etc., and choose a background color or image for the window.

2. **List View (⌘ + 2):**

   o **Appearance:** Presents items in a neat, spreadsheet-like list with columns for different attributes. Folders can be expanded (click the triangle ▶) to show their contents inline.

   o **Pros:** Excellent for seeing detailed information at a glance, easy to sort by any column, efficient use of space for many items, allows selection of multiple non-contiguous items easily.

   o **Cons:** Less visually engaging than Icon or Gallery view, requires horizontal scrolling if you have many columns enabled.

   o Customization (View > Show View Options or ⌘ + J): You can choose which columns are visible (Name, Date Modified, Date Created, Size, Kind, Tags, Comments, Version, etc.), change the text size, toggle icon previews, show relative dates (e.g., "Yesterday"), and calculate all sizes (useful but can slow down browsing large folders). You can also rearrange column order by dragging the column headers, and resize columns by dragging the divider lines between headers.

   o **Sorting:** Simply click a column header (like "Date Modified" or "Size") to sort all items in the list by that attribute. Click again to reverse the sort order.

Common List View Column	Information Displayed
Name	File or folder name
Date Modified	When the item was last saved or changed
Date Created	When the item was originally created
Size	File size (folders might show "--" or calculate size)
Kind	Type of item (Folder, PDF Document, JPEG image, App, etc.)
Tags	Color-coded tags assigned to the item
Comments	Spotlight comments added via Get Info
Version	Application version number (for apps)

1. **Column View (⌘ + 3):**

   o **Appearance:** Displays your folder hierarchy in a series of cascading columns from left to right. Clicking a folder in one column reveals its contents in the next column immediately to its right.

   o **Pros:** Fantastic for quickly navigating through nested folders (deep hierarchies), always shows you the path you took, provides a preview and details for the selected file in the rightmost column.

   o **Cons:** Can require significant horizontal screen space for deep folders, might feel less intuitive initially than Icon or List view.

   o Customization (View > Show View Options or ⌘ + J): Options are fewer here, mainly text size, showing icons, and showing the preview column. You can resize columns by dragging the divider handles at the bottom between columns.

2. **Gallery View (⌘ + 4):**

   o **Appearance:** Features a large preview of the selected file at the top, with a horizontally scrolling row of thumbnails for all items in the folder underneath. A sidebar often appears on the right showing detailed metadata about the selected file.

   o **Pros:** Ideal for visually browsing media files like photos and videos, provides quick access to metadata (like camera settings, image dimensions), allows quick scrubbing through video previews.

   o **Cons:** Not very space-efficient for non-visual files or large numbers of items, navigation relies heavily on the thumbnail strip.

o Customization (View > Show View Options or ⌘ + J): You can choose whether to show the preview sidebar and what metadata it displays (e.g., EXIF tags for photos).

Experiment with each view mode! You'll likely find yourself switching between them depending on the type of files you're working with and what you need to accomplish. Setting a default view for all folders or specific views for individual folders is also possible via the View Options panel (⌘ + J).

Customizing the Toolbar

Don't forget you can tailor the Toolbar to include the actions you use most often. Right-click (or Control-click) on an empty area of the Toolbar and select **"Customize Toolbar..."**. A sheet will drop down showing a palette of available buttons (like Eject, Burn, Delete, New Folder, Get Info, Quick Look, Connect to Server, and many more). Simply drag buttons onto the Toolbar where you want them, drag them off to remove them, or drag them around to rearrange. You can also choose whether to show icons only, text only, or icons and text for the toolbar items. Make it work for you!

Organizing Files: Folders, Tags, Smart Folders, and Stacks

A clean digital workspace is a productive workspace. As you start creating documents, downloading files, and saving photos, your MacBook Air M4 can quickly accumulate a lot of data. Taking a little time to organize your files using Finder's tools will save you significant time and frustration later when you need to find something specific. Let's explore the key organizational methods: Folders, Tags, Smart Folders, and Stacks.

Folders: The Foundation of Organization

Folders are the most fundamental way to group related items together. Just like physical file folders in a cabinet, they provide structure to your storage.

- **Creating Folders:**
    - **Menu Bar:** Navigate to the location where you want the new folder (e.g., your Documents folder), make sure no files are selected, then go to **File > New Folder**.

    - **Keyboard Shortcut:** Press Shift + Command (⌘) + N.

    - **Right-Click:** Right-click (or Control-click) in an empty space within a Finder window or on the Desktop and choose **New Folder** from the contextual menu.

    - A new folder named "untitled folder" will appear. Its name will be highlighted, ready for you to type a more descriptive name.

- **Naming and Renaming:**
    - When you first create a folder, just start typing the name you want and press Return (Enter).
    - To rename an existing folder (or file), click its icon once to select it, wait a brief moment, then click *directly on its name.* The name will become editable. Type the new name and press Return. Alternatively, select the folder and press the Return key to enter renaming mode.
    - Choose clear, descriptive names for your folders (e.g., "Budget Spreadsheets 2025," "Vacation Photos - Italy," "University Course Notes").
- **Moving Items into Folders:** Simply click and drag the file(s) or other folder(s) you want to move directly onto the icon of the destination folder. Release the mouse button, and the items will be moved inside. You can also use Cut/Copy (⌘ + X / ⌘ + C) and Paste (⌘ + V) commands, although dragging is often more intuitive for moving.
- **Creating Hierarchies:** You can create folders inside other folders to build a logical structure (e.g., Documents > Work > Projects > Project Alpha > Reports). Plan a structure that makes sense for how you work or think about your files. Common top-level folders might include Work, Personal, Finances, Photos, Music, Projects, etc.

Tags: Flexible, Color-Coded Categorization

While folders provide a rigid hierarchy (a file can only be in one folder at a time), **Tags** offer a much more flexible way to categorize and find files, regardless of where they are stored. Think of them like keywords or labels you can attach to any file or folder.

- **What are Tags?** Tags are essentially metadata labels, often associated with colors, that you can assign to items. A single file can have multiple tags. For example, a photo from your Italy trip could be tagged "Vacation," "Italy," "Photos," and "Favorites."
- **Default Tags:** macOS comes with a set of default colored tags:

Color	Default Name (Can be changed)
Red	Red
Orange	Orange
Yellow	Yellow
Green	Green
Blue	Blue

Purple	Purple
Gray	Gray

1. **Assigning Tags:**

   o **Drag to Sidebar:** Select a file or folder and drag it onto the desired Tag name listed in the **Tags** section of the Finder Sidebar.

   o **Toolbar Button:** Select the item(s), then click the **Tags button** (looks like a price tag or circle) in the Finder window's Toolbar. A popover appears where you can type an existing tag name, select from recent/favorite tags, or click on the colored dots.

   o **Right-Click Menu:** Right-click (or Control-click) the item(s) and choose **Tags...** from the contextual menu. This brings up the same popover as the toolbar button. You can also directly select one of the colored dots shown lower down in the contextual menu.

   o **Get Info Window:** Select the item, press Command (⌘) + I (or File > Get Info). In the Info window, there's an "Add Tags..." section where you can type or select tags.

2. **Creating Custom Tags:** Don't like the default names or need more categories?

   o Go to **Finder > Settings...** (⌘ + ,).

   o Click the **Tags** tab.

   o You'll see the list of existing tags. Click the **plus (+) button** at the bottom to add a new tag. Type its name.

   o To change a tag's color, right-click it in the list and choose a new color from the palette.

   o To rename a tag, double-click its name in the list and type the new name.

   o You can drag tags in this list to reorder them or drag your most-used tags into the "Favorite Tags" section at the bottom for quicker access in the Sidebar and contextual menus.

3. **Finding Files by Tag:** This is where tags shine! Simply click on a Tag name in the **Tags** section of the Finder Sidebar. The main Finder window will instantly display *all* files and folders that have been assigned that tag, no matter which folders they actually live in. You can also type tag:[tagname] (e.g., tag:Urgent) into the Spotlight search bar.

Tags are fantastic for cross-referencing items. A report might live in Documents > Work > Projects > Project Alpha but also be tagged "Urgent" and "Review Needed." You can find it either by navigating the folder structure or by clicking the "Urgent" tag.

Smart Folders: Your Automatic Search Assistants

Imagine having folders that automatically update themselves to show files matching specific criteria you set. That's exactly what **Smart Folders** do! They aren't actual folders that hold files; instead, they are saved searches that dynamically display items meeting your rules.

1. **How They Work:** You define criteria (like file type, date created/modified, keywords in the name, tags, etc.), and the Smart Folder continuously searches your Mac (or specific locations) and displays any matching items. The original files remain in their actual locations.

2. **Creating a Smart Folder:**
   o Make sure Finder is the active application.
   o Go to **File > New Smart Folder**. A new Finder window will open with a search bar active below the toolbar.
   o **Define Criteria:** Start defining your search. You can:
      ▪ Type keywords into the search bar (e.g., "presentation").
      ▪ Click the **plus (+) button** to the right of the search bar to add specific attribute criteria.
      ▪ Use the dropdown menus that appear. The first menu lets you choose an attribute (e.g., Kind, Last opened date, Name, Contents, Tags). The second menu provides modifiers (e.g., is, is not, contains, is before, is after, matches). The third field lets you enter the value (e.g., PDF, yesterday, "report", "Vacation").
      ▪ Add multiple criteria by clicking the '+' button again. You can specify whether *All* or *Any* of the criteria must be met.
   o **Set Search Scope:** Just below the criteria, choose where Finder should search: "This Mac" or the specific folder you were previously viewing (e.g., "Documents"), or "Shared".
   o **Save the Smart Folder:** Once the search results look correct, click the **Save** button near the top right.
   o A dialog box appears. Give your Smart Folder a descriptive name (e.g., "Recent Invoices," "Unfinished Reports," "Photos from 2025"). Choose where to save it (the default "Saved Searches" folder is fine, accessible via Go > Go to Folder > ~/Library/Saved Searches). Crucially, check the **"Add to Sidebar"** box if you want easy access to this Smart Folder directly from the Finder Sidebar.
   o Click **Save**.

3. **Examples of Useful Smart Folders:**
   o "All PDF Documents modified in the last 7 days." (Kind is PDF, Last modified date is within last 7 days)
   o "Word documents containing 'Budget'." (Kind is Word Document, Contents contains 'Budget')

- o "Images tagged 'Final' but not 'Approved'." (Kind is Image, Tag is 'Final', Tag is not 'Approved')

- o "Large Files over 500MB." (Size is greater than 500 MB)

4. **Using Smart Folders:** Simply click the Smart Folder's name in your Finder Sidebar (or wherever you saved it). It will instantly display all current files matching the criteria you set – no manual searching required!

Smart Folders are incredibly powerful for staying organized and quickly accessing dynamic sets of files without having to constantly rearrange your primary folder structure.

Stacks: Tidying Your Desktop Automatically

We briefly mentioned Stacks in section 2.1, but let's reiterate its role specifically for organization. Stacks are primarily a **Desktop organization feature**. They don't change where your files are stored, but they dramatically clean up the visual clutter on your Desktop itself.

- **Enabling/Disabling:** Right-click (Control-click) anywhere on your empty Desktop background and choose **Use Stacks**. Click it again to turn Stacks off.

- **How it Works:** When enabled, all the files scattered on your Desktop are instantly grouped into neat stacks based on certain criteria.

- **Grouping Stacks:** Right-click the Desktop again and hover over **Group Stacks By**. You can choose to group them by:
  - o **Kind:** (Default) Stacks for Documents, Images, PDFs, Movies, Screenshots, etc.
  - o **Date Last Opened, Date Added, Date Modified, Date Created:** Stacks for Today, Previous 7 Days, Previous 30 Days, etc.
  - o **Tags:** Stacks for each color tag you've used on Desktop items.

- **Interacting with Stacks:**
  - o Click a stack once to expand it, fanning out the files it contains.
  - o Click the stack icon again (or elsewhere on the Desktop) to collapse it.
  - o Hovering over a collapsed stack might let you scrub through previews of the items inside (especially for images).

Stacks are purely about visual organization *on the Desktop*. They don't affect files stored in other folders like Documents or Downloads. If your Desktop tends to become a dumping ground for temporary files or screenshots, enabling Stacks is a fantastic way to keep it manageable automatically.

By combining the structural organization of **Folders**, the flexible categorization of **Tags**, the dynamic searching power of **Smart Folders**, and the Desktop tidiness of **Stacks**, you have a comprehensive toolkit within Finder to manage your digital world effectively on your MacBook Air M4.

Quick Look: Instant Previews for Almost Any File

Imagine needing to check the contents of a document, glance at a photo, or even watch a short video clip, but you don't want to wait for the full application (like Microsoft Word, Photos, or QuickTime Player) to launch. This is where one of macOS's most convenient and time-saving features comes in: **Quick Look**. It lets you peek inside a file instantly without opening it in its native app.

What is Quick Look?

Quick Look is a built-in preview technology in macOS. When invoked, it opens a dedicated, lightweight window that displays the contents of the selected file(s). It's incredibly fast and supports a surprisingly wide variety of common file types. It's perfect for quickly identifying if a file is the one you're looking for before committing to opening it fully.

How to Activate Quick Look

Using Quick Look is incredibly simple. First, select the file you want to preview by clicking it once in a Finder window or on your Desktop. Then, do one of the following:

1. **Press the Spacebar:** This is the easiest and most common method. Just tap the Spacebar once. Boom! The Quick Look preview window appears. Press the Spacebar again to close it.

2. **Use the Keyboard Shortcut:** Press Command (⌘) + Y. This also opens the Quick Look window. Pressing it again closes the window.

3. **Use the Toolbar:** If your Finder Toolbar includes the **Action button (gear icon)**, click it and select "Quick Look [filename]" from the menu.

4. **Use the Menu Bar:** Go to the **File** menu in the Menu Bar and choose "Quick Look [filename]".

The Spacebar method is the one most people use due to its speed and convenience.

The Quick Look Window: More Than Just a Static Preview

The window that pops up isn't just a simple image. Depending on the file type, it offers several interactive features:

*   **Content Display:** The main area shows the file's content – the text of a document, the image itself, the first page of a PDF, the player interface for audio/video, etc.

*   **Navigation (Multiple Files):** If you selected *multiple* files in Finder *before* hitting the Spacebar, the Quick Look window will display the first selected item, and you'll see navigation arrows (< and >) appear near the top left. Use these arrows (or the arrow keys on your keyboard) to cycle through the previews of all the selected files without closing the window.

- **Index Sheet View:** When previewing multiple files, you'll also see a button with a grid icon (four small squares). Clicking this **Index Sheet** button shows thumbnails of all the selected items, allowing you to quickly jump to a specific file's preview. Click the button again (or double-click a thumbnail) to return to the single-item preview.

- **Full Screen Button:** A button with two diagonal arrows lets you take the Quick Look preview full screen for a more immersive view, especially useful for photos and videos. Press Esc or click the corresponding button to exit full screen.

- **Markup Button (Pencil Tip Icon):** For many image file types (JPEG, PNG, TIFF, etc.) and PDF documents, a **Markup** button appears in the Quick Look toolbar. Clicking this opens a set of annotation tools *directly within Quick Look*. You can quickly draw shapes, add text, sign documents, crop images, and more without needing to open Preview or another editing app. (We'll explore Markup tools in more detail later). This is incredibly handy for quick annotations.

- **Open With [Application Name] Button:** Usually located near the top right, this button clearly indicates the default application for the file type (e.g., "Open with Preview," "Open with Pages"). Clicking it closes the Quick Look window and launches the file in that designated application for full editing capabilities.

- **Share Button:** The standard macOS Share icon allows you to send the file via Mail, Messages, AirDrop, add it to Notes, etc., directly from the Quick Look window.

- **Zooming and Scrolling:** For images and documents, you can often zoom in and out using pinch gestures on your trackpad or keyboard shortcuts (Command + Plus (+) / Command + Minus (-)) . Use standard scrolling gestures (two fingers on trackpad) or the scroll bar (if visible) to navigate through multi-page documents (like PDFs or Word files) or large images.

- **Audio/Video Playback:** If you Quick Look an audio (MP3, AAC, etc.) or video (MP4, MOV, etc.) file, the window displays playback controls (play/pause, timeline scrubbing, volume control). You can watch or listen directly within Quick Look.

What File Types Does Quick Look Support?

The beauty of Quick Look is its broad compatibility. While it might not work for every obscure or highly specialized file format, it handles most common types beautifully:

File Category	Common Supported Examples	Notes
Images	JPEG, PNG, GIF, TIFF, HEIC, PSD (Photoshop), AI (Illustrator)	Often includes basic metadata display. Markup tools available.
Documents	PDF, DOC/DOCX (Word), PAGES (Pages), TXT, RTF	Multi-page navigation, text selection often possible. Markup for PDFs.
Presentations	PPT/PPTX (PowerPoint), KEY (Keynote)	View slides sequentially.
Spreadsheets	XLS/XLSX (Excel), NUMBERS (Numbers), CSV	View spreadsheet content (might show first sheet).
Audio	MP3, AAC, M4A, AIFF, WAV	Includes playback controls.
Video	MP4, MOV, M4V, AVI (with correct codecs)	Includes playback controls, scrubbing.
Web Files	HTML, Webarchives	Renders a basic preview of the webpage.
Archives	ZIP	Shows a list of the files contained within the archive.
Developer Files	Various code files (PY, JS, SWIFT, etc.), JSON, XML	Often shows syntax-highlighted code.
Font Files	TTF, OTF	Displays sample text using the font.
Contact Cards	VCF	Shows contact information.
Calendar Events	ICS	Displays event details.

This list isn't exhaustive, and support can sometimes depend on installed applications that provide Quick Look "generators." But for everyday file types, Quick Look is remarkably versatile.

The Benefits of Using Quick Look

Incorporating Quick Look into your workflow offers several advantages:

- **Saves Time:** Instantly see file contents without waiting for large applications to load.

- **Reduces Clutter:** Avoid opening multiple application windows just to glance at different files.

- **Quick Identification:** Easily confirm if a vaguely named file is the one you actually need.

- **Fast Edits/Annotations:** Make quick markups on images or PDFs without leaving the preview.

- **Efficient Browsing:** Quickly cycle through previews of multiple selected files.

Start using the Spacebar on your files – you'll quickly wonder how you ever managed without Quick Look! It's a simple yet profoundly useful tool for navigating your digital world on the Mac.

Spotlight Search: Finding Files, Apps, Info, and More

Your MacBook Air M4, like all Macs, comes equipped with an incredibly powerful and fast system-wide search technology called **Spotlight**. Forget manually digging through folders trying to remember where you saved that file from six months ago. Spotlight acts like your personal search engine for everything on your Mac – and even extends to the web for quick info, calculations, and conversions. Learning to leverage Spotlight can dramatically speed up how you find information and launch applications.

Accessing Spotlight

There are two primary ways to summon the Spotlight search interface:

1. **Click the Magnifying Glass Icon:** Look for the magnifying glass icon (Q) in the right section of your Menu Bar. Click it once.

2. **Use the Keyboard Shortcut:** Press Command (⌘) + Spacebar. This is the method most experienced Mac users prefer because it's incredibly fast and can be done from within any application without reaching for the mouse.

Either method will cause the Spotlight search bar to appear, usually centered on your screen, ready for your query. To dismiss Spotlight without performing an action, just press the Esc key or click anywhere outside the search bar and results window.

Performing a Search: Just Start Typing!

Using Spotlight is as simple as it gets: just start typing what you're looking for into the search bar. Spotlight begins searching *instantly* as you type, refining the results with each character you add. You don't even need to press Return/Enter initially.

What Can Spotlight Find? (Almost Anything!)

Spotlight's power lies in the vast range of information it indexes and can retrieve for you. Here are just some examples:

- **Files and Folders:** Type any part of a file or folder name (e.g., "budget spreadsheet," "Italy photos," "project alpha report"). Spotlight searches not only filenames but often the *content* of documents (like text within PDFs or Word files) as well.

- **Applications:** The fastest way to launch an application is often via Spotlight. Just type the first few letters of the app's name (e.g., "saf" for Safari, "pag" for Pages, "sys" for System Settings). The application will usually appear as the Top Hit; just press Return to launch it.

- **System Settings:** Can't remember where the Bluetooth or Display settings are? Type "bluetooth" or "display" into Spotlight, and it will provide a direct link to open that specific pane in System Settings.

- **Contacts:** Type a person's name, email address, or phone number to pull up their contact card from your Contacts app.

- **Calendar Events:** Search for appointments by name or keyword (e.g., "doctor appointment," "meeting with Sarah").

- **Mail Messages:** If you use Apple's Mail app, Spotlight indexes your emails. You can search for subjects, senders, recipients, or keywords within the email body (e.g., "email from Bob about invoice").

- **Music:** Find songs, artists, or albums in your Music library.

- **Dictionary Definitions:** Type a word, and Spotlight will often show its definition directly in the results. You can also explicitly type define [word].

- **Calculations:** Perform quick math without opening the Calculator app. Just type the equation directly into Spotlight (e.g., $(145 + 390) * 2 / 5$, $sqrt(144)$). The answer appears instantly in the results.

- **Unit and Currency Conversions:** This is incredibly handy! Type things like:
  - 15 kg in lbs
  - 5 miles in km
  - 100 USD in CHF (using local currency example for Switzerland)
  - 32 degrees C in F

- Spotlight performs the conversion on the fly.

- **Web Searches:** If Spotlight doesn't find a direct match on your Mac or for its built-in functions, it will offer web search suggestions or a direct link to perform the search in your default web browser.

- **And More:** Depending on your location and installed apps, Spotlight might also find movie showtimes, nearby points of interest, stock quotes ("AAPL stock"), weather ("weather Zurich"), flight information, and more.

Navigating Spotlight Results

As you type, Spotlight presents results in a list, typically categorized for clarity.

- **Categorized List:** You'll see headings like Top Hit (Spotlight's best guess), Applications, Documents, Folders, System Settings, Mail Messages, Web Suggestions, Definition, Calculator, etc.

- **Selection:** Use the **Up (↑)** and **Down (↓)** arrow keys on your keyboard to move through the list of results.

- **Preview Pane:** As you highlight different results with the arrow keys, the right side of the Spotlight window dynamically updates to show a **preview** or more information about the selected item. This is like a built-in Quick Look! You can often see a document preview, contact details, map location, definition, calculation result, etc., without leaving Spotlight.

- **Opening Items:** Once the item you want is highlighted, press the Return (Enter) key to open it (launch the app, open the file/folder, go to the System Setting, perform the web search, etc.).

- **Revealing Files in Finder:** If you highlight a file or folder result and want to see where it's located on your Mac, press Command (⌘) + R. This will close Spotlight and open a Finder window with the item selected. You can also press Command (⌘) + Return to achieve the same thing.

- **Getting More Info:** For some items like files, pressing Command (⌘) + I while they are highlighted in Spotlight will open the standard "Get Info" window for that item.

Refining Your Searches: Getting More Specific

While just typing keywords often works, you can make Spotlight even more powerful by using more specific search techniques:

- **Natural Language:** Spotlight understands some natural language queries. Try searching for things like:
  - documents I worked on yesterday
  - photos from August 2024
  - emails from lisa about project phoenix
  - presentations created last month

- **Keywords and Operators:** For more precise control, you can use specific keywords (often called metadata attributes):
  - kind:[file type]: Narrows results to a specific type. Examples: kind:pdf, kind:image, kind:audio, kind:movie, kind:presentation, kind:folder, kind:application. You can combine this with other terms: report kind:pdf.

- date:[when]: Filters by date. Examples: date:today, date:yesterday, date:this week, date:last month, date:04/15/2025, date:>01/01/2025, date:<12/31/2024. **Combine it:** invoice date:this month.

- tag:[tag name or color]: Finds items with specific Finder tags. Examples: tag:Urgent, tag:red. **Combine it:** contract tag:Approved.

- author:[name] or from:[name]: Finds documents by author or emails/messages from a specific person.

- title:[word] or subject:[word]: Searches specifically within file titles or email subjects.

- **Boolean Operators:** Use AND, OR, NOT (must be uppercase) to combine search terms:

  - "vacation photos" AND "italy" (Finds items containing both phrases)

  - report OR presentation (Finds items containing either word)

  - invoice NOT "paid" (Finds items containing "invoice" but not "paid")

- **Quotation Marks:** Use quotes " " around phrases to search for that exact sequence of words.

Customizing Spotlight

You can tailor Spotlight's behavior slightly to better suit your needs:

1. Go to **System Settings > Siri & Spotlight**.

2. Select **Spotlight Privacy...** at the bottom if you want to prevent Spotlight from searching specific folders or external drives (e.g., backup drives, folders with sensitive information). Click the '+' button to add locations to exclude.

3. Back in the main "Siri & Spotlight" section, scroll down to **Search results**. Here, you can uncheck categories you *don't* want Spotlight to include in its results (e.g., if you never want to see Bookmarks or Calculator results). You can also drag the categories in the list to change the order in which they appear in the Spotlight results window.

Why Spotlight is Indispensable

Spotlight is arguably one of the most powerful and frequently used features of macOS for efficient users.

- **Speed:** It's incredibly fast at finding files and launching apps.

- **Convenience:** Perform calculations, conversions, and definitions without opening separate apps.

- **Comprehensiveness:** Searches filenames, file contents, metadata, system settings, contacts, emails, and more.

- **Reduces Reliance on Folder Structure:** Even if your folders aren't perfectly organized, Spotlight can usually find what you need based on name or content.

Make Command (⌘) + Spacebar your reflex action whenever you need to find something or launch an app on your MacBook Air M4. It will quickly become an essential part of your workflow!

Essential Built-in Productivity Apps

Now that you're comfortable navigating the macOS interface and managing your files with Finder, let's turn our attention to the core applications Apple includes to help you get things done right out of the box. Your MacBook Air M4 comes equipped with powerful, efficient, and well-integrated apps for browsing the web, handling email, managing your schedule, and keeping track of tasks and ideas. In this chapter, we'll take a deep dive into Safari, Mail, Calendar, Reminders, and Notes – the essential toolkit for your daily productivity. These apps are designed to work seamlessly together and sync effortlessly across your Apple devices via iCloud.

Browsing the Web Intelligently with Safari Features

Safari is Apple's very own web browser, pre-installed on your MacBook Air. It's known for its impressive speed, energy efficiency (which translates to longer battery life on your M4 Air – a huge plus!), and strong focus on user privacy and security. Let's explore how to make the most of it.

Launching Safari and the Interface

You can launch Safari by clicking its compass icon in your Dock or by finding it in your Applications folder or via Launchpad/Spotlight. When you open it, you'll notice its clean interface:

- **Smart Search Field (Top Center):** This single bar acts as both the website address (URL) bar and the search bar. Just type a web address or your search query here.

- **Tabs (Below Smart Search Field):** Safari uses tabs to let you view multiple webpages within a single window. You'll see a tab for each open page.

- **Toolbar (Below Tabs):** Contains essential navigation and action buttons. By default, this usually includes:

  - **Back/Forward Buttons (< >):** Navigate through your browsing history within the current tab.

  - **Sidebar Button:** Toggles the sidebar open or closed, revealing Bookmarks, Reading List, and History.

  - **Tab Group Button (Optional):** If using Tab Groups, this shows the current group name and lets you switch between them.

  - **Share Button:** Share the current page via Mail, Messages, AirDrop, etc.

  - **New Tab Button (+):** Opens a new, empty tab.

  - **Show All Tabs Button (Overlapping Squares):** Gives you an overview of all open tabs.

- **Start Page:** When you open a new tab or window, Safari displays a customizable Start Page. By default, it might show Favorites, Frequently Visited sites, Privacy Report summary, Reading List items, iCloud Tabs from your other devices, and Siri Suggestions. You can customize what appears here by clicking the settings icon in the bottom-right corner of the Start Page. You can even set a custom background image!

Core Browsing: Tabs, Bookmarks, Reading List, History

Let's look at the fundamental features for navigating the web:

1. **Working with Tabs:**

   - **Creating:** Click the '+' button in the toolbar or press Command (⌘) + T.

   - **Switching:** Click the tab you want to view, or use Control + Tab (next tab) / Control + Shift + Tab (previous tab).

   - **Closing:** Click the 'x' on the tab or press Command (⌘) + W. To close all tabs *except* the current one, right-click (Control-click) the current tab and choose "Close Other Tabs."

   - **Reordering:** Click and drag tabs left or right.

   - **Pinning Tabs:** If you have websites you visit constantly (like webmail or a project management tool), you can "pin" them. Right-click a tab and choose "Pin Tab." Pinned tabs shrink to just an icon on the far left of the tab bar, stay there permanently (until unpinned), and load automatically when you open Safari. This saves space and keeps important sites readily available.

2. **Tab Groups: Organizing Your Browsing Sessions:** This is a powerful feature for keeping related tabs together. Imagine having one group for "Work Projects," another for "Vacation Planning," and another for "News Sites."

   - **Creating:** Click the downward arrow next to the Sidebar button (or the current Tab Group name) in the toolbar and choose "New Tab Group" or "New Tab Group with [X] Tabs" (to group your currently open tabs). Give the group a name.

   - **Switching:** Use the same dropdown menu to switch between your different Tab Groups. Each group remembers its own set of tabs.

   - **Managing:** You can rename, delete, or share Tab Groups (collaborate on a set of tabs with others via iCloud). Tab Groups also sync across your Apple devices signed into the same iCloud account.

3. **Smart Search Field:** Type a website address (like www.apple.com) and press Return to go there. Type a search query (like "best hiking trails Switzerland") and press Return – Safari will use your default search engine (like Google,

DuckDuckGo, etc., configurable in Safari Settings) to find results. Safari often provides search suggestions as you type.

4. **Bookmarks: Saving Your Favorite Sites:** Found a site you want to visit again easily? Bookmark it!

   o **Adding:** Click the Share button in the toolbar and choose "Add Bookmark..." or press Command (⌘) + D. Choose where to save it (Favorites or another bookmark folder) and optionally rename it.

   o **Favorites Bar:** You can choose to show a Favorites Bar below the main toolbar (View > Show Favorites Bar) for one-click access to your most important bookmarks. Add sites here when creating the bookmark or by dragging them onto the bar from the Bookmarks editor.

   o **Viewing/Managing:** Click the Sidebar button in the toolbar and select the Bookmarks tab (looks like an open book). Here you can see all your bookmarks, organize them into folders, edit names/addresses, and delete unwanted ones. Bookmarks sync via iCloud.

5. **Reading List: Saving Articles for Later:** See an interesting article but don't have time to read it now? Add it to your Reading List. Safari saves a version of the page for offline reading.

   o **Adding:** Click the Share button and choose "Add to Reading List," or press Shift + Command (⌘) + D. You can also hover over a link, click and hold, and choose "Add Link to Reading List."

   o **Viewing:** Click the Sidebar button and select the Reading List tab (eyeglasses icon). Click an item to read it. Items you've read are dimmed. You can swipe left on an item in the list to save it offline or remove it. Reading List also syncs via iCloud.

6. **History: Retracing Your Steps:** Need to find that page you visited yesterday?

   o **Viewing:** Click the Sidebar button and select the History tab (clock icon). It shows pages visited, grouped by date. You can also access History via the "History" menu in the Menu Bar.

   o **Searching:** Use the search field at the bottom of the History sidebar to find specific pages.

   o **Clearing:** Go to the History menu > Clear History... Choose the time frame (last hour, today, all history) you want to clear. Be aware this also clears related website data like cookies.

Focus on Privacy and Security

Safari includes several features designed to protect your privacy and keep you safe online:

- **Intelligent Tracking Prevention (ITP):** Works automatically in the background to identify and limit the ability of websites to track your browsing activity across different sites (cross-site tracking), primarily by restricting third-party cookies and other tracking methods. You don't need to do anything to enable it; it's built-in.

- **Privacy Report:** Want to see who's been trying to track you? Click the shield icon in the toolbar (or go to Safari menu > Privacy Report...). It shows a summary of the known trackers Safari has prevented from profiling you on the current site and over the last 30 days. It's quite eye-opening!

- **Private Browsing:** For sessions where you don't want Safari to remember your history, cookies, or autofill information, use Private Browsing. Go to **File > New Private Window** (or Shift + Command (⌘) + N). The Smart Search Field turns dark gray to indicate you're in a private session. In macOS Sequoia, you can even set Private Browsing windows to lock when you're not using them, requiring Touch ID or your password to reopen.

- **Password Management & Passkeys:** Safari integrates tightly with **iCloud Keychain** (which we mentioned in Chapter 1). It can securely generate strong, unique passwords for new website accounts, save them to your encrypted Keychain, and automatically fill them in when you return. You can view and manage saved passwords in Safari Settings > Passwords (requires Touch ID or login password). Safari also supports the newer, more secure **Passkeys** standard, allowing passwordless logins on supported sites using Touch ID or your iPhone.

- **Fraudulent Website Warning:** Safari maintains a list of known phishing and malware websites. If you try to navigate to a suspected dangerous site, Safari will display a prominent warning before loading the page.

Safari Privacy Feature	Primary Benefit	How to Access/Use
Intelligent Tracking Prevention	Limits cross-site tracking by advertisers and data brokers.	Always active; works automatically in the background.
Privacy Report	Shows which trackers were blocked on the current site & over time.	Click shield icon in toolbar or Safari menu > Privacy Report...
Private Browsing	Prevents saving history, cookies, autofill for the session.	File > New Private Window (Shift + ⌘ + N). Window locks when inactive (Sequoia).
iCloud Keychain Integration	Securely saves & autofills passwords/passkeys. Generates strong passwords.	Active when signed into iCloud. Manage in Safari Settings > Passwords.

Fraudulent Website Warning	Protects against known phishing and malware sites.	Automatic; displays a warning if a suspected dangerous site is visited.

Efficiency and Convenience Features

Beyond the basics, Safari offers tools to make browsing smoother:

- **Reader View:** On webpages with articles (like news sites or blogs), a small icon with horizontal lines often appears on the left side of the Smart Search Field. Clicking this **Reader View** icon strips away ads, navigation bars, and other clutter, presenting just the main text and images in a clean, easy-to-read format. You can customize the font, size, and background color within Reader View. Click the icon again to exit.

- **Handoff:** If you're viewing a webpage in Safari on your Mac and need to step away, you can instantly open the same page on your nearby iPhone or iPad (and vice versa). Just look for the Safari icon that appears on the far left of the Dock on your Mac (if coming from iOS/iPadOS) or in the App Switcher on your iPhone/iPad (if coming from Mac). Requires Bluetooth, Wi-Fi, Handoff enabled, and devices signed into the same iCloud account.

- **Safari Extensions:** You can add extra features to Safari using Extensions developed by third parties. These might include ad blockers, password managers (though Keychain is excellent), grammar checkers, shopping tools, etc. Find and manage extensions in **Safari > Settings... > Extensions**. You can browse for more extensions in the App Store. Be mindful of the permissions extensions request.

- **Profiles (macOS Sequoia & later):** If you want to keep your work browsing separate from your personal browsing, Profiles are fantastic. Go to **Safari > Settings... > Profiles**. You can create different profiles (e.g., "Work," "Personal"). Each profile maintains its own separate history, cookies, website data, extensions, Tab Groups, Favorites, and Start Page settings. You can easily switch between profiles using a button in the toolbar or the File menu. This is great for maintaining focus and separating contexts without needing multiple user accounts on your Mac.

Safari is a deep, capable browser that balances performance, features, and industry-leading privacy protections. Take the time to explore its settings and features to make your web browsing experience on the MacBook Air M4 truly excellent.

Mastering Email Communication with the Mail App

Email remains a cornerstone of communication for work and personal life. Your MacBook Air M4 comes with Apple's **Mail** application, a powerful yet user-friendly client designed to manage all your email accounts in one place. Whether you use iCloud Mail, Gmail, Microsoft Outlook/Exchange, Yahoo, or other standard email providers, Mail can handle them all.

Launching Mail and the Interface

Find the Mail icon (looks like a postage stamp) in your Dock or Applications folder and click it to launch. The Mail window typically presents a three-pane view:

1. **Sidebar (Left):** This is your navigation hub. It lists all your configured email accounts and their associated **Mailboxes**. Common default mailboxes include:

   - **Inbox:** Where new incoming messages arrive.

   - **VIPs:** Messages from contacts you've designated as VIPs.

   - **Flagged:** Messages you've marked with a flag.

   - **Sent:** A copy of messages you've sent.

   - **Drafts:** Messages you've started composing but haven't sent yet.

   - **Junk:** Where Mail automatically filters suspected spam messages.

   - **Trash:** Messages you've deleted (usually kept temporarily).

   - **Archive:** A place to store messages you want to keep but remove from your Inbox.

   - You'll also see sections for each email account you've added (e.g., "iCloud," "Gmail") and any custom folders you create within those accounts or under "On My Mac."

2. **Message List (Middle):** This pane displays the list of emails within the mailbox currently selected in the Sidebar. You'll typically see columns for sender, subject, date received, and potentially flags or attachments. You can customize these columns by right-clicking the header row.

3. **Message Preview Pane (Right):** When you select a message in the Message List, its full content is displayed here for reading. You can resize these panes by dragging the divider lines between them. You can also switch to a "Classic Layout" (Message List on top, Preview Pane below) via Mail > Settings > Viewing.

4. **Toolbar (Top):** Contains buttons for common email actions:

   - **Get Mail:** Manually check all accounts for new messages.

   - **New Message:** Opens a window to compose a new email.

   - **Reply / Reply All / Forward:** Actions for the selected message.

   - **Archive:** Moves the selected message(s) to the Archive mailbox.

- ○ **Delete (Trash Can):** Moves the selected message(s) to the Trash.
- ○ **Junk:** Marks the selected message(s) as junk/spam.
- ○ **Flag:** Apply or remove a flag from the selected message(s).
- ○ **Move To:** Move the selected message(s) to a different mailbox/folder.
- ○ **Filter:** Toggles message filtering based on criteria like unread status.
- ○ **Search Bar:** Search for messages within the current mailbox or all mailboxes.

Setting Up Your Email Accounts

If you signed into iCloud during the initial Mac setup, your @icloud.com email address might already be configured in Mail. Adding other accounts is easy:

1. If Mail prompts you upon first launch, follow the instructions.

2. Otherwise, go to the **Mail** menu > **Add Account...**.

3. Select your email provider type (iCloud, Microsoft Exchange, Google, Yahoo!, AOL, Other Mail Account...).

4. Click **Continue**.

5. Enter the required information (usually your name, email address, and password). For major providers like Google or Microsoft, you might be redirected to their sign-in page for authentication (often using secure methods like OAuth instead of just your password).

6. Choose the apps you want to use with this account (Mail is usually selected by default, but you might also see options for Contacts, Calendars, Notes depending on the provider).

7. Click **Done**.

Your account will appear in the Sidebar, and Mail will start downloading your messages. You can also manage accounts later via **System Settings > Internet Accounts**.

Reading and Managing Your Mail

With your accounts set up, let's manage that inbox:

1. **Reading Mail:** Select a mailbox in the Sidebar. Click a message in the Message List to view it in the Preview Pane. Unread messages usually have a blue dot next to them.

2. **Conversations:** Mail automatically groups related messages (replies and forwards) into **Conversations**. You'll see a number next to the latest message in the list indicating how many messages are in the thread. Click it to expand or collapse the conversation in the Preview Pane. You can turn conversation view off in Mail > Settings > Viewing > "Organize by Conversation."

3. **Sorting:** Click the column headers in the Message List (like "From," "Subject," "Date Received") to sort messages by that criteria. Click again to reverse the order.

4. **Filtering:** Click the small Filter icon (looks like a funnel) at the top of the Message List to quickly show only unread messages, messages with attachments, flagged messages, etc.

5. **Searching:** The Search bar in the toolbar is very powerful. Start typing a name, subject keyword, or content snippet. Mail suggests search terms and scopes (Current Mailbox, All Mailboxes, specific people, subjects). Click a suggestion or press Return to perform the search.

6. **Mailboxes and Folders:** Don't let your Inbox overflow! Create folders to organize messages.

   o Right-click (Control-click) on an account name or existing folder in the Sidebar and choose **New Mailbox....** Give it a name and choose its location.

   o Drag messages from the Message List into the desired folder in the Sidebar.

   o **Smart Mailboxes:** Similar to Smart Folders in Finder, these automatically gather messages based on criteria you set (e.g., "Emails from Family," "Unread Today," "Messages with Attachments"). Go to **Mailbox > New Smart Mailbox...** to create one. They appear in the Sidebar with a gear icon.

7. **Flags:** Use flags to mark messages that need follow-up or are important. Click the Flag button in the toolbar or right-click a message and choose a flag color. Access all flagged messages via the "Flagged" mailbox in the Sidebar.

8. **Marking Read/Unread:** Select a message and go to **Message > Mark > As Unread** (or As Read). The blue dot indicator will update.

Composing and Sending Emails

Ready to write?

- **New Message:** Click the "New Message" button (pencil on paper icon) in the toolbar or press Command (⌘) + N. A new composition window appears.

- **Addressing:** Enter recipient email addresses in the "To:" field. Start typing a name from your Contacts, and Mail will suggest matches. Add recipients to "Cc:" (Carbon copy) or "Bcc:" (Blind carbon copy – recipients in Bcc are hidden from others) as needed. Choose the sending account using the "From:" dropdown if you have multiple accounts configured. Enter a clear **Subject**.

- **Formatting:** Use the formatting bar above the message body to change fonts, sizes, colors, alignment, create lists (bulleted/numbered), and adjust indentation.

- **Attachments:** Click the **Paperclip icon** in the toolbar to attach files, or simply drag files from Finder directly into the message body.

- **Signatures:** Set up personalized signatures for each account in **Mail > Settings > Signatures**. Mail can automatically add your chosen signature to new messages.

- **Replying/Forwarding:** Select the message you want to respond to and click the **Reply** (single back arrow), **Reply All** (double back arrow), or **Forward** (single forward arrow) button in the toolbar.

- **Undo Send:** Made a mistake right after hitting send? For a brief period (usually 10-30 seconds, configurable in Mail Settings > Composing), an "Undo Send" button appears at the bottom of the Sidebar. Click it quickly to retract the email!

- **Schedule Send:** Don't want to send that email immediately? Click the small downward arrow next to the Send button. You can choose suggested times (like "Send Tonight" or "Send Tomorrow Morning") or select "Send Later..." to pick a specific date and time. Mail will hold the message in a "Send Later" mailbox and send it automatically at the scheduled time (your Mac needs to be on and connected).

- **Mail Drop:** If you attach a very large file (often over 20MB, depending on your provider), Mail might automatically offer to use **Mail Drop**. This uploads the attachment securely to iCloud (doesn't count against your storage) and puts a download link in the email for the recipient. It's great for sending large videos or presentations without hitting attachment size limits.

Exploring More Advanced Mail Features

Once you're comfortable with the basics, Mail offers more tools:

- **Rules:** Automate email processing. Go to **Mail > Settings > Rules**. You can create rules like "If From contains 'newsletter@example.com', then Move Message to mailbox 'Newsletters'."

- **VIPs:** Mark important senders as VIPs (hover over their name in a message header and click the star). Their messages appear in the VIPs mailbox for quick access, and you can set custom notification settings for them.

- **Mute Conversations:** Overwhelmed by replies in a long email thread you no longer need to follow closely? Select the conversation and go to **Message > Mute** (or click the Mute button). You'll stop getting notifications for new replies in that thread.

- **Hide My Email (iCloud+ feature):** When composing a new message, if you click in the "From:" field, you might see an option to use "Hide My Email." This creates a unique, random @icloud.com address that forwards to your real inbox, protecting your actual email address.

Apple Mail is a robust client that effectively balances simplicity with powerful features. By setting up your accounts and exploring its organizational tools, you can turn email from a chore into a manageable part of your digital workflow.

Organizing Your Schedule with Calendar

Keeping track of appointments, meetings, birthdays, and deadlines is crucial. The built-in **Calendar** app on your MacBook Air M4 is designed to help you manage your time effectively and visualize your schedule clearly. Like Mail and Notes, it syncs seamlessly with iCloud, ensuring your schedule is consistent across your Mac, iPhone, and iPad.

Launching Calendar and the Interface

Open the Calendar app from your Dock or Applications folder. The main window typically includes:

- **Main Calendar View:** This large area displays your events in one of several formats:
    - **Day View:** Shows a single day's schedule, usually broken down by hour.
    - **Week View:** Displays the entire week, typically with days as columns and time slots as rows.
    - **Month View:** Provides an overview of the entire month, showing event indicators on specific days. Clicking a day often shows its events in a list.
    - **Year View:** Shows the whole year, highlighting days with events (less detailed).
- **Toolbar (Top):** Contains buttons for switching between Day/Week/Month/Year views, navigating to the previous/next period (day, week, month), jumping to "Today," adding a New Event (+), and searching for events.
- **Sidebar (Left):**
    - **Calendar List:** Shows all the calendars you have access to (both your own and any you're subscribed to or sharing), grouped by account (e.g., iCloud, Google). Each calendar has a checkbox to toggle its visibility in the main view and a distinct color.
    - **Mini-Month Navigator:** Small calendars for the current and next month, allowing quick date selection.

Managing Your Calendars

You likely have at least one default calendar (e.g., "Home" or "Work" under your iCloud account). You can create more to organize different types of events:

- **Creating New Calendars:** Go to **File > New Calendar**. Choose the account (e.g., iCloud) where you want it stored, give it a name (e.g., "Family," "Projects," "Fitness"), and press Return.
- **Changing Calendar Colors:** Right-click (Control-click) a calendar name in the Sidebar and choose a new color from the palette. Assigning distinct colors helps visually differentiate events in the main view.

- **Showing/Hiding Calendars:** Simply check or uncheck the box next to a calendar name in the Sidebar to show or hide its events in the main view. This is useful for focusing on specific schedules (e.g., only showing work events during the workday).

- **Subscribing to Calendars:** You can add public calendars for holidays, sports team schedules, etc. Go to **File > New Calendar Subscription...** and paste the web address (URL) of the calendar feed (often ending in .ics).

- **Sharing Calendars (iCloud):** You can share your iCloud calendars with family, friends, or colleagues. Right-click an iCloud calendar in the Sidebar, choose **Sharing Settings...**, and add people via their email address or phone number. You can choose whether they can view only or also edit events.

Creating and Editing Events

Adding events to your schedule is quick and flexible:

1. **Quick Event Creation:**
   - Click the **New Event (+) button** in the toolbar.
   - Double-click directly on a time slot in Day or Week view.
   - Click and drag across time slots in Day or Week view to set the duration.
   - A small popover appears. Start typing the event details. Calendar supports **natural language input**. Try typing things like:
     - Meeting with Marketing Team Friday 3pm-4pm
     - Lunch with David tomorrow at noon at The Corner Cafe
     - Dentist appointment May 10th 9:30 AM

2. Calendar will often parse the details (title, date, time, location) automatically. Press Return to create the event quickly.

3. **Editing Event Details:** Double-click an existing event, or select it and press Command (⌘) + I (or click the 'i' info button if visible) to open the detailed event inspector window. Here you can refine all aspects:
   - **Title:** The name of the event.
   - **Location:** Add an address or place name. Calendar often suggests locations from Maps and can add travel time estimates.
   - **All-day:** Check this box for events that span the entire day (like birthdays or holidays).
   - **Starts/Ends:** Adjust the date and time precisely. Set the time zone if needed.
   - **Repeat:** Set up recurring events (daily, weekly, monthly, yearly, custom patterns).
   - **Travel Time:** Add estimated travel time before the event (Calendar can sometimes calculate this based on location and current traffic).

- Calendar: Choose which calendar this event belongs to (using the color-coded dropdown).
- Invitees: Enter email addresses of people you want to invite (works best with iCloud or Exchange accounts). Invitees receive an invitation they can accept or decline.
- Alert: Set reminders for the event (e.g., 15 minutes before, 1 day before). You can add multiple alerts.
- Show As: Mark your availability during the event as Busy or Free.
- Notes: Add any relevant details, agendas, or links.
- Attachment: Attach related files to the event.

Viewing and Navigating Your Schedule

- **Switching Views:** Use the Day, Week, Month, Year buttons in the toolbar to change how your schedule is displayed. Choose the view that best suits the level of detail you need. Month view is great for planning, while Day or Week view is better for seeing exact timings.
- **Navigating:** Use the arrow buttons (< >) in the toolbar to move to the previous or next day, week, or month. Click the "Today" button to instantly jump back to the current date. Use the mini-month calendars in the Sidebar to quickly select any date.
- **Searching:** Use the Search bar in the toolbar to find events by title, invitee, location, or notes.

Integration with Other Apps

Calendar works nicely with other macOS apps:

- **Mail:** Mail can sometimes detect dates and times mentioned in emails and offer to create a Calendar event directly from the email.
- **Contacts:** Uses your Contacts app to suggest invitees and their availability (if shared).
- **Maps:** Integrates with Maps for location suggestions and travel time calculations.
- **Reminders:** You can choose to show items from the Reminders app directly within your Calendar view (go to Calendar > Settings > General > "Show Reminders Calendar"). This lets you see your tasks alongside your appointments.
- **Siri:** You can ask Siri to create events, check your schedule, or find appointments (e.g., "Hey Siri, schedule a meeting with John for 3 PM tomorrow," "Hey Siri, what's on my calendar for Friday?").

By using Calendar consistently to track your commitments, set reminders, and visualize your time, you can stay organized and make the most of your busy schedule.

Beyond scheduled appointments, daily life involves countless tasks, ideas, lists, and bits of information we need to capture and manage. Your MacBook Air M4 includes two excellent apps for this: **Reminders** for trackable to-do items, and **Notes** for freeform information capture. Both sync via iCloud, keeping your tasks and thoughts accessible everywhere.

Reminders: Your Smart To-Do List

The Reminders app helps you create lists of tasks and get notified so you don't forget important things.

1. **Interface Overview:**
   - **Sidebar (Left):** Shows your **Lists**. By default, you have **Smart Lists** that automatically group reminders:
     - *Today:* Items due today.
     - *Scheduled:* Items with a specific date assigned.
     - *All:* Every reminder across all your lists.
     - *Flagged:* Reminders you've marked with a flag.
     - *Completed:* Items you've checked off.
     - Below the Smart Lists, you'll see your **Custom Lists** (e.g., Groceries, Work Tasks, Project X). You can group custom lists together.
   - **Main Area (Right):** Displays the reminders within the list currently selected in the Sidebar.
   - **Toolbar (Top):** Contains a Search bar and buttons to show/hide the Sidebar or show item details.

2. **Creating Reminders and Lists:**
   - **New List:** Click "Add List" at the bottom of the Sidebar. Give it a name, choose a color, and select an icon to personalize it.
   - **New Reminder:** Select the list you want to add to, then click the **plus (+) button** in the toolbar or simply click on an empty line in the main area and start typing. Press Return to save the reminder.

3. **Adding Details to Reminders:** Simply typing the task name is often enough, but Reminders offers much more:
   - Select a reminder, then click the small **'i' (info) button** that appears next to it (or press Command (⌘) + I). This opens the details inspector:
     - **Notes:** Add extra details or context.
     - **URL:** Add a relevant web link.

- **Date & Time:** Set a specific due date and optionally a time for an alert. You can choose common options or set a custom date/time.

- **Repeat:** Make the reminder recurring (daily, weekly, specific days, etc.).

- **Location:** Get reminded when you arrive at or leave a specific location (e.g., "Remind me to buy milk when I arrive at the grocery store"). Requires Location Services for Reminders to be enabled.

- **When Messaging:** Get reminded when you're messaging a specific person in the Messages app (e.g., "Remind me to ask Sarah about the report when I message her").

- **Flag:** Mark the reminder as important.

- **Priority:** Set a priority level (Low, Medium, High).

- **List:** Change which list the reminder belongs to.

- **Subtasks:** Break down a larger reminder into smaller, manageable steps.

- **Image:** Add an image to the reminder.

- **Tags:** Add #tags directly in the reminder title (e.g., "Call plumber #home #urgent"). Tags become clickable filters and appear in the Tag Browser at the bottom of the Sidebar.

4. **Completing Reminders:** Click the empty circle next to a reminder to mark it as complete. It will usually move to the "Completed" section.

5. **Using Siri:** Reminders works great with Siri. Try saying things like:

   o "Hey Siri, remind me to call Mom tonight at 7 PM."

   o "Hey Siri, add 'buy bread' to my Groceries list."

   o "Hey Siri, remind me about this email tomorrow morning" (while viewing an email in Mail).

Reminders is perfect for everything from simple shopping lists to complex project tasks with deadlines and subtasks.

Notes: Your Digital Notebook

The Notes app is your go-to place for capturing thoughts, brainstorming ideas, saving snippets of information, creating checklists, sketching, and much more. It's incredibly versatile.

1. **Interface Overview:**

   o **Sidebar (Left):** Organizes your notes. You'll see sections for:

      - *iCloud / On My Mac:* Depending on where your notes are stored.

- *Folders:* Create folders to group related notes (e.g., "Meeting Notes," "Recipes," "Journal"). You can create folders within folders.
- *Smart Folders:* Automatically group notes based on criteria like tags, date created, mentions, etc.
- *Tags:* A Tag Browser showing all the #tags you've used across your notes.

- **Note List (Middle):** Shows a list of notes within the selected folder, Smart Folder, or tag. You can choose between Gallery view (visual previews) or List view.
- **Note Editor (Right):** The main area where you view and edit the content of the selected note.
- **Toolbar (Top):** Contains buttons for Sidebar toggle, creating a New Note, formatting options, attaching media, collaboration/sharing, and searching notes.

2. **Creating and Formatting Notes:**
   - Click the **New Note button** (pencil on paper icon) in the toolbar or press Command (⌘) + N.
   - Just start typing! Use the **Format button (Aa)** or the Format menu to apply styles:
     - Title, Heading, Subheading styles.
     - Bold, Italic, Underline, Strikethrough.
     - Body font choices.
     - Lists: Bulleted (* or - followed by space), Dashed, Numbered (1. followed by space), Checklist (great for tasks within a note).
   - **Checklists:** Use the Checklist button in the toolbar to create interactive checklists. Click circles to mark items done.
   - **Tables:** Insert simple tables using the Table button in the toolbar.

3. **Organizing Your Notes:**
   - **Folders:** Right-click in the Sidebar under your account and choose **New Folder**. Drag notes from the Note List into folders.
   - **Tags:** Simply type a hashtag followed by a keyword (e.g., #idea, #projectX, #recipe) anywhere within the body of your note. That tag automatically becomes clickable and appears in the Tag Browser in the Sidebar. Clicking a tag in the browser shows all notes containing that tag. You can use multiple tags per note.
   - **Smart Folders:** Go to **File > New Smart Folder**. Define criteria based on tags, date created/edited, mentions, checklists, attachments, locked status, etc. This is powerful for automatically grouping notes (e.g., "Notes tagged #idea created this month").

- **Pinning Notes:** Right-click a note in the Note List and choose **Pin Note**. Pinned notes always stay at the top of the list within their folder for quick access.

- **Locking Notes:** For sensitive information, you can lock individual notes. Select the note, click the **Lock button** (padlock icon) in the toolbar, and set a separate password (or use your Mac login password/Touch ID). Locked notes require authentication to view. Be careful not to forget your Notes password if you set a custom one!

4. **Adding More Than Text:**

- **Photos & Videos:** Drag image/video files directly into a note, or click the **Media Browser button** (photo icon) in the toolbar.

- **Sketches:** Click the **Markup button (pencil tip)** and choose "Add Sketch." You can draw with your trackpad or use your nearby iPhone or iPad as a drawing tablet via Continuity Sketch.

- **Scanned Documents:** Use the Markup button > "Scan Documents" to use your iPhone/iPad camera to scan a document directly into your note. It automatically corrects perspective.

- **Web Links:** Paste a web address (URL), and Notes often creates a rich preview with an image and title.

5. **Collaboration and Sharing:**

- Click the **Share button** (or Collaboration icon) on a note or folder. You can invite people via Mail, Messages, or by copying a link.

- Choose whether collaborators can make changes or only view.

- In shared notes, you can type @ followed by a collaborator's name (@David) to mention them, triggering a notification.

- The **Activity view** (person icon with lines) shows recent changes made by collaborators in shared notes.

6. **Quick Note:** macOS has a feature called Quick Note designed for instant note-taking. By default, moving your cursor to the bottom-right corner of the screen often reveals a small tab; clicking it opens a new Quick Note window. You can jot down a thought, add links from Safari, etc., without even opening the main Notes app. Quick Notes are saved in a dedicated folder within Notes. You can configure the Hot Corner trigger in System Settings > Desktop & Dock > Hot Corners...

Notes is far more than a simple text editor; it's a flexible digital scrapbook and information hub. Combined with Reminders for actionable tasks, these two apps provide a robust system for capturing and organizing the important details of your work and life.

By becoming proficient with Safari, Mail, Calendar, Reminders, and Notes, you'll be well on your way to using your MacBook Air M4 as a true productivity machine.

Multitasking and Optimizing Your Workflow

As you start using your MacBook Air M4 for more complex tasks, you'll inevitably find yourself working with multiple applications and windows open simultaneously. While the M4 chip provides the power to run many things at once, managing that digital workspace effectively is key to staying productive and avoiding feeling overwhelmed. macOS Sequoia offers several elegant and powerful tools designed specifically for multitasking and organizing your windows. In this chapter, we'll explore Mission Control and Spaces for a bird's-eye view and virtual desktops, Split View for working with two apps side-by-side, the focus-oriented Stage Manager, and essential tips for efficient app switching and window handling. Mastering these techniques will significantly enhance your workflow.

Using Mission Control and Managing Multiple Desktops (Spaces)

Imagine your screen filled with overlapping windows from your web browser, email client, word processor, and maybe a messaging app. Finding the specific window you need can become a visual scavenger hunt. This is where **Mission Control** comes to the rescue. It provides an instant "zoom-out" perspective, showing you all your open windows, desktop spaces, and full-screen apps at a glance.

Accessing Mission Control: Your Overview Command

There are several ways to activate Mission Control, catering to different preferences:

1. **Keyboard Shortcut (Default):** Press the **F3 key** (the key with three rectangles on it, often located above the number 3 or 4 key on your MacBook Air keyboard). If you have function keys set to standard functions, you might need to press Fn + F3. An alternative default shortcut is often Control (^) + Up Arrow.

2. **Trackpad Gesture:** This is often the quickest and most intuitive method. **Swipe up with three or four fingers** simultaneously on your trackpad. (The exact number of fingers depends on your settings in System Settings > Trackpad > More Gestures > Mission Control).

3. **Magic Mouse Gesture:** Double-tap firmly on the surface of your Magic Mouse with two fingers.

4. **Hot Corner:** You can configure a corner of your screen to activate Mission Control when you move your mouse pointer there. Go to **System Settings > Desktop & Dock**, scroll down and click the **"Hot Corners..."** button. Choose "Mission Control" for your desired corner.

5. **Application Icon:** You can launch the Mission Control application directly from your Applications folder or via Launchpad. You could even drag its icon to your Dock for one-click access.

Experiment with these methods to find the one that feels most natural for you. The trackpad gesture or keyboard shortcut are typically the most efficient.

Understanding the Mission Control View

When you activate Mission Control, your screen transforms to show you this organized overview:

- **Spaces Bar (Top Edge):** Running along the very top is the Spaces Bar. This crucial area displays small thumbnail previews of all your different **Desktops**, which Apple calls **Spaces**. You'll see your main Desktop (usually labeled "Desktop 1"), any additional Desktops you've created ("Desktop 2," etc.), and thumbnails representing any applications currently running in **Full Screen** mode or paired up in **Split View**. The Space you are currently viewing is usually highlighted or slightly larger.

- **Application Windows (Main Area):** Below the Spaces Bar, Mission Control displays thumbnail previews of all the open windows *from the applications currently visible on that specific Desktop Space*. By default (this is configurable), windows belonging to the same application are often grouped together visually. If you have many windows open, macOS might neatly tile them so you can see as many as possible. Hovering your cursor over a window thumbnail might slightly enlarge it.

- **Desktop Preview:** The main area essentially provides a zoomed-out view of the windows on your current Space.

Using Mission Control for Window Management

1. **Finding and Switching Windows:** Simply locate the thumbnail of the window you want to switch to in the main area and click on it. Mission Control will dismiss, and that window will become the active, frontmost window on your Desktop.

2. **App Exposé (Viewing Windows of a Single App):** Sometimes you don't need to see *all* windows, just the different windows belonging to one specific application (e.g., all your open Safari windows or Word documents). You can activate **App Exposé** in a couple of ways:

   - **Keyboard:** Press Control (^) + Down Arrow.
   - **Trackpad:** Swipe *down* with three or four fingers (the opposite of the Mission Control gesture).
   - Dock: Right-click (Control-click) an app's icon in the Dock and choose "Show All Windows."

App Exposé clears away windows from other applications and neatly arranges thumbnails of only the active application's windows, making it easy to pick the specific document or browser window you need.

Multiple Desktops (Spaces): Organizing Your Work Zones

Perhaps the most powerful aspect integrated with Mission Control is the concept of **Spaces**, or multiple virtual Desktops. Instead of cramming all your application windows onto a single screen, you can create separate Desktop environments for different tasks or types of work, keeping things much more organized and focused.

- **The Concept:** Imagine having one Desktop dedicated entirely to your work project (e.g., word processor, spreadsheet, research browser windows), another Desktop for communication (email, messages, video calls), and perhaps a third for personal Browse or creative hobbies. Spaces allow you to create these distinct work zones.

- **Creating New Spaces:**
  - Enter Mission Control (e.g., swipe up with three/four fingers).
  - Move your mouse pointer up to the **Spaces Bar** at the top.
  - Move your pointer towards the right end of the Spaces Bar. A **plus (+) button** will appear.
  - Click the '+' button. A new, empty Desktop thumbnail (e.g., "Desktop 2") will be added to the Spaces Bar. You can create multiple Spaces this way.

- **Switching Between Spaces:** Once you have multiple Spaces, moving between them is seamless:
  - **Mission Control:** Enter Mission Control and simply click on the thumbnail of the Space you want to switch to in the Spaces Bar.
  - **Trackpad Gesture: Swipe left or right with three or four fingers** across your trackpad. This fluidly slides you from one Space to the next. This is arguably the fastest method.
  - **Keyboard Shortcuts:** Use Control (^) + Right Arrow (→) to move to the Space on the right, and Control (^) + Left Arrow (←) to move to the Space on the left. You can also often use Control (^) + [Number] (e.g., Control + 1 for Desktop 1, Control + 2 for Desktop 2) if enabled in settings.

- **Moving Windows Between Spaces:** You have an app window on Desktop 1 but want it on Desktop 2? Easy:
  - **Mission Control Drag:** Enter Mission Control. Click and drag the window thumbnail from the main area *up* onto the desired Desktop thumbnail in the Spaces Bar. Release the mouse button. The window will now belong to that Space.
  - **Window Drag (Edge):** While viewing a normal window (not in Mission Control), click and hold its title bar, drag it to the absolute left or right edge of your screen, and *hold it there* for a moment. The screen should slide over to the adjacent Space, bringing the window with it.

(This requires the "Displays have separate Spaces" option to be enabled in Mission Control settings, which is usually the default).

- **Arranging Spaces:** Don't like the order of your Spaces? Enter Mission Control and simply click and drag the Space thumbnails in the Spaces Bar left or right to reorder them.

- **Assigning Applications to Specific Spaces:** If you always want a particular app (like Mail) to open on a specific Space (e.g., your "Communication" Space, maybe Desktop 2), you can assign it:
    o Make sure the app is open and you are on the Desktop Space where you want it to live.
    o Right-click (Control-click) the application's icon in the **Dock**.
    o Hover over **Options**.
    o Under the "Assign To" section, choose "This Desktop".

- Now, whenever you launch that app or switch to it, macOS will automatically take you to its assigned Space. You can also choose "All Desktops" (the app window appears on every Space) or "None" (the default, opens on the currently active Space).

- **Closing Spaces:** If you no longer need an extra Desktop Space, enter Mission Control, hover your mouse pointer over its thumbnail in the Spaces Bar, and click the **'X'** button that appears in the corner. Any windows currently residing in that Space will be automatically moved to an adjacent Desktop Space (usually the one to the left). You cannot close the original "Desktop 1".

- **Full-Screen Apps and Spaces:** When you put an application into Full Screen mode (by clicking the green button in its title bar), macOS automatically creates a dedicated Space just for that application. You switch to and from full-screen apps using the same methods you use to switch between regular Desktop Spaces (trackpad swipe, keyboard shortcuts, Mission Control).

Customizing Mission Control Behavior

You can tweak how Mission Control and Spaces behave slightly:

1. Go to **System Settings > Desktop & Dock**.

2. Scroll down to the **Mission Control** section.

3. Key options include:
    o **Automatically rearrange Spaces based on most recent use:** If checked, macOS might reorder your Spaces in the bar depending on which one you used last. Many users prefer to *uncheck* this to keep Spaces in a fixed, predictable order.

    o **When switching to an application, switch to a Space with open windows for the application:** If checked (default), switching to an app (e.g., via Command+Tab) will automatically take you to a Space where that app already has windows open.

- **Group windows by application:** When checked (default), Mission Control shows window thumbnails clustered by their parent application. Unchecking it spreads all windows out individually.

- **Displays have separate Spaces:** If checked (default and usually recommended, especially with multiple monitors), each monitor connected to your Mac can have its own independent set of Spaces. The Menu Bar and Dock appear on the active screen. Unchecking this links displays, making Spaces span across all monitors (less common now).

4. You can also reassign the **Keyboard Shortcuts** for Mission Control and App Exposé here if the defaults conflict with other apps or you prefer different combinations.

Action	Common Method(s)	Notes
Enter Mission Control	F3 key / Ctrl + Up Arrow / Swipe up (3 or 4 fingers)	Choose your favorite.
Enter App Exposé	Ctrl + Down Arrow / Swipe down (3 or 4 fingers)	Shows windows of the active app only.
Create New Space	Enter Mission Control, move pointer to Spaces Bar, click '+'.	
Switch Between Spaces	Swipe left/right (3 or 4 fingers) / Ctrl + Left/Right Arrow	Trackpad swipe is often fastest.
Move Window to Another Space	Enter Mission Control, drag window thumbnail onto Space thumbnail.	Or drag window to screen edge and hold.
Close a Space	Enter Mission Control, hover over Space thumbnail, click 'X'.	Cannot close Desktop 1.

Mission Control combined with Spaces is a fundamental macOS workflow for managing multiple windows and tasks efficiently. It might take a little practice to get used to swiping between Spaces, but once you do, it can feel much more organized than having dozens of windows piled onto a single Desktop.

Working with Two Apps Side-by-Side using Split View

Sometimes, you need to actively work with two applications simultaneously without them overlapping or requiring constant switching. Maybe you're writing a report in Pages while referencing data from a Numbers spreadsheet, translating text from a webpage into a document, or taking notes while watching an online lecture. For these scenarios, macOS offers **Split View**, which neatly places two apps side-by-side, filling the entire screen without distractions.

Entering Split View

Putting two apps into Split View is quite straightforward:

1. **Start with an Open Window:** Have at least one of the application windows you want to use open and visible.

2. **Hover Over the Green Button:** Move your mouse cursor over the **green full-screen button** (the leftmost of the three "traffic light" buttons) in the top-left corner of the window's title bar. **Don't click yet!** Just hover for a moment.

3. **Choose Tiling Option:** A small menu will appear with options like:
    o "Enter Full Screen"
    o "Tile Window to Left of Screen"
    o "Tile Window to Right of Screen"
    o (Sometimes "Move Window to [Other Display]" if you have multiple monitors)

4. **Select Tiling:** Choose either **"Tile Window to Left of Screen"** or **"Tile Window to Right of Screen"**.

5. **Select the Second App:** The first window will snap to occupy the chosen half of the screen. The other half of the screen will then display thumbnails of all your other open, eligible windows (similar to Mission Control). Simply click on the window thumbnail for the second application you want to use in Split View.

6. **You're in Split View!** The two chosen applications now sit perfectly side-by-side, filling the entire screen. macOS has automatically created a new, dedicated Space just for this Split View pair, which you can see as a combined thumbnail in the Mission Control Spaces Bar.

Working Effectively in Split View

Once you have your two apps arranged:

- **Adjusting the Split:** Notice the thick **black vertical divider line** running between the two applications. Click and drag this divider left or right to resize the space allocated to each app. You can make one app wider and the other narrower, but they will always collectively fill the screen.

- **Switching Focus:** To work within one of the apps, simply click anywhere inside its portion of the screen. Its Menu Bar menus will become active at the top of the screen (though the Menu Bar might auto-hide depending on your settings – just move your cursor to the top edge to reveal it). You can type, click buttons, and use commands within the currently active app. Click the other app's area to switch focus back.

- **Using the Menu Bar:** As mentioned, the Menu Bar at the top dynamically reflects whichever of the two apps is currently active. So, if you're active in Pages on the left and Safari on the right, clicking in the Pages section shows the Pages, File, Edit, etc., menus, while clicking in the Safari section shows the Safari, File, Edit, History menus.

- **Swapping Sides:** Want the app on the left to be on the right, and vice-versa? Click and hold on the **top edge/title bar area** (where the window buttons would normally be, though they might be hidden until hover) of one of the apps, then drag it horizontally across towards the other side. The apps should smoothly swap positions.

- **Replacing an App in Split View:** Decide you want to swap out one of the apps for a different one?
    - Enter **Mission Control** (swipe up with 3/4 fingers or press F3/Ctrl+Up).
    - You'll see the Split View pair as a single thumbnail in the Spaces Bar.
    - Find the window thumbnail (in the main Mission Control area below the Spaces Bar) of the *new* application you want to bring into the split.
    - Drag that new window thumbnail *up* from the main area and drop it directly *onto* the half of the Split View thumbnail (in the Spaces Bar) that contains the app you want to *replace*. The apps should swap places.

Exiting Split View

When you're finished working with the two apps side-by-side:

1. **Use the Green Button:** Move your cursor to the top of the screen to reveal the hidden title bar and traffic light buttons for either of the apps currently in Split View. Click the **green button** on one of the apps. That app will exit Split View and usually return to being a standard window on your main Desktop Space. The *other* app from the Split View pair will typically transition into its own, standard full-screen Space.

2. **Use Mission Control:** Enter Mission Control. Hover your cursor over the Split View pair's thumbnail in the Spaces Bar. A small icon with two arrows pointing away from each other might appear; clicking this exits Split View. Alternatively, you can simply drag one of the window thumbnails *out* of the Split View pair thumbnail in the Spaces Bar and onto another Desktop Space. This also breaks the Split View.

Considerations for Split View

- **App Compatibility:** While most modern Mac apps work well with Split View, some older applications or those with fixed window sizes might not support tiling or might behave unexpectedly.

- **Full Screen Nature:** Remember that Split View operates within the full-screen environment. The Menu Bar might auto-hide, and accessing the Dock typically requires moving your cursor to the bottom edge of the screen. It's designed for focused work on those two specific apps.

Action	How to Do It
Enter Split View	Hover over green window button, choose "Tile Window to Left/Right", click second window on other side.
Adjust Space Between Apps	Click and drag the black vertical divider line.
Swap App Positions	Click and drag the top edge/title area of one app to the other side.
Replace an App	Enter Mission Control, drag new window thumbnail onto the app-to-be-replaced within the Split View thumbnail.
Exit Split View	Move cursor to top, click green button on either app. OR Enter Mission Control and drag one window out.

Split View is an excellent tool for specific tasks requiring simultaneous reference or interaction between two applications, providing a clean, distraction-free environment on your MacBook Air's screen.

Focusing Your Workspace with Stage Manager

Introduced in macOS Ventura, **Stage Manager** offers a different approach to managing multiple applications and windows, aiming to keep you focused on your current task while making recently used apps easily accessible. It arranges your workspace with one central app (or group of apps) and a visual strip of recent apps on the side. It's quite different from the traditional overlapping windows or the Mission Control/Spaces model.

Enabling and Disabling Stage Manager

You can turn Stage Manager on or off easily:

1. **Via Control Center:** Click the Control Center icon (two switches) in your Menu Bar. Find the **Stage Manager** module and click its toggle switch to turn it On or Off.

2. **Via System Settings:** Go to **System Settings > Desktop & Dock**. Scroll down to the **Stage Manager** section and use the toggle switch there.

When you enable Stage Manager, your screen layout will change noticeably.

Understanding the Stage Manager Interface

Stage Manager organizes your screen into two main areas:

1. **Center Stage:** This is the primary focus area in the center of your screen. It displays the window(s) of the application you are currently actively working on. Unlike traditional full-screen modes, windows on the Center Stage can often still be resized and repositioned to some extent, though Stage Manager tends to keep them fairly centered.

2. **The Stage (Left Strip):** Along the left edge of your screen (by default), you'll see a vertical strip containing small, live thumbnail previews of your other recently used applications or window groups. These represent the apps waiting "in the wings."

Working with Stage Manager

Interacting with apps in Stage Manager involves switching focus between the Center Stage and the left strip:

- **Switching Apps:** To bring a different application to the forefront, simply click its thumbnail in the **left strip (the Stage)**. That application (or group) will smoothly move to the Center Stage, and the application(s) you were just using will move into a thumbnail on the left strip.

- **Grouping Windows/Apps:** Stage Manager allows you to create sets of apps that work together. If you want to bring an app from the left strip and use it alongside the app(s) currently on the Center Stage:

- **Drag from Strip:** Click and drag the thumbnail of the app you want to add from the left strip *onto* the Center Stage area. Release it, and it should join the current app(s) there, forming a group. This group will now move together between the Center Stage and the left strip.

- **Shift-Click:** While viewing an app on the Center Stage, hold down the Shift key and click on an app thumbnail in the left strip. That app will be added to the Center Stage group.

- **From Mission Control:** You can also drag window thumbnails from Mission Control onto the Stage Manager strip or the Center Stage area.

- **Accessing the Desktop:** Need to grab a file from your Desktop? By default, clicking on the empty Desktop background will slide the Center Stage windows smoothly off to the side, revealing your Desktop icons and files. Click an app thumbnail in the left strip (or the hidden center windows) to bring them back. (Note: This behavior can be changed in settings).

- **Window Management on Center Stage:** While Stage Manager encourages focus on one app or group, you can still generally resize and overlap the windows that are currently on the Center Stage, much like in the standard desktop environment, though Stage Manager might try to keep them somewhat organized.

Customizing Stage Manager's Behavior

You can tweak how Stage Manager looks and functions:

1. **Via Control Center:** Click the Control Center icon, then click the small arrow (>) or the text label on the Stage Manager module. This often gives quick toggles for "Show Recent Apps" (the left strip) and "Hide Desktop Items."

2. **Via System Settings:** Go to **System Settings > Desktop & Dock**. Find the **Stage Manager** section and click the **"Customize..."** button. This reveals more detailed options:

   - **Show Recent Applications:** This checkbox toggles the visibility of the entire left strip of app thumbnails. Turning it off means you'd switch apps using other methods (like Command+Tab or the Dock) while Stage Manager primarily manages the centering of the active window.

   - **Show Desktop Items:** Controls whether clicking the Desktop background reveals your Desktop files or does nothing (requiring you to access Desktop files via Finder). If you frequently drag files from the Desktop onto app windows, you'll likely want this enabled.

   - **Show windows from an application:** This important setting determines how Stage Manager handles multiple windows from the same app:

     - **"All at Once":** When you click an app's thumbnail in the left strip, *all* of that application's open windows are brought to the Center Stage together (often overlapping).

- **"One at a Time":** When you click an app's thumbnail, only its most recently used window comes to the Center Stage. To access other windows from the same app, you click its thumbnail in the left strip *again* to cycle through them. This promotes more focus on a single window.

  o **Multiple Displays:** If you use external monitors, you can configure how Stage Manager behaves across them (e.g., whether the strip appears on each display).

Stage Manager Customization Option	Effect	Consideration
Show Recent Applications	Toggles the visibility of the app thumbnail strip on the left.	Turning off removes the main visual switching method of Stage Manager.
Show Desktop Items	Toggles whether clicking the Desktop background reveals Desktop files.	Enable if you frequently access Desktop files; disable for less visual change.
Show windows from an application	Choose "All at Once" or "One at a Time" for handling multiple windows of the same app.	"One at a Time" enhances focus; "All at Once" behaves more like traditional window layering.

Is Stage Manager Right for You?

Stage Manager presents a distinct workflow that appeals to some users more than others:

- **Pros:** Can help maintain focus on the primary task, keeps recent apps visually accessible without cluttering the main workspace, grouping related app windows together can be useful for specific projects.

- **Cons:** Takes up screen real estate with the left strip (especially noticeable on the smaller MacBook Air screen), the workflow feels different and takes some adjustment, might feel less flexible than traditional window management for users who like precise manual placement of many overlapping windows.

The best way to know if Stage Manager fits your style is to try it out! Enable it via Control Center, use it for a while, experiment with grouping windows and customizing the settings. You might find it's the perfect way to stay organized, or you might prefer the flexibility of Mission Control and Spaces, or even just traditional window layering. macOS gives you the choice.

Tips for Efficient App Switching and Window Management

So far, we've explored several powerful macOS features for managing your workspace: Mission Control, Spaces, Split View, and Stage Manager. However, woven into the fabric of macOS are also faster, often keyboard-driven methods for switching between applications and managing individual windows. Combining these techniques with the visual tools can lead to a highly efficient workflow.

Recap: The Tools in Your Arsenal

Just to quickly summarize the main visual/spatial methods we've covered:

- **Dock Clicking:** Simple launching and switching for frequently used apps.
- **Mission Control:** Bird's-eye view of all windows and Spaces.
- **Spaces (Multiple Desktops):** Organizing windows into task-specific virtual desktops.
- **Split View:** Two apps side-by-side in full screen.
- **Stage Manager:** Focus on center app(s) with recent apps accessible on the side.

Now, let's add some classic and essential keyboard/shortcut techniques:

The App Switcher (Command + Tab): The Classic Power Move

This is perhaps the most fundamental and widely used method for quickly switching between *running* applications.

1. Press and Hold Command (⌘): Keep the Command key held down.

2. Tap Tab: While holding Command, tap the Tab key once. An overlay panel appears on your screen, showing large icons of all your currently running applications, ordered roughly by recent use. The currently highlighted icon represents the app you'll switch to if you release Command now.

3. **Cycle Through Apps:**

   o To move *forward* (usually left to right) through the app icons in the switcher, keep holding Command and tap the Tab key repeatedly.

   o To move *backward* through the icons, keep holding Command and tap the tilde/grave accent key (~). This key is usually located above the Tab key on most keyboards.

   o Alternatively, while holding Command, you can use the **Left (←)** and **Right (→)** arrow keys to navigate the highlighted selection.

4. Release Command: When the icon of the application you want to switch to is highlighted, simply release the Command key. The App Switcher disappears, and that application becomes active, bringing its windows to the front.

5. **Bonus App Switcher Tricks:**

   o **Hide App:** While the App Switcher is active and an app icon is highlighted, press the H key (while still holding Command). This will switch to the app *and* hide its windows simultaneously.

   o **Quit App:** While the App Switcher is active and an app icon is highlighted, press the Q key (while still holding Command). This will quit that application entirely without even switching to it first. Very handy for closing background apps quickly.

Mastering Command + Tab is crucial for fast navigation between your open applications without taking your hands off the keyboard.

Switching Windows Within an App (Command + ~)

This shortcut is the essential companion to Command + Tab. While Command + Tab switches between *different applications*, Command + ~ (Command key plus the tilde/grave accent key) switches between ***different open windows of the same application***.

For example, if you have three Safari windows open, pressing Command + ~ will cycle focus between those three Safari windows, without bringing Mail or Pages to the front. This is incredibly useful when working with multiple documents in Word, multiple browser windows, or several Finder windows. If Command + ~ doesn't work, check your Keyboard settings for conflicting shortcuts, but this is the standard default. Shift + Command + ~ typically cycles in the reverse direction.

Hiding Windows vs. Minimizing vs. Closing

Understanding the difference between these actions is key to managing window clutter effectively:

- Hiding (Command + H): This makes all windows of the currently active application instantly disappear from the screen, but the application itself keeps running in the background (its dot remains under the Dock icon). This is fantastic for temporarily reducing clutter to focus on another app or see your Desktop. To bring the hidden app's windows back, simply click its Dock icon or use Command + Tab to switch back to it.

  o Hide Others (Option + Command + H): This hides the windows of *all applications EXCEPT* the one you are currently working in. It's an excellent command for instant focus.

- Minimizing (Command + M): This takes the *frontmost active window* and shrinks it down into the Dock (either as a separate preview near the Trash or into the application's icon, depending on your Dock settings). The application keeps running. To restore a minimized window, you need to click its preview in the Dock.

- **Why Hiding is Often Better:** Many users find Hiding (⌘ + H) more efficient than Minimizing (⌘ + M). Hidden apps are easily brought back with a single click on the Dock icon or via ⌘ + Tab. Restoring minimized windows requires specifically clicking their preview in the Dock, which can become cumbersome if you minimize many windows. Hiding keeps your Dock cleaner.

- Closing a Window (Command + W): This closes the frontmost active window. For document-based apps (like Pages, Word, TextEdit), this might close the document but leave the application running if other documents are open. For apps like Safari or Finder, it closes the current tab or window. The application itself *usually remains running* (check for the dot under the Dock icon).

- Quitting an Application (Command + Q): This completely shuts down the application and all its associated windows and processes. Use this when you are finished working with an application to free up system resources.

Generally, use Hide (⌘ + H) for temporary clutter removal, Close Window (⌘ + W) when finished with a specific document or task within an app, and Quit (⌘ + Q) when you are completely done using the application for your current session. Avoid excessive minimizing if you find hiding works better for your flow.

Other Useful Tips

- **Keyboard Navigation:** Within dialog boxes or windows with multiple fields or buttons, often the Tab key will move focus between elements, Shift + Tab moves backward, and the Spacebar can "click" the highlighted button.

- **Trackpad Gestures:** Don't forget the gestures we discussed: swipe up for Mission Control, swipe left/right for Spaces/full-screen apps. Practice these until they become second nature. Check **System Settings > Trackpad** to review and customize all available gestures.

- **Combine Techniques:** The real power comes from mixing these methods. You might use Command + Tab to quickly switch to Safari, then Command + ~ to find the right Safari window, use a trackpad swipe to move that window to a different Space alongside your Notes app, and then use Option + Command + H to hide everything else for focused work.

Finding Your Flow

There's no single "right" way to manage windows and switch apps on macOS. The best approach depends on your personal preferences, the task at hand, and how many applications you typically juggle.

- **For simple task switching:** The Dock and Command + Tab might be sufficient.

- **For organizing different projects or contexts:** Mission Control and Spaces are excellent.

- **For focused side-by-side work:** Split View is ideal.

- **For keeping recent apps accessible while focusing:** Stage Manager offers a unique alternative.

- **For maximum speed and keyboard control:** Rely heavily on Command + Tab, Command + ~, Command + H, and Command + Q.

Experiment with all these tools and techniques provided in macOS Sequoia. Pay attention to which methods feel fastest and most intuitive for *you*. Building efficient window and application management habits will make using your powerful MacBook Air M4 an even more enjoyable and productive experience.

Staying Connected: Networking & Communication

Your MacBook Air M4 is a powerful machine, but its true potential is unlocked when it's connected – to the internet, to your peripherals, and to other people. macOS Sequoia provides robust and user-friendly ways to manage these connections. In this chapter, we'll cover the essentials of getting online with Wi-Fi (including the advanced Wi-Fi 6E capability of your M4 Air), pairing wireless accessories using Bluetooth, effortlessly sharing files with nearby Apple devices using AirDrop, and communicating through text, audio, and video using the built-in Messages and FaceTime apps, taking advantage of that upgraded 12MP Center Stage camera.

Connecting to Wi-Fi Networks (Leveraging Wi-Fi 6E)

Getting your MacBook Air online is usually the first step after setup. Wi-Fi (Wireless Fidelity) allows your Mac to connect to the internet and your local network without needing any physical cables, using radio waves broadcast by a wireless router.

Connecting to a Wi-Fi Network: Step-by-Step

There are a few easy ways to connect:

- **Using the Menu Bar (Quickest):**
  - Look for the **Wi-Fi icon** (looks like concentric arcs, like a fan) in the top-right corner of your Menu Bar.
  - Click the Wi-Fi icon. A dropdown menu will appear.
  - If Wi-Fi is off, click the toggle switch to turn it on.
  - The menu will list nearby available Wi-Fi networks under "Other Networks" or "Known Networks." Networks with a padlock icon require a password.
  - Click the name of the network you want to join.
  - If prompted, carefully enter the **network password** (sometimes called the WPA key or passphrase – it's often printed on your router). Check the "Show password" box if you want to see what you're typing.
  - Click **Join**.
  - If the connection is successful, the Wi-Fi icon in the Menu Bar will turn solid black (or white, depending on your theme), and the network name will have a checkmark next to it in the dropdown menu.

- **Using Control Center:**
  - Click the **Control Center icon** (two switches) in the Menu Bar.
  - Click the **Wi-Fi module**.
  - Ensure the Wi-Fi toggle at the top right of the module is blue (On).

- Click the arrow (>) next to the Wi-Fi text or the network name to expand the module.
- Select the desired network from the list and enter the password if required.

- **Using System Settings:**
  - Open **System Settings** (Gear icon in Dock or Apple menu □ > System Settings...).
  - Click **Wi-Fi** in the sidebar.
  - Make sure the **Wi-Fi toggle** at the top is switched On (green).
  - Your Mac will scan for networks. Find the desired network name under "Other Networks" or "Known Networks."
  - Click the network name. If it requires a password, a dialog box will appear. Enter the password and click **Join**.

Once connected, your Mac will usually remember the network and its password, automatically reconnecting whenever you're in range (unless you tell it not to).

Understanding Wi-Fi Status Icons

The Wi-Fi icon in your Menu Bar provides quick visual feedback:

Icon Appearance	Meaning
(Solid Black/White Arcs)	Connected to a Wi-Fi network. The fullness indicates signal strength.
(Empty Arcs Outline)	Wi-Fi is On, but not connected to any network.
(Arcs with Exclamation)	Problem connecting to the network.
(Grayed Out/Slash)	Wi-Fi is turned Off.
(Animating Arcs)	Actively searching for or connecting to a network.

Managing Known Networks

Your Mac keeps a list of networks you've previously joined. You can manage this list:

1. Go to **System Settings > Wi-Fi**.
2. Scroll down to the **Known Networks** section. You'll see networks you've joined before.

3. Click the **three dots (...)** button next to a network name for options:

   o **Forget This Network:** Removes the network and its password from your Mac's memory. You'll need to manually rejoin and re-enter the password next time. Useful for networks you no longer use or if connection details have changed.

   o **Auto-Join:** Toggle this On (default) to have your Mac automatically connect to this network when it's in range. Turn it Off if you prefer to connect manually (e.g., for a public network).

   o **Details...:** Opens a panel with more technical information about the network connection and options like TCP/IP settings (usually leave these on Automatic unless you know what you're doing).

4. **Preferred Network Order:** While macOS generally connects to the strongest known network, you can influence the preference slightly by managing the order, though this is less direct now. Forgetting less-preferred networks in a location with multiple known networks can help ensure connection to the desired one.

Leveraging Wi-Fi 6E on Your MacBook Air M4

Your MacBook Air M4 comes equipped with the latest generation of Wi-Fi technology: **Wi-Fi 6E**. But what does that mean for you?

1. **Wi-Fi Generations:** Think of Wi-Fi standards like generations of mobile networks (3G, 4G, 5G). Each new generation brings improvements in speed, capacity, and efficiency. You might have heard of Wi-Fi 5 (802.11ac) and Wi-Fi 6 (802.11ax). Wi-Fi 6E is an extension of Wi-Fi 6.

2. **The 6 GHz Advantage:** Previous Wi-Fi standards primarily used the 2.4 GHz and 5 GHz radio bands. These bands can get crowded with signals from your neighbors' networks, microwave ovens, Bluetooth devices, and older cordless phones, leading to interference and slower speeds. **Wi-Fi 6E introduces access to a brand new, wide-open 6 GHz frequency band.**

3. **Benefits of 6 GHz (with Wi-Fi 6E):**

   o **Less Interference:** Far fewer devices currently use the 6 GHz band, meaning significantly less congestion and interference, leading to a more stable connection.

   o **Higher Potential Speeds:** The wider channels available in the 6 GHz band allow for faster data transfer rates compared to the crowded 2.4 GHz and 5 GHz bands.

   o **Lower Latency:** Reduced interference and improved efficiency can lead to lower latency (less delay), which is beneficial for video calls, online gaming, and real-time applications.

4. **The Catch: You Need a Wi-Fi 6E Router!** To actually experience the benefits of Wi-Fi 6E and connect using the 6 GHz band, your **wireless router must also be a Wi-Fi 6E compatible router**. If you have an older router (Wi-Fi 5 or Wi-Fi 6 without the 'E'), your MacBook Air M4 will still connect perfectly fine using the 5 GHz or 2.4 GHz bands, but it won't be able to utilize the exclusive 6 GHz band. Think of it like having a car capable of high speeds – you still need a clear, open highway (the 6 GHz band provided by a 6E router) to reach those speeds.

If you have a Wi-Fi 6E router, your MacBook Air M4 should automatically connect using the 6 GHz band when appropriate for the best performance. There isn't usually a specific setting you need to change on the Mac itself, beyond simply connecting to the Wi-Fi 6E network broadcast by your router.

Basic Wi-Fi Troubleshooting

If you're having trouble connecting:

1. **Check the Basics:** Is Wi-Fi turned on (check Menu Bar/Control Center)? Are you selecting the correct network name? Are you typing the password correctly (case-sensitive)?

2. **Toggle Wi-Fi:** Turn Wi-Fi off on your Mac, wait a few seconds, then turn it back on.

3. **Restart:** Restart your MacBook Air. Also, try restarting your Wi-Fi router (unplug it from power, wait 30 seconds, plug it back in, wait a few minutes for it to fully boot up).

4. **Forget and Rejoin:** Forget the network in System Settings > Wi-Fi > Known Networks, then try connecting again as if it were a new network.

5. **Check Range:** Ensure you're within reasonable range of your Wi-Fi router. Walls and distance weaken the signal.

6. **Run Wireless Diagnostics:** Hold down the **Option (⌥)** key on your keyboard and *then* click the Wi-Fi icon in the Menu Bar. You'll see extra options, including **Open Wireless Diagnostics....** Follow the on-screen instructions for a more in-depth check of your connection.

Getting connected via Wi-Fi is usually straightforward, and with Wi-Fi 6E support, your M4 Air is ready for the next generation of wireless performance when paired with compatible network hardware.

Pairing and Managing Bluetooth Devices (Keyboards, Mice, Headphones)

Bluetooth is a wireless technology designed for connecting devices over short distances. It's perfect for peripherals like wireless keyboards, mice, trackpads, headphones, speakers, game controllers, and even for features like Handoff and AirDrop between Apple devices. Bluetooth is generally very power-efficient, making it ideal for battery-powered accessories. Your MacBook Air M4 has the latest Bluetooth 5.3 standard built-in.

Turning Bluetooth On or Off

You need Bluetooth enabled on your Mac to connect to Bluetooth devices.

- **Control Center:** Click the Control Center icon in the Menu Bar, then click the **Bluetooth module** to toggle it On (blue) or Off (gray).

- **Menu Bar Icon (If Added):** If you've added the Bluetooth icon to your Menu Bar (via System Settings > Control Center), click it to toggle On/Off or access connected devices.

- **System Settings:** Go to **System Settings > Bluetooth** and use the main toggle switch at the top.

Pairing a New Bluetooth Device

"Pairing" is the process of establishing a secure, initial connection between your Mac and a new Bluetooth device.

1. **Make the Device Discoverable:** First, put your Bluetooth device (keyboard, mouse, headphones, etc.) into **pairing mode** or **discoverable mode**. The exact steps vary greatly depending on the device – you'll need to **consult the device's manual**. Often, it involves pressing and holding a specific button until a light starts flashing in a particular way.

2. **Open Bluetooth Settings on Mac:** Go to **System Settings > Bluetooth**. Make sure Bluetooth is turned On.

3. **Wait for Discovery:** Your Mac will automatically scan for nearby discoverable Bluetooth devices. Wait a few moments for your device to appear in the **"Nearby Devices"** list. It should show the device's name (e.g., "Logitech MX Master 3S," "AirPods Pro," "Bose QuietComfort 45").

4. **Connect:** Once your device appears, click the **Connect** button next to its name.

5. **Follow Prompts (If Any):**

   o For some devices (like keyboards), your Mac might display a numeric code (passkey) on the screen and ask you to type that same code on the Bluetooth keyboard itself, followed by pressing Enter/Return on the Bluetooth keyboard to complete the pairing.

o   For other devices, you might just see a confirmation on the Mac or the device itself. AirPods and Beats headphones with Apple chips often have an even simpler pairing process when near devices signed into your iCloud account.

6. **Paired!** Once successfully paired, the device will move from "Nearby Devices" to the "My Devices" list and show a "Connected" status. Your wireless keyboard, mouse, or headphones should now be working with your Mac.

Managing Paired and Connected Devices

Once a device is paired, it's remembered by your Mac. You can manage these devices in **System Settings > Bluetooth**:

1. **Connecting/Disconnecting:** Paired devices don't always connect automatically (especially headphones or speakers). In the "My Devices" list, find the device. If it's disconnected, there might be a "Connect" button next to it. If it's already connected, hover over it, and a "Disconnect" button might appear. You can also often right-click (Control-click) the device name for Connect/Disconnect options.

2. **Device Options (Info Icon):** Click the small circled 'i' icon next to a device name in the "My Devices" list to see more options:

   o   **Name:** You can sometimes rename the device as it appears on your Mac (e.g., rename "WH-1000XM4" to "My Sony Headphones").

   o   **Disconnect:** Temporarily disconnects the device.

   o   **Forget This Device...:** This *unpairs* the device completely. It removes it from your Mac's memory. If you want to use it again, you'll need to go through the full pairing process from the beginning. Use this if you're giving the device away, selling it, or having persistent connection problems that other troubleshooting hasn't fixed.

   o   **Device-Specific Options:** Depending on the device type (especially Apple devices like AirPods), you might see additional options here, such as controls for noise cancellation, spatial audio, microphone settings, or automatic switching behavior.

3. **Battery Level:** For many Bluetooth devices (especially mice, keyboards, headphones), their battery level is displayed next to their name in the Bluetooth settings list when connected. You might also be able to add a Battery widget to your Notification Center or see it by adding the Bluetooth icon to your Menu Bar.

Adding the Bluetooth Menu Bar Icon

For quick access to Bluetooth status and connected devices without opening System Settings:

1. Go to **System Settings > Control Center**.
2. Scroll down to the **Other Modules** section.
3. Find **Bluetooth**.
4. Use the dropdown menu next to it to select **"Show in Menu Bar"**.
5. The Bluetooth icon (stylized 'B') will now appear in your Menu Bar. Clicking it shows connection status, lists nearby/connected devices (with battery levels), and allows quick connecting/disconnecting or opening Bluetooth settings.

Common Bluetooth Peripherals	Examples	Primary Use
Keyboards	Apple Magic Keyboard, Logitech MX Keys	Wireless typing
Mice	Apple Magic Mouse, Logitech MX Master	Wireless pointing and clicking
Trackpads	Apple Magic Trackpad	Wireless multi-touch gestures, pointing
Headphones/Earbuds	AirPods, Beats, Bose, Sony, etc.	Wireless audio listening, microphone for calls
Speakers	Portable Bluetooth speakers, soundbars	Wireless audio playback
Game Controllers	PlayStation DualSense, Xbox Wireless Controller	Playing games on Mac
Phones/Tablets	iPhone, iPad, Android devices	File transfer (limited), Personal Hotspot
Other	Fitness trackers, styluses (for iPad Sidecar)	Data syncing, specific functionalities

Basic Bluetooth Troubleshooting

Wireless connections can sometimes be finicky. If your Bluetooth device isn't connecting or working properly:

1. **Check Power & Range:** Ensure the Bluetooth device is turned on, sufficiently charged, and within range of your Mac (typically around 10 meters / 30 feet, but walls can interfere).

2. **Toggle Bluetooth:** Turn Bluetooth off on your Mac (via Control Center or System Settings), wait a few seconds, and turn it back on. Do the same on the Bluetooth device itself if possible.

3. **Check Connection Status:** Look in System Settings > Bluetooth. Is the device listed under "My Devices"? Does it say "Connected"? If not, try clicking "Connect."

4. **Interference:** Other wireless devices (microwaves, older cordless phones, even some USB 3.0 devices) can potentially interfere with Bluetooth. Try moving devices around or temporarily turning off other wireless equipment.

5. **Forget and Re-pair:** If problems persist, try unpairing the device. Click the 'i' icon next to it in Bluetooth settings and choose "Forget This Device...". Then, put the device back into pairing mode and go through the initial pairing process again.

6. **Restart Your Mac:** A simple restart can often resolve temporary glitches.

7. **Check for Software Updates:** Ensure both macOS and your Bluetooth device's firmware (if applicable) are up to date.

Bluetooth makes it easy to declutter your desk and enjoy wireless freedom with your favorite accessories on your MacBook Air M4.

Seamless File Sharing with AirDrop

Need to quickly send a photo from your Mac to a friend's iPhone? Or maybe transfer a document from your iPad to your MacBook Air without emailing it or using a USB drive? **AirDrop** is Apple's magical solution for effortless, direct, wireless file sharing between nearby Apple devices. It uses a combination of Bluetooth and Wi-Fi, making it fast and convenient, and it doesn't require an internet connection between the devices.

How AirDrop Works (The Simple Version)

1. **Discovery:** AirDrop uses Bluetooth Low Energy (BLE) to broadcast and discover other AirDrop-enabled Apple devices nearby.

2. **Connection:** When you choose to send a file, the devices establish a direct peer-to-peer Wi-Fi connection between themselves. This makes the actual file transfer very fast, even for large files.

3. **Security:** The connection is encrypted, and Apple uses identifiers linked to your Apple ID (for Contacts Only mode) or device information to manage discovery securely.

Setting Your AirDrop Discoverability

Before others can send files *to* you via AirDrop, you need to decide who can "see" your Mac. This is an important privacy setting.

You can adjust your discoverability in two main places:

1. **Control Center:**
   - Open Control Center (click the two-switches icon in the Menu Bar).
   - Click the **AirDrop module**.
   - Choose one of the three options:
     - **Receiving Off:** Your Mac won't be visible to anyone trying to share via AirDrop. You can still *send* files, however.
     - **Contacts Only:** Only people who are in your Contacts app (and whose Apple ID email or phone number is listed in your contact card for them, and vice-versa for them having your info) can see your Mac when they try to AirDrop. This is generally the recommended setting for privacy. Both devices usually need to be signed into iCloud.
     - **Everyone for 10 Minutes:** For the next 10 minutes, *any* nearby Apple device using AirDrop will be able to see your Mac. After 10 minutes, it automatically reverts to "Contacts Only" (or "Receiving Off" if that was your previous setting). Use this setting temporarily when you need to receive a file from someone not in your contacts.

2. **Finder:**
   - Open a Finder window.
   - Click **AirDrop** in the Favorites section of the Sidebar (or choose **Go > AirDrop** from the Menu Bar).
   - At the bottom of the AirDrop window, you'll see the text "Allow me to be discovered by:" followed by the same three options (No One, Contacts Only, Everyone). Click the blue text to change the setting.

AirDrop Discoverability	Who Can See Your Mac	Recommended Use
Receiving Off / No One	Nobody	When you don't want to receive any AirDrop files.
Contacts Only	People in your Contacts	Everyday use for best privacy among known contacts.
Everyone for 10 Minutes	Anyone nearby	Temporarily, to receive from someone not in contacts.

Sending Files and Content with AirDrop

Sharing from your Mac using AirDrop is integrated into many apps and the Finder itself.

1. **Select the Item(s):** Find the file, photo, document, web link, contact card, or other piece of content you want to share. You can select multiple items in Finder.

2. **Initiate Sharing:** Do one of the following:
   - **Right-Click (Control-Click):** Right-click the selected item(s), hover over the **Share** submenu, and choose **AirDrop**.
   - **Share Button (Toolbar/App):** Click the **Share button** (looks like a square with an arrow pointing up) in the Finder toolbar or within the application (e.g., Photos, Safari, Contacts). Choose **AirDrop** from the sharing options.
   - **Finder AirDrop Window:** Open the AirDrop window in Finder (Go > AirDrop or click in Sidebar). Drag the file(s) directly onto the icon of the recipient device shown in the window.

3. **Choose the Recipient:** An AirDrop sheet or window will appear, showing nearby discoverable Apple devices represented by circles with the user's name, device name, or profile picture. Click the circle representing the person/device you want to send to.

4. **Wait for Acceptance:** The recipient will receive a notification on their device asking them to Accept or Decline the transfer (unless you are sending between your *own* devices signed into the same Apple ID, in which case it often transfers automatically without prompting). On your Mac, you'll see a "Waiting..." status under their icon, which changes to "Sending..." once they accept. A progress bar appears for larger files. You'll get a "Sent" confirmation when it's complete.

Receiving Files with AirDrop

When someone sends you a file via AirDrop:

1. **Notification:** A notification will pop up on your Mac screen (usually in the top-right corner) showing a preview of the file (if possible) and who is sending it.

2. **Accept or Decline:** You'll have buttons to **Accept** or **Decline** the transfer.

3. **Saving:** If you click **Accept**, the file transfer begins. Once complete, the file is automatically saved to your **Downloads** folder. Finder might even open a window showing you the downloaded file. If a web link or contact card is sent, it might offer to open directly in Safari or Contacts.

Troubleshooting Common AirDrop Issues

Sometimes AirDrop doesn't seem to work. Here are the most common things to check on *both* the sending and receiving devices:

1. **Wi-Fi and Bluetooth On:** Ensure both Wi-Fi and Bluetooth are turned on for both devices, even if not connected to a specific network. AirDrop uses both technologies.

2. **Discoverability Settings:** Double-check the "Allow me to be discovered by" setting on the *receiving* device. If it's set to "Contacts Only," ensure both parties are logged into iCloud and have each other's correct Apple ID email/phone number in their respective Contacts apps. Try setting both devices to "Everyone" temporarily to see if discovery works.

3. **Proximity:** Make sure the devices are relatively close to each other, ideally within about 9 meters (30 feet) and not separated by thick walls.

4. **Devices Awake:** Ensure both devices are awake with their screens on. AirDrop often doesn't work if one device is asleep.

5. **Personal Hotspot Off:** Sometimes, having Personal Hotspot enabled on either device can interfere with AirDrop. Try turning it off temporarily.

6. **Firewall Settings (Mac):** On the receiving Mac, go to **System Settings > Network > Firewall**. If the firewall is On, click "Options..." and ensure that "Block all incoming connections" is *unchecked*, and check if "Automatically allow built-in software to receive incoming connections" and "Automatically allow downloaded signed software to receive incoming connections" are checked. You might need to specifically allow sharingd if issues persist.

7. **Restart Devices:** A simple restart of both devices can often resolve temporary glitches.

AirDrop is a remarkably simple and efficient way to move files between your Apple ecosystem devices, saving you the hassle of cables, emails, or cloud uploads for quick transfers.

Communicating via Messages and FaceTime (Utilizing the 12MP Center Stage Camera)

Beyond file sharing, your MacBook Air M4 is a fantastic communication hub, thanks to the built-in **Messages** and **FaceTime** applications, tightly integrated with macOS and iCloud. You can seamlessly continue text conversations from your iPhone, or make high-quality video calls leveraging the significantly upgraded camera hardware in your M4 Air.

Messages: More Than Just Text

The Messages app lets you send and receive text messages, photos, videos, audio clips, and more. It supports two main types of messaging:

- **iMessage (Blue Bubbles):** This is Apple's own secure messaging service that works over Wi-Fi or cellular data between Apple devices (Macs, iPhones, iPads, Apple Watches). iMessages offer features like end-to-end encryption, read receipts, typing indicators, message effects (balloons, lasers!), Tapback reactions (like a thumbs-up on a message), and higher quality media sharing. You need to be signed in with your Apple ID to use iMessage.

- **SMS/MMS (Green Bubbles):** These are standard cellular text messages (SMS for text, MMS for multimedia like photos). Messages on your Mac can send and receive these *if* you have an iPhone and set up **Text Message Forwarding**. This routes the standard texts through your iPhone to appear in the Messages app on your Mac.

Setting Up Messages:

1. Launch the Messages app (speech bubble icon in Dock/Applications).

2. If prompted, sign in with the **Apple ID** you use for iMessage on your other devices. Enable syncing in iCloud settings if needed (System Settings > [Your Name] > iCloud > Show All > Messages in iCloud > Sync this Mac).

3. **To enable SMS/MMS:** On your **iPhone**, go to **Settings > Messages > Text Message Forwarding**. You should see your MacBook Air listed. Turn the toggle On for your Mac. You might need to enter a confirmation code displayed on your Mac into your iPhone.

Using Messages:

1. **Interface:** The main window shows a list of your conversations in the left sidebar and the selected conversation's chat history in the main pane on the right.

2. **Starting a New Conversation:** Click the **Compose button** (pencil in a square) near the top of the sidebar. In the "To:" field, start typing a contact's name, phone number, or email address associated with their iMessage account. Select the contact from the suggestions.

3. **Sending:** Type your message in the input field at the bottom and press Return.

  o **Photos/Videos:** Drag files directly into the input field or click the App Store icon next to the input field to access photos or other iMessage apps.

  o **Tapbacks:** Right-click (Control-click) a message bubble you received and choose "Tapback..." to react with a heart, thumbs up/down, Ha Ha, !!, or ?.

  o **Effects:** Type your message, then click and *hold* the blue Send arrow (for iMessage). You can choose Bubble effects (Slam, Loud, Gentle, Invisible Ink) or Screen effects (Balloons, Confetti, Lasers, etc.).

  o **Audio Messages:** Click the audio wave icon next to the input field, record your message, and send.

4. **Managing Conversations:**

  o **Pinning:** Right-click a conversation in the sidebar and choose "Pin." Pinned chats stay at the top for easy access.

  o **Muting:** Right-click a conversation and choose "Hide Alerts" to silence notifications for that specific chat.

  o **Group Chats:** Add multiple people to the "To:" field to start a group chat. For iMessage groups, you can name the group, add/remove people (if everyone is using iMessage), and mention people (@Name).

  o **Searching:** Use the search bar at the top of the sidebar to find specific text within your conversations.

FaceTime: High-Quality Video and Audio Calls

FaceTime is Apple's service for making free, high-quality video and audio calls to other Apple device users over Wi-Fi or cellular data.

Making and Receiving Calls:

1. Launch the FaceTime app (green icon with a white video camera).

2. Sign in with your Apple ID if prompted.

3. To make a call:

  o Click "New FaceTime."

  o Enter the name, email address, or phone number of the person(s) you want to call in the entry field. You can add multiple people for a Group FaceTime call.

  o Click the green **FaceTime** button (choose Audio or Video if prompted, or click the specific icons).

4. To receive a call: A notification will appear on your screen. Click **Accept** to answer or **Decline** to reject the call. You might also see options to reply with a message.

Leveraging the M4 Air's 12MP Center Stage Camera

Your MacBook Air M4 features a significant camera upgrade to a **12 Megapixel Ultra Wide camera**. This enables a fantastic feature called **Center Stage**.

- **What is Center Stage?** During a FaceTime video call (and in some other video conferencing apps that support it), Center Stage uses the ultra-wide camera lens and machine learning (powered by the M4 chip's Neural Engine) to automatically keep you **centered in the frame**. If you move around slightly, the camera digitally pans and zooms to follow you. If someone else joins you in front of the camera, Center Stage intelligently zooms out to include them in the shot as well.

- **Benefits:** It makes video calls feel much more dynamic and natural. You don't have to worry about staying perfectly still in front of the camera. It ensures you (and anyone with you) are always well-framed for the person on the other end.

- **Control:** Center Stage is usually enabled by default for FaceTime. You can typically toggle it (and other video effects) on or off during a call by clicking the **Video icon** that appears in your Menu Bar when the camera is active, then selecting Center Stage under the Effects section.

Video Effects and Audio Modes (macOS Sequoia)

macOS Sequoia enhances video calls further:

- **Video Effects:** Access these via the Video icon in the Menu Bar during a call:
  - **Portrait Mode:** Blurs the background, keeping you in sharp focus (similar to Portrait mode on iPhone photos).
  - **Studio Light:** Dims the background slightly and brightens your face for a more professional look.
  - **Reactions:** Use hand gestures (like making a heart shape with your hands, giving a thumbs up/down, peace sign) to trigger fun full-screen animations like hearts, fireworks, rain, etc. You can also click icons in the Video menu to trigger them manually.

- **Microphone Modes:** Access these via the **Microphone icon** in Control Center during a call:
  - **Standard:** Default microphone behavior.
  - **Voice Isolation:** Prioritizes your voice and significantly reduces background noise (like vacuum cleaners, dogs barking). Excellent for noisy environments.
  - **Wide Spectrum:** Captures more ambient sound, useful if multiple people are talking near the Mac or you want to capture environmental audio like music playing in the room.

Feature	Description	Benefit
Center Stage	Camera automatically pans/zooms to keep you centered.	More natural calls; no need to stay perfectly still; includes others nearby.
Portrait Mode	Blurs the background during video calls.	Focuses attention on you, hides messy backgrounds.
Studio Light	Dims background, illuminates your face.	Creates a more professional lighting look, even in poor lighting.
Reactions	Trigger screen effects (hearts, thumbs up, etc.) with hand gestures or clicks.	Adds fun and expressiveness to video calls.
Voice Isolation	Mic mode that suppresses background noise.	Clearer audio for the listener, even in noisy places.
Wide Spectrum	Mic mode that captures more ambient sound.	Useful for group calls around one Mac or sharing environmental audio.

Other FaceTime Features:

- **Screen Sharing:** During a call, click the Screen Sharing button to share your entire screen or just a specific application window with the person(s) you're talking to. Great for collaboration or getting tech support.

- **SharePlay:** Watch movies, listen to music, or even use compatible apps together *in sync* during a FaceTime call. Start playing content in a supported app (like Apple TV+, Music), and you'll see an option to SharePlay it. Playback controls are shared.

- **FaceTime Links:** Want to invite people who don't have Apple devices (or aren't in your contacts) to a call? Open FaceTime, click "Create Link," and share that web link. Participants can join via their web browser on Android or Windows devices.

- **Handoff:** Seamlessly transfer an ongoing FaceTime call between your Mac and your iPhone or iPad. Just open the FaceTime app on the other device, and you should see an option to switch the call over.

With Messages handling your texts and iMessages, and FaceTime providing high-quality audio/video calls enhanced by the M4 Air's superior camera and macOS Sequoia's effects, your MacBook Air is a powerful communication tool connecting you to colleagues, friends, and family.

Media Consumption & Entertainment

Beyond productivity, your MacBook Air M4 is a fantastic device for enjoying music, movies, TV shows, podcasts, audiobooks, and ebooks. macOS Sequoia includes dedicated apps designed to manage and play your media content seamlessly, often syncing your libraries and progress across all your Apple devices via iCloud. In this chapter, we'll explore the Music app for your tunes, the TV app for visual entertainment, the Podcasts app for your favorite shows, and the Books app for both ebooks and audiobooks. Let's dive into how you can relax and be entertained.

Managing and Enjoying Your Music Library with the Music App

Whether you have a vast collection of digital music files accumulated over years, purchase tracks from the iTunes Store, or subscribe to the Apple Music streaming service, the **Music** app is your central hub for listening on your Mac.

Launching Music and the Interface

Find the Music app icon (a musical note, often red or white) in your Dock or Applications folder. The main window presents a clean interface, typically structured like this:

- **Sidebar (Left):** Your main navigation area, divided into sections:
  - **Library:** Contains music you own or have added to your personal collection. Subsections include Recently Added, Artists, Albums, Songs, Genres, Compilations, Composers, Music Videos, Home Sharing.
  - **Store:** Provides access to the iTunes Store for purchasing music tracks or albums (if you prefer owning files over streaming).
  - **Apple Music (If Subscribed):** Sections dedicated to the streaming service appear here, such as Listen Now (personalized recommendations), Browse (discover new releases, charts, genres), and Radio (live stations like Apple Music 1 and algorithmic stations).
  - **Devices:** Shows connected devices like iPhones or iPads if you manage their music syncing manually (less common now with iCloud Music Library).
  - **Playlists:** All your created playlists (standard and Smart) and playlist folders are listed here.
- **Main Content Area (Center/Right):** Displays the content based on your selection in the Sidebar (e.g., list of songs, album grid, playlist tracks, Apple Music recommendations).
- **Playback Controls & Up Next (Top):** At the very top, you'll find:
  - Standard playback controls: Play/Pause, Previous/Next Track buttons.
  - Volume slider.

- Now Playing area: Shows the current track/artist/album art. Clicking the album art often reveals the Up Next queue and playback history.
- AirPlay button (looks like a triangle pointing into concentric circles): Stream audio to compatible speakers, Apple TVs, or other Macs.
- Lyrics button (speech bubble with quotes): Shows time-synced lyrics for supported songs (primarily from Apple Music).
- Up Next button (three dots and lines): Shows the queue of upcoming songs.

- **Search Bar (Top Left of Sidebar):** Search your Library, Apple Music, or the iTunes Store.

Building Your Music Library

There are several ways to populate your Music app:

1. **Importing Existing Files:** If you have music files (like MP3, AAC, ALAC, WAV, AIFF) already on your Mac or an external drive:
   - Go to **File > Import...** and navigate to the folder containing your music files. Select the files/folders and click Open.
   - Alternatively, simply **drag and drop** the music files or folders directly from Finder into the main Music app window (onto the Library section in the Sidebar or the Songs list).
   - **Organization Settings:** By default, Music might copy imported files into its designated media folder and keep it organized. You can check/change these settings in **Music > Settings... > Files**. Options include "Keep Music Media folder organized" and "Copy files to Music Media folder when adding to library." Keeping these checked usually results in a tidier library structure managed by the app.

2. **Purchasing from the iTunes Store:** Click **Store** in the Sidebar. You can browse or search for music and purchase individual tracks or albums using your Apple ID. Purchased music automatically appears in your Library.

3. **Adding from Apple Music (Subscription Required):** If you subscribe to Apple Music:
   - **Adding:** Browse the vast streaming catalog in the Browse or Listen Now sections. When you find a song, album, or playlist you like, click the **plus (+) button** or the **"Add"** button. This adds it to your personal Music Library section for easy access alongside your owned music. Note that this *doesn't* download the file by default; it just links the streaming version to your library.
   - **Downloading:** To listen offline, you need to download the added Apple Music tracks. Click the **download icon (cloud with a downward arrow)** that appears next to a song, album, or playlist after you've added it to your library. Downloaded tracks can be played even without an internet connection.

Playing Your Music

- **Basic Playback:** Double-click a song, album, or playlist to start playing. Use the **playback controls** at the top of the window to Play/Pause, skip tracks (Command + Right/Left Arrow), adjust volume, etc.

- **Shuffle & Repeat:** Buttons for Shuffle (play tracks in random order) and Repeat (repeat one song or the current album/playlist) are usually located near the playback controls or in the Now Playing/Up Next view.

- **Up Next Queue:** Click the **Up Next button (three dots and lines)** to see what songs are scheduled to play next. You can drag songs within this queue to reorder them, remove songs, or clear the queue. You can also add songs or albums to play next or later by right-clicking them and choosing "Play Next" or "Play Later."

- **AirPlay:** Click the **AirPlay icon** to stream the audio output to compatible devices on your network, like HomePods, Apple TV, Sonos speakers, or other AirPlay-enabled receivers.

- **Lyrics:** For many songs (especially on Apple Music), clicking the **Lyrics button (speech bubble)** displays time-synced lyrics that scroll along with the music, perfect for sing-alongs.

- **Spatial Audio & Lossless (Apple Music):** If you subscribe to Apple Music and have compatible hardware (like AirPods Pro/Max or using the MacBook Air M4's built-in speakers with supported content), you can experience **Spatial Audio with Dolby Atmos**, which creates an immersive, three-dimensional soundstage. Apple Music also offers **Lossless Audio** for higher fidelity sound quality. You can manage these settings in **Music > Settings... > Playback**.

Organizing with Playlists

Playlists are essential for curating your music for different moods, activities, or genres.

- **Standard Playlists:**
  - Go to **File > New > Playlist** (or Command + N).
  - Give your playlist a name in the Sidebar.
  - Find songs or albums you want to add (from your Library or Apple Music) and simply **drag them** onto the playlist name in the Sidebar.
  - You can drag songs within the playlist view to reorder them.

- **Smart Playlists:** These automatically populate based on rules you define.
  - Go to **File > New > Smart Playlist...** (Option + Command + N).
  - Define criteria using the dropdown menus (e.g., "Genre" contains "Rock," "Year" is "1990-1999," "Play Count" is greater than "10," "Rating" is 5 stars).
  - Add multiple rules using the '+' button and specify if *All* or *Any* rules must match.

- You can limit the playlist by number of items, total time, or size, and choose how items are selected (e.g., random, most recently added).
- Check "Live updating" to have the playlist automatically refresh as your library changes.
- Click OK and give the Smart Playlist a name. Examples: "Top Rated Rock," "Recently Added Jazz," "Workout Mix."

- **Playlist Folders:** If you have many playlists, you can group them into folders. Go to **File > New > Playlist Folder**. Drag existing playlists into the folder in the Sidebar.
- **Collaborative Playlists (Apple Music):** You can invite friends who also subscribe to Apple Music to add, remove, and reorder songs in a shared playlist. Create a standard playlist, then click the collaboration icon (person with a plus) to get a sharing link or invite contacts.

Music App Section/Feature	Description	Key Use
Library (Artists, Albums, Songs)	Music you own (imported/purchased) or added from Apple Music.	Accessing your personal music collection.
Store	iTunes Store for purchasing music.	Buying music tracks/albums to own permanently.
Apple Music (Listen Now, Browse, Radio)	Streaming service features (requires subscription).	Discovering new music, listening to curated playlists, radio stations.
Playlists	User-created lists of songs (Standard, Smart, Collaborative).	Curating music for specific moods, activities, genres, or sharing with friends.
Up Next Queue	The list of songs scheduled to play next.	Seeing and modifying the upcoming playback order.
AirPlay	Wirelessly stream audio to compatible speakers/devices.	Listening on better speakers or multi-room audio.
Spatial Audio/Lossless	Enhanced audio formats (requires Apple Music & compatible hardware).	Immersive 3D sound (Spatial) or higher fidelity audio (Lossless).

The Music app provides a comprehensive way to manage and enjoy your entire music world, whether it's files you've collected over years or the vast catalog available through Apple Music.

Watching Movies and Shows with the TV App

Just as the Music app handles your audio, the **TV** app is Apple's central destination for visual entertainment on your Mac. It brings together movies and TV shows you've purchased or rented from Apple, content from the **Apple TV+** subscription service, and access to other streaming services via **Apple TV Channels**.

Launching the TV App and the Interface

Open the TV app (black icon with a white Apple logo and 'TV') from your Dock or Applications folder. The interface is designed for browsing and watching:

- **Sidebar (Left, optional - can be hidden):** Provides primary navigation:
  - **Search Bar:** Find specific movies, shows, actors, or genres.
  - **Watch Now:** Your personalized hub, featuring the "Up Next" queue and recommendations.
  - **Apple TV+:** Dedicated section for Apple's original streaming content (requires subscription).
  - **Store:** Browse, buy, or rent movies and TV shows.
  - **Library:** Access all your purchased and rented content.
  - **Channels & Apps:** Sections for Apple TV Channels you subscribe to or links to integrated third-party apps.
- **Main Content Area (Center/Right):** Displays content based on your Sidebar selection – rows of recommendations, featured items, your library grid, etc.
- **Up Next Queue (Prominently in Watch Now):** This dynamic row shows movies you've started or TV show episodes you're currently watching, making it easy to resume playback right where you left off across all your devices signed into the same Apple ID.

Ways to Watch

The TV app consolidates several types of content:

1. **Your Library:** Click **Library** in the Sidebar to see all the movies and TV shows you have purchased or rented from Apple (previously the iTunes Store). Content is usually categorized by Movies, TV Shows, Recently Purchased, Genres, etc. Click an item to see its details page and play button.

2. **Apple TV+:** If you subscribe to Apple TV+, clicking this section reveals all the exclusive original series (like Ted Lasso, Severance, Foundation) and films available through the service. Browse by genre or featured collections. Click a show or movie to start watching.

3. **Store:** Click **Store** to browse the vast catalog of movies and TV shows available for purchase or rent. You can browse new releases, top charts, collections, deals, and different genres. Clicking an item takes you to its product page with trailers, descriptions, cast/crew info, Rotten Tomatoes scores, and Buy/Rent options. Rented movies typically give you 30 days to start watching and 48 hours to finish once started.

4. **Apple TV Channels:** Apple allows you to subscribe to certain third-party streaming services *directly within* the TV app (availability varies significantly by region – check the Store or Channels section). Examples might include Paramount+, Starz, MUBI, etc. If you subscribe via Channels, that service's content integrates directly into your Watch Now feed and library, offering a unified viewing experience without needing separate apps for those specific services.

Playback Experience

When you start playing a movie or show:

1. **Playback Controls:** Standard controls appear when you move your cursor: Play/Pause, scrubbable timeline, volume slider, skip forward/backward 10 seconds buttons.

2. **Subtitles and Audio Options:** Look for a speech bubble or gear icon in the playback controls. This lets you select different audio languages, turn on subtitles or closed captions (SDH), and choose audio output devices (like connected AirPods or speakers via AirPlay).

3. **Picture Quality (4K, HDR):** The TV app supports high-quality video formats. If the content is available in 4K, HDR10, HDR10+, or Dolby Vision, and your MacBook Air M4's display supports it (which it generally does for HDR), the app will attempt to play it in the best possible quality for your screen. Quality might also depend on your internet speed and playback settings.

4. **Spatial Audio (Dolby Atmos):** For content mastered with Dolby Atmos and when using compatible audio hardware (like third-generation AirPods, AirPods Pro, AirPods Max, or even the M4 Air's built-in speakers in many cases), you can experience immersive Spatial Audio. This creates a surround-sound-like effect where sound seems to come from all around you, even above. Look for the Dolby Atmos logo on the content's detail page. You can manage Spatial Audio settings related to AirPods in Bluetooth settings, and sometimes audio track selection in the TV app's playback controls.

5. **Downloads for Offline Viewing:** Want to watch on the go without internet? For most purchased content, rentals (after starting playback), and Apple TV+ shows/movies, you'll see a **download icon (cloud with downward arrow)** on the item's detail page or next to an episode listing. Click it to download the video file to your Mac's storage. Downloaded items appear in the Library

section and can be played offline. Manage downloads and quality settings in TV > Settings... > Playback.

Content Source in TV App	Description	Access Requirement	Offline Viewing?
Library	Movies & TV shows purchased or rented from Apple.	Purchase/Rental via Apple ID	Yes (Purchased)
Apple TV+	Apple Original series and films.	Active Apple TV+ subscription	Yes
Store	Catalog of movies & TV shows available to buy or rent.	Apple ID for transactions	Yes (Rentals limited time)
Apple TV Channels	Third-party streaming services subscribed to *within* the TV app.	Separate subscription fee for each channel	Often Yes (depends on channel)
Up Next Queue	Dynamic list tracking shows/movies you're currently watching.	Based on your viewing activity across linked services	N/A

The TV app aims to be your one-stop shop for premium video content, offering a unified library, high-quality playback features, and access to both purchased media and streaming services like Apple TV+.

Listening to Podcasts and Audiobooks

For spoken-word entertainment and information, macOS provides the dedicated **Podcasts** app and integrates audiobook playback into the **Books** app.

Podcasts App: Your Gateway to Shows

The Podcasts app makes it easy to discover, subscribe to, and listen to hundreds of thousands of free podcasts on countless topics.

- **Interface:** Similar to Music, it features:
    - **Sidebar (Left):** Library sections (Listen Now, Shows you Follow, Saved Episodes, Downloaded Episodes), plus options to browse Channels (groups of shows from creators) and Categories.
    - **Main Content Area:** Displays recommendations in Listen Now, featured shows in Browse, top charts, or the episodes of a selected show.
    - **Search Bar (Top Left):** Search for specific shows, episodes, or topics.

- **Playback Controls (Top):** Play/Pause, skip forward/backward (customizable duration), volume, AirPlay, playback speed, sleep timer.

- **Finding and Following Shows:**
  - **Browse:** Explore curated collections and categories.
  - **Top Charts:** See what's popular.
  - **Search:** Look for shows by name, host, or topic.
  - **Follow:** When you find a show you like, click the **"Follow"** button (often a plus '+' sign or explicitly says Follow) on its page. New episodes will then automatically appear in your Listen Now feed and the Shows section. Following is free. Some podcasts might offer paid subscriptions via Apple Podcasts Subscriptions for bonus content or ad-free listening, which would be clearly indicated.

- **Listening to Episodes:**
  - Click an episode in Listen Now, from a Show's page, or from the Saved/Downloaded sections to start playing.
  - Use the playback controls at the top: adjust **playback speed** (e.g., 1.5x, 2x), set a **sleep timer** to automatically stop playback after a certain duration, skip ahead or back (usually 15 or 30 seconds).
  - **Up Next Queue:** Like Music, Podcasts maintains an Up Next queue. You can see it by clicking the queue button (three dots and lines) near the playback controls. Add episodes manually or let it auto-play from a show.
  - **Downloading Episodes:** To listen offline, click the **download icon (cloud with arrow)** next to an episode listing, or configure a show's settings (click the '...' button on a show page > Settings...) to automatically download new episodes. Downloaded episodes appear in the Downloaded section.

- **Managing Your Library:**
  - **Unfollow:** Go to the Shows section, right-click a show, and choose "Unfollow Show."
  - **Saved Episodes:** Click the bookmark icon on an episode to save it for easy access later in the Saved section.
  - **Managing Downloads:** Control automatic downloads per show or manually delete played/unneeded episodes from the Downloaded section or within System Settings > General > Storage > Manage...

Podcasts sync your followed shows, episode playback positions, and saved episodes across your devices via iCloud.

Audiobooks (in the Books App)

Unlike podcasts, audiobooks purchased from Apple are managed and played within the **Books** app (which we'll cover fully next). There isn't a separate Audiobooks app on macOS.

- **Finding Your Audiobooks:** Open the **Books** app. Look for the **Audiobooks** section in the Sidebar or Library view. All audiobooks purchased with your Apple ID will appear here.

- **The Audiobook Player:** When you click an audiobook to play it:
  - A dedicated player interface appears, often at the top or bottom of the Books window.
  - **Controls:** You get Play/Pause, skip forward/backward (often by chapter or a set time interval like 15 seconds), a scrubbable timeline showing chapters, volume control, and an AirPlay button.
  - **Playback Speed:** Look for a button labeled "1x" (or similar) to adjust the narration speed (e.g., 1.25x, 1.5x, 2x, 0.75x).
  - **Sleep Timer:** Usually accessible via a moon icon, this lets you set playback to stop after a certain time or at the end of the current chapter.
  - **Chapter Navigation:** An icon often resembling a list or table of contents lets you jump directly to specific chapters.

- **Syncing:** Your listening progress (where you left off) syncs automatically via iCloud, so you can start listening on your Mac and seamlessly pick up at the same spot on your iPhone's Books app later.

- **Purchasing:** You buy new audiobooks through the **Audiobook Store** tab within the Books app.

Feature	Podcasts App	Audiobooks (in Books App)
Primary Content	Episodic shows (usually free)	Full-length narrated books (usually purchased)
Discovery	Browse categories, charts, search, follow shows	Browse Audiobook Store, search
Playback Speed	Variable speed control (e.g., 0.5x - 2x)	Variable speed control (e.g., 0.75x - 2x)
Sleep Timer	Yes (by time or end of episode)	Yes (by time or end of chapter)
Offline	Download individual episodes or auto-download	Purchased audiobooks are downloaded
Organization	Followed Shows, Saved Episodes, Downloads	Library section, Collections

Syncing	Subscriptions, playback position via iCloud	Library, playback position via iCloud

Whether you prefer informative interviews, captivating stories in podcast form, or having books read to you, your MacBook Air M4 has you covered with the Podcasts and Books apps.

Reading Books and PDFs with the Books App

The **Books** app is your digital library on the Mac, serving as the home for ebooks purchased from Apple, your own imported ePub and PDF files, and the audiobooks we just discussed. It provides a comfortable reading experience and keeps your library organized and synced.

Launching Books and the Interface

Open the Books app (orange icon with an open white book) from your Dock or Applications folder. Its interface is generally straightforward:

- **Sidebar (Left):** Organizes your content:
  - **Library:** Sections like All, Books, PDFs, Audiobooks, plus any custom Collections you create.
  - **My Purchases:** Shows items bought from the Stores.
  - **Store:** Tabs for the Book Store and Audiobook Store.
- **Main Library View (Center/Right):** Displays your books, PDFs, and audiobooks, usually as a grid of covers or a list. You can switch between views and sort items (by Recent, Title, Author, Manually).
- **Search Bar (Top Right):** Search your library or the stores.
- **Reading/Listening Pane:** When you open an item, it either takes over the main window (for reading) or displays playback controls (for audiobooks).

Building Your Digital Library

1. **Book Store / Audiobook Store:** Click these tabs in the Sidebar to browse Apple's extensive collection. You can explore recommendations, charts, genres, and search for specific titles or authors. Purchase items using your Apple ID. They are automatically added to your Library and available for download.

2. **Importing Your Own Files:** Books isn't just for purchased content! You can add your own DRM-free ePub files (a common ebook format) and PDF documents.
   - Go to **File > Add to Library...** and select the ePub or PDF file(s).
   - Alternatively, simply **drag and drop** ePub or PDF files from Finder directly into the Books app window (onto the Library section).

- Imported ePubs appear in the "Books" section, while PDFs go into the dedicated "PDFs" section.

The Reading Experience (eBooks and PDFs)

When you double-click an ebook (ePub) or PDF in your library to open it:

1. **Navigation:**
   - **Turn Pages:** Swipe left/right with two fingers on the trackpad, click near the left/right edges of the page, or use the Left/Right arrow keys. For PDFs, you can also scroll vertically.
   - **Table of Contents:** Look for an icon with lines or dots (often near the top) to open the book's table of contents for quick chapter navigation.
   - **Scrubber (Bottom):** A bar at the bottom shows your progress and allows you to quickly scrub to different parts of the book.

2. **Appearance Customization (Aa Button):** Click the **"Aa" button** (usually in the top toolbar when reading an ebook) to adjust the reading appearance:
   - **Font Size:** Increase or decrease the text size.
   - **Font Style:** Choose from various built-in fonts optimized for reading.
   - **Background Color:** Select White, Sepia (often easier on the eyes), Gray, or Night (white text on black).
   - **Brightness:** Adjust screen brightness directly within the app.

3. **Bookmarks, Highlights, and Notes:**
   - **Bookmarks:** Click the **Bookmark icon** (usually a ribbon) at the top right to mark your current page. Access all bookmarks via the Table of Contents/Notes panel.
   - **Highlighting:** Select text with your cursor. A popover menu appears; choose a highlight color.
   - **Adding Notes:** Select text, choose "Add Note" from the popover. Type your note. Highlighted text with notes gets a small indicator.
   - **Viewing Notes/Highlights:** Access the dedicated Notes/Highlights panel (often via the Table of Contents button) to see all your annotations in one place. These sync via iCloud.

4. **Search:** Use the search field within the reading view to find specific words or phrases within the current book or PDF.

5. **PDF Specifics:** When viewing PDFs, you might also see options for viewing thumbnails of all pages, changing the view (Single Page, Two Pages), and accessing Markup tools (similar to Quick Look/Preview) for annotation.

Organizing Your Library

Keep your growing collection tidy:

- **Collections:** These are like custom shelves or folders within your Books library.

    o Go to **File > New Collection**.

    o Give the collection a name (e.g., "Sci-Fi," "Cookbooks," "Research Papers").

    o Drag books or PDFs from your main library view onto the collection name in the Sidebar. An item can belong to multiple collections.

- **Sorting and Viewing:** Use the controls at the top of the main library view to switch between Grid (covers) and List view, and to sort your items by Most Recent, Title, Author, or Manually (allowing you to drag items into your preferred order within the selected view).

Syncing Across Devices

- One of the best features of using Books is iCloud syncing. When enabled (System Settings > [Your Name] > iCloud > iCloud Drive > Options... > ensure Books is checked), the following sync automatically across your Mac, iPhone, and iPad:

- Your library contents (purchased and imported).

- Your reading progress in ebooks and listening progress in audiobooks.

- Bookmarks, highlights, and notes you've added.

- Your custom collections.

This means you can start reading a book on your MacBook Air, make some highlights, then pick up your iPad later and continue reading from the exact same spot with all your annotations intact.

The Books app provides a comfortable and organized environment for enjoying both written and spoken literature on your Mac, seamlessly integrated with the broader Apple ecosystem.

Unleashing Your Creativity

Your MacBook Air M4 isn't just a tool for productivity and communication; it's also a fantastic platform for expressing your creativity. Whether you're passionate about photography, interested in making home movies, or dreaming of composing your own music, macOS Sequoia includes powerful yet accessible applications to get you started. In this chapter, we'll explore the Photos app for managing and enhancing your images and videos, dive into the basics of video editing with iMovie, take our first steps into music creation with GarageBand, and finally, understand how the advanced M4 chip inside your Mac specifically boosts these creative endeavors.

Organizing, Editing, and Sharing Photos with the Photos App

In an age where we capture countless photos and videos on our iPhones and cameras, managing that ever-growing library is essential. The **Photos** app on your Mac is designed to be the central hub for your entire visual collection. It helps you organize, find, edit, and share your precious memories, and with iCloud Photos enabled, it keeps everything seamlessly synced across all your Apple devices.

Launching Photos and the Interface

Open the Photos app (icon with a colorful flower pinwheel) from your Dock or Applications folder. The main window typically includes:

- **Sidebar (Left):** Your primary navigation tool. Key sections include:
  - **Library:** Different ways to view your entire collection, automatically organized by **Years, Months, Days,** and **All Photos**.
  - **Memories:** Automatically curated collections of photos and videos set to music, based on dates, locations, or people.
  - **People & Pets:** Automatically detects and groups photos based on recognized faces of people and pets.
  - **Places:** Displays your photos on an interactive world map based on their embedded location data.
  - **Albums:** Contains subsections for:
    0. *My Albums:* Albums and folders you create manually.
    1. *Shared Albums:* Albums you've created to share with others or that others have shared with you via iCloud.
    2. *Media Types:* Automatically groups items by type (Videos, Selfies, Live Photos, Portrait, Screenshots, RAW, etc.).
    3. *Imports:* Shows photos recently imported.
    4. *Utilities:* Hidden Album, Duplicates.

- **Main Viewing Area (Center/Right):** Displays thumbnails or individual photos/videos based on your selection in the Sidebar.
- **Toolbar (Top):** Contains buttons for navigating library views, zooming, searching, accessing editing tools (Edit), creating projects (slideshows, books - though some project types are being phased out), sharing, getting info, and marking items as Favorites (heart icon).

Bringing Your Photos and Videos In

Getting your visual memories into the Photos app is usually straightforward:

1. **From iPhone/iPad (iCloud Photos):** This is the easiest and most recommended method. If you enable **iCloud Photos** on both your iPhone/iPad (Settings > [Your Name] > iCloud > Photos > Sync this [Device]) and your Mac (Photos > Settings... > iCloud > iCloud Photos), any photo or video you take on your mobile device will automatically upload to iCloud and appear in the Photos app on your Mac (and vice versa). Edits also sync. This keeps your library consistent everywhere. Make sure you have enough iCloud storage for your library size.

2. **From iPhone/iPad (Manual Import):** Connect your iPhone or iPad to your Mac using a USB cable. Open the Photos app on your Mac. Your device should appear under the "Devices" section in the Sidebar. Click it. You'll see thumbnails of photos/videos on the device. Select the ones you want to import and click the "Import Selected" or "Import All New Items" button. You can choose to delete items from the device after importing.

3. **From Cameras/SD Cards:** Connect your digital camera via USB or insert its SD card into a card reader connected to your Mac. The device or card should appear under "Devices" in the Photos Sidebar. Click it and follow the same import process as for an iPhone.

4. **From Finder Folders:** If you have photo/video files already organized in folders on your Mac or an external drive, you can import them. Go to **File > Import...** in the Photos app and navigate to the folder, or simply **drag and drop** the folder(s) or individual files from Finder directly into the Photos app window. By default, Photos copies the items into its own library package file (managed internally). You can change this behavior in Photos > Settings... > General > Importing (uncheck "Copy items to the Photos library"), but managing the library yourself is generally more complex.

Organizing Your Ever-Growing Library

With potentially thousands of photos, organization is key:

1. **Navigating Library Views:** Use the **Years, Months, Days,** and **All Photos** views in the Sidebar for different levels of overview. Days view often highlights the best shots and plays short video clips automatically, providing a dynamic summary. All Photos shows everything chronologically.

2. **Creating Albums:** Group related photos manually. Go to **File > New Album** (or Command + N). Give the album a name in the Sidebar under "My Albums." Then, find the photos/videos you want to add (from any library view) and drag their thumbnails onto the album name in the Sidebar. A photo can be in multiple albums without duplicating the file.

3. **Using Folders for Albums:** If you have many albums, organize them into folders. Go to **File > New Folder**. Name the folder, then drag existing albums into it in the Sidebar.

4. **Smart Albums:** Create albums that automatically update based on criteria. Go to **File > New Smart Album...**. Define rules using dropdowns (e.g., "Photo" "is" "Favorite," "Date Captured" "is in the range" "01/01/2024 to 12/31/2024," "Keyword" "is" "Vacation," "Person" "includes" "Anna"). This is powerful for finding specific types of photos automatically.

5. **Keywords:** Add descriptive keywords for better searching. Select one or more photos, press Command (⌘) + I to open the Info window, and type keywords into the "Add a Keyword" field. You can manage your keyword list via **Window > Keyword Manager**. Search for keywords using the main search bar.

6. **People & Pets Album:** Photos uses facial recognition (and pet recognition!) to automatically find and group photos of the same individuals or animals. Go to the **People & Pets** section in the Sidebar. Photos might suggest names based on your Contacts, or you can click "Add Name" below a face circle. As you name people/pets, Photos gets better at recognizing them. Clicking a person's circle shows all photos identified as containing them.

7. **Places Album:** If your photos have location data (most photos taken on smartphones do), click **Places** in the Sidebar to see your photos pinned on an interactive world map. Zoom in to specific locations to see photos taken there.

8. **Favorites:** See a photo or video you absolutely love? Select it and click the **Heart icon (♡)** in the toolbar (or press the Period . key). All favorited items appear in the automatically generated "Favorites" album for quick access.

Editing Your Photos and Videos (The Basics)

Photos includes a surprisingly powerful set of editing tools suitable for most everyday adjustments.

1. **Enter Edit Mode:** Select the photo or video you want to enhance and click the **Edit** button in the top-right corner of the toolbar.

2. **Editing Interface:** The view changes, showing the image/video prominently with adjustment tools typically appearing in a sidebar on the right. You'll usually see tabs for **Adjust, Filters,** and **Crop**.

3. **Auto Enhance (Magic Wand):** Often the first thing to try! Click the **Magic Wand icon (□)** at the top of the Adjust pane. Photos analyzes the image and automatically applies adjustments to light and color that it thinks will improve the shot. It's often a great starting point, and you can always fine-tune afterwards or revert.

4. **Adjust Tab:** This is where the detailed controls live. You'll find sliders and options grouped by category:

   - **Light:** Controls overall brightness and tone (Exposure, Brilliance, Highlights, Shadows, Contrast, Black Point). Experiment with these sliders. Brilliance is often a good one to try first for overall pop.

   - **Color:** Adjusts color intensity and balance (Saturation, Vibrance, Cast). Saturation affects all colors equally; Vibrance boosts muted colors more. Cast helps correct color tints.

   - **Black & White:** Convert to monochrome with controls for intensity, neutrals, tone, and grain.

   - **White Balance:** Correct unrealistic color casts by setting a neutral gray point or adjusting Temperature (cool/warm) and Tint (green/magenta).

   - **Curves & Levels:** More advanced tools for fine-tuning tonal range and contrast (might be hidden initially; click the disclosure triangles).

   - **Definition, Noise Reduction, Sharpen:** Tools to enhance clarity, reduce graininess (especially in low light shots), and sharpen edges.

   - **Vignette:** Darkens or lightens the edges of the photo for artistic effect.

   - **Retouch (Healing Brush):** Click this tool (looks like a bandage), adjust the brush size ([and] keys), and click or drag over small blemishes, spots, or unwanted objects. Photos intelligently samples surrounding areas to blend them away. Option-click to manually select a source area to sample from.

5. **Filters Tab:** Apply pre-set looks (like Vivid, Dramatic, Mono, Silvertone) with adjustable intensity. Good for quick stylistic changes.

6. **Crop Tab:** Straighten horizons (drag the dial or use Auto), adjust aspect ratio (Original, Square, 16:9, custom), crop the image by dragging the corners/edges, flip the image horizontally.

7. **Video Editing:** When editing a video clip, the Adjust tab offers similar Light and Color adjustments. The main difference is you'll see a filmstrip timeline at the bottom. You can **Trim** the video by dragging the yellow handles at the beginning or end of the timeline to shorten the clip.

8. **Revert/Compare:** While editing, you can often click and hold the image itself to see the original version temporarily. There's also usually a "Revert to Original" button if you want to undo all changes. Edits are non-destructive; you can always go back.

9. **Done:** Click **Done** in the toolbar when you're finished editing.

Photos Editing Tool	Primary Function	Good For
Auto Enhance (□)	Automatically adjusts light and color.	Quick improvements, good starting point.
Light Adjustments	Control exposure, highlights, shadows, contrast, etc.	Fixing photos that are too dark/bright, improving overall tone.
Color Adjustments	Control saturation, vibrance, color cast.	Making colors pop, correcting unrealistic color tints.
Crop & Straighten	Change aspect ratio, trim edges, level horizon.	Improving composition, fixing tilted photos.
Filters	Apply pre-set stylistic looks.	Quickly changing the mood or style of a photo.
Retouch	Remove small blemishes or unwanted spots.	Cleaning up portraits or removing distracting elements.
Video Trim	Shorten the start or end point of a video clip.	Removing unwanted footage from the beginning or end of a video.

Sharing Your Creations

Once your photos look great, share them! Select one or more photos/videos, then:

- Click the **Share button** (square with upward arrow) in the toolbar.
- Choose your sharing method:
  - **AirDrop:** Send directly to nearby Apple devices.
  - **Messages / Mail:** Share via text or email.
  - **Shared Albums:** Create or add to an album shared with specific people via iCloud. Collaborators can often add their own photos, videos, and comments. Great for family events or trips.
  - **Add to other Apps:** Send directly to Notes, Reminders, etc.
  - **Social Media (via Extensions):** If you have sharing extensions installed, options for platforms like Flickr might appear.
- **Exporting:** To get standard image/video files you can use anywhere, go to **File > Export**. You can choose "Export [X] Photos/Videos..." (offers format options like JPEG/TIFF/PNG, quality settings, metadata inclusion) or "Export Unmodified Original...".

Memories and Slideshows

- **Memories:** Click **Memories** in the Sidebar. Photos automatically creates short movies from related photos and videos in your library, set to music. You can play them, customize the music and mood, edit the included photos, and share them.

- **Slideshows:** Select an album or a group of photos, go to **File > Create > Slideshow > Photos**. Choose a theme, add music, customize timings, and play a classic photo slideshow.

The Photos app is a powerful tool for managing your entire visual history. Leveraging iCloud Photos makes it effortless, while the built-in organization and editing tools allow you to curate and perfect your memories right on your MacBook Air.

Creating and Editing Videos with iMovie Basics

Want to turn those video clips from your vacation, family gathering, or school project into a polished movie? Apple's **iMovie** is the perfect place to start. It comes free with your Mac and offers a surprisingly powerful yet intuitive interface for editing videos, adding titles, music, and effects, without the steep learning curve of professional editing software.

Launching iMovie and the Interface

Find iMovie (purple star icon with a video camera) in your Applications folder or Launchpad. When you open it, you'll typically see the Projects browser. Let's look at the main editing interface you'll use when working on a project:

- **Browser (Top Left):** This area displays the source media (video clips, photos, audio) that you've imported into your current iMovie library or project. You can organize media here using Events.

- **Viewer (Top Right):** This is where you watch your video clips and preview your edited movie as you assemble it. Playback controls appear here.

- **Timeline (Bottom):** The heart of the editing process. This is where you arrange your video clips, photos, audio tracks, titles, and transitions in sequence to build your movie. You'll see video thumbnails, audio waveforms, and layers for titles and background music.

- **Toolbar (Top):** Contains buttons for importing media, accessing libraries (like Photos, Music), adding Titles, Backgrounds, Transitions, and sharing your finished movie.

Starting a New Project

1. From the Projects browser view, click the large **"Create New"** button.

2. Choose your project type:

   o **Movie:** This gives you a blank timeline where you have complete creative control to assemble clips, add music, titles, etc. This is what we'll focus on for basic editing.

   o **Trailer:** Provides pre-made templates with Hollywood-style graphics, music, and placeholders for specific types of shots (action, group, close-up). Fun for creating quick, stylized trailers, but less flexible than a Movie project.

3. Select **Movie**. A new, empty project opens in the editing interface.

Importing Your Media

Before you can edit, you need to bring your raw footage and photos into iMovie:

1. Click the **Import Media button** (downward arrow icon) in the toolbar, OR go to **File > Import Media...** (Command + I).

2. An import window appears. Use the sidebar to navigate:

   o **Cameras:** Connect your camera or insert its SD card. Select the device to see its clips.

   o **Photos Library:** Access your entire Apple Photos library directly within iMovie! Select "Photos" in the sidebar, browse your albums or moments, and select the photos/videos you want.

   o **Mac Folders:** Navigate to folders on your Mac or connected drives containing your media files.

3. Select the video clips, photos, or audio files you want to import. You can select multiple items.

4. Choose which **Event** to import into (Events are like organizational folders within your iMovie library; you can create a new one).

5. Click **Import Selected**. The media will appear in the Browser pane.

Basic Editing on the Timeline

This is where your movie takes shape:

1. **Adding Clips to the Timeline:** Select a video clip or photo in the Browser. You can select a portion of a video clip by clicking and dragging across the thumbnail to create a yellow selection box. Then, simply **drag the selected clip or photo down** from the Browser into the Timeline at the bottom. Place it where you want it in the sequence.

2. **Arranging Clips:** Once clips are in the Timeline, click and drag them left or right to change their order.

3. **Trimming Clips:** Need to shorten a clip? Move your cursor over the beginning or end edge of a clip in the Timeline. The cursor changes to a trim tool (a vertical bar with arrows). Click and drag the edge inward to remove unwanted footage from the start or end. The Viewer updates to show the new start/end frame.

4. **Splitting Clips:** Want to cut a clip into two pieces (e.g., to remove a section from the middle)? Position the **playhead** (the vertical white line in the Timeline that indicates the current playback position) where you want to make the cut. Select the clip, then right-click (Control-click) and choose **Split Clip**, or go to **Modify > Split Clip**, or press Command (⌘) + B. The clip is now split into two independent clips at the playhead position. You can then trim or delete the unwanted section.

5. **Adding Transitions:** To smooth the cut between two adjacent clips, add a transition. Click **Transitions** in the Toolbar above the Browser. Browse effects like Cross Dissolve, Fade to Black, Wipes, etc. Drag the transition thumbnail *between* two clips in the Timeline. You can adjust the duration of the transition by double-clicking it in the Timeline. Use transitions sparingly for a more professional look.

6. **Adding Titles:** Need text overlays for introductions, lower thirds (identifying someone), or credits? Click **Titles** in the Toolbar. Browse the various styles. Drag a title style onto a clip in the Timeline (it will appear as a layer above the video). Select the title bar in the Timeline, then type your text directly into the Viewer where the placeholder text appears. Use the controls above the Viewer to change font, size, color, and duration.

7. **Adding Backgrounds & Maps:** Click **Backgrounds** in the Toolbar to access solid colors, gradients, patterns, or **Animated Maps**. Drag a map style to the Timeline. Double-click it to customize the route (start/end locations) and style. Great for travel videos!

Working with Audio

Sound is crucial for a good movie:

1. **Adjusting Clip Volume:** Select a video clip in the Timeline. A horizontal line representing the audio level appears across its audio waveform (usually below the video thumbnail). Drag this line up or down to increase or decrease the volume for that specific clip. You can also select the clip and click the **Volume button (speaker icon)** above the Viewer for a slider.

2. **Adding Background Music:**

   o Click **Audio** in the Toolbar. You can access **Sound Effects** built into iMovie, or choose **Music** to access your library from the Music app (be mindful of copyright if sharing publicly!).

   o Drag the desired audio file or sound effect into the **background music well** below the main video track in the Timeline.

   o Adjust the background music volume (often lowering it slightly so it doesn't overpower dialogue) using the volume line on the audio clip.

3. **Detaching Audio:** If you want to edit the audio of a video clip independently (e.g., use the audio over a different visual), right-click the video clip and choose **Detach Audio**. The audio appears as a separate green region below the video clip, which you can now move, trim, or delete independently.

4. **Recording Voiceovers:** Position the playhead where you want the narration to start. Click the **Microphone icon** below the Viewer. Choose your microphone input, adjust the level, and click the red **Record button**. Speak your narration. Click Record again to stop. The recording appears as a new audio track in the Timeline.

Enhancing Your Video

iMovie offers tools to improve the look and feel:

1. **Color Correction & Filters:** Select a clip. Click the **Color Balance button (palette icon)** or **Color Correction button (filter icon)** above the Viewer. Use Auto-Enhance, match color between clips, adjust white balance, or tweak skin tones. The filter button offers Instagram-style preset looks.

2. **Stabilization:** If you have shaky handheld footage, select the clip and click the **Stabilization button (shaky camera icon)** above the Viewer. Check "Stabilize Shaky Video" and adjust the amount. iMovie will analyze the clip (this can take time) to smooth out the bumps.

3. **Speed Adjustments:** Select a clip and click the **Speed button (speedometer icon)** above the Viewer. Choose Slow, Fast, Freeze Frame, or Custom to create slow-motion or time-lapse effects.

4. **Cropping & Ken Burns:** Select a clip and click the **Cropping button (square crop icon)** above the Viewer.

   o **Fit:** Shows the entire frame.

   o **Crop to Fill:** Lets you drag a rectangle to crop the video frame.

   o **Ken Burns:** Allows you to set a start rectangle and an end rectangle, creating a smooth pan-and-zoom effect across a still photo or video clip. Very useful for adding motion to photos in your movie.

Exporting Your Finished Movie

Once you're happy with your edit:

1. Click the **Share button** (square with upward arrow) in the top-right corner of the iMovie window.

2. Choose your desired output method:

   o **Export File:** This is the most common option for saving a high-quality video file to your Mac. You can choose:

     ▪ Format (Video and Audio, or Audio Only).

- Resolution (e.g., 720p, 1080p HD, 4K). Choose the highest resolution appropriate for your source footage and intended viewing.
- Quality (Low, Medium, High, Best - ProRes for very high quality if needed). Higher quality means larger file size.
- Compression (Faster or Better Quality).
  - **Email:** Prepares a smaller version suitable for emailing.
  - **YouTube & Vimeo:** Upload directly to these platforms (requires signing in).
  - **Save Current Frame:** Exports a still image of the frame currently under the playhead.

3. Click **Next...**, give your exported file a name, choose where to save it, and click **Save**. iMovie will render (export) your movie, which can take some time depending on the length, complexity, and chosen quality. A progress indicator appears in the top-right corner.

iMovie Feature	Purpose	Location/Access
Browser	View imported source media (video, photos, audio).	Top Left Pane
Viewer	Preview clips and the edited movie.	Top Right Pane
Timeline	Assemble and arrange clips, audio, titles, transitions.	Bottom Pane
Import Media	Bring video, photos, audio into iMovie.	Toolbar Button (down arrow) / File Menu
Trim/Split Clips	Adjust clip duration or cut clips apart.	Drag edges in Timeline / Cmd+B or Modify Menu
Transitions	Add effects (dissolves, wipes) between clips.	Transitions Button in Toolbar, drag to Timeline
Titles	Add text overlays (intros, lower thirds, credits).	Titles Button in Toolbar, drag to Timeline
Audio Adjustments	Change volume, add music/sound effects, record voiceover.	Audio Button in Toolbar / Volume line on clips / Mic icon
Video Enhancements	Color correction, stabilization, speed changes, cropping/Ken Burns.	Buttons above Viewer (palette, filter, camera, speed, crop)
Share/Export	Save finished movie as a file or upload to platforms.	Share Button in Toolbar / File Menu

iMovie provides an excellent starting point for video editing on your Mac. It's capable enough for impressive results while remaining accessible for beginners.

Exploring Music Creation with GarageBand Basics

Ever wanted to record your own songs, create beats, or experiment with musical ideas? **GarageBand** transforms your MacBook Air M4 into a surprisingly powerful music creation studio, and just like iMovie, it comes free with your Mac. It's designed for both beginners using pre-made loops and more experienced musicians recording instruments and vocals.

Launching GarageBand and the Interface

Find GarageBand (icon with a guitar) in your Applications folder or Launchpad. When you first launch it, you might be prompted to download essential sounds. Then, you'll likely see the project chooser.

- **Choosing a Project Template:** GarageBand offers templates to get you started:
  - **Empty Project:** Starts with a completely blank slate.
  - **Keyboard Collection, Amp Collection, Voice, Ringtone, Songwriter, Electronic:** These provide pre-configured tracks and settings suited for specific genres or tasks.
  - Learn to Play: Interactive piano and guitar lessons (requires download).

- For learning the basics, starting with an Empty Project or one of the genre templates is often best.

- **Main Window Interface:** Once a project is open, the main elements are:
  - **Tracks Area (Main Section):** This is where your musical arrangement takes shape. Each instrument or audio recording lives on its own horizontal **Track**. Time moves from left to right. You'll add **Regions** (colored blocks representing MIDI notes or audio recordings) to these tracks.
  - **Control Bar (Top):** Contains essential transport controls (Record, Play, Go to Beginning, Cycle), the LCD display (showing tempo, time signature, key, playback position), buttons for the Library, Smart Controls, Editors, Loop Browser, and master volume.
  - **Library (Left Pane):** When a Software Instrument track is selected, the Library appears here, letting you choose different instrument sounds (pianos, synths, drums, guitars, orchestral, etc.) and presets.
  - **Smart Controls (Bottom Pane, optional):** Provides an easy-to-use set of knobs and buttons visually tailored to the selected instrument, allowing you to quickly tweak the sound (e.g., adjust reverb, cutoff filter, amp settings) without deep diving into complex plugins.

- Editors (Bottom Pane, optional): When you double-click a region in the Tracks area, the Editor pane opens here, showing either:
  0. *Piano Roll:* For editing MIDI notes (pitch, timing, velocity) for Software Instruments.
  1. *Score Editor:* Shows MIDI notes as traditional music notation.
  2. *Audio Region Editor:* Shows the waveform for audio recordings, allowing editing like trimming, flex time (adjusting timing), and pitch correction.
- Loop Browser (Top Right Button): Opens a pane for finding and previewing thousands of pre-made Apple Loops.

Working with Different Track Types

GarageBand primarily uses three types of tracks:

1. **Software Instrument Tracks:** These tracks play sounds generated by virtual instruments within GarageBand.
   - **Creating:** Click the '+' button above the track headers or go to **Track > New Track...** and choose "Software Instrument."
   - **Choosing Sounds:** With the track selected, browse the **Library** pane on the left to pick an instrument category (e.g., Piano, Synthesizer, Drum Kit, Guitar) and then a specific sound preset.
   - **Playing/Recording:**
     - *MIDI Keyboard:* If you have a USB MIDI keyboard connected, you can play notes directly.
     - *Musical Typing:* Press Command (⌘) + K to bring up the Musical Typing window, which turns your computer keyboard into a piano keyboard.
     - *Recording:* Select the track header, position the playhead (vertical line) where you want to start, click the red **Record button** in the Control Bar, and play your part using your MIDI keyboard or Musical Typing. Click the **Stop button** (square) when finished. A new MIDI region appears on the track.
   - **Drummer Tracks:** A special type of Software Instrument track that features virtual drummers playing various styles and kits. Create one via **Track > New Drummer Track**. Select the Drummer track header, then use the controls in the Editor pane (which becomes the Drummer Editor) to choose a drummer, style, kit, and adjust parameters like complexity, fills, and swing. GarageBand generates a realistic drum part automatically!

2. **Audio Tracks (Real Instruments/Vocals):** These tracks are for recording sound from external sources.

   - **Creating:** Click '+' or **Track > New Track...** and choose "Audio" (microphone or guitar input).

   - **Setting Up Input:** Select the track header. In the Smart Controls pane (or Track Info pane), choose the correct **Input Source** (e.g., Built-in Microphone, or your connected audio interface channel if using one). If recording guitar direct, you might enable "Monitor" to hear the processed sound while playing (use headphones to avoid feedback!).

   - **Recording:** Position the playhead, click **Record**, and perform your part (sing, play guitar, etc.). Click **Stop**. A new audio region (waveform) appears on the track.

3. **Apple Loops:** These are pre-recorded snippets of music (drum beats, bass lines, guitar riffs, sound effects) designed to loop seamlessly and automatically match your project's tempo and key. They are fantastic for quickly building song ideas, especially for beginners.

   - **Opening the Loop Browser:** Click the **Loop Browser button** (looks like a loop) in the top-right corner of the Control Bar, or press the O key.

   - **Finding Loops:** Browse by Instrument, Genre, or Mood using the buttons at the top, or use the search bar. Click a loop name to preview it.

   - **Adding Loops:** Simply **drag** the loop you like from the Loop Browser directly onto an empty area in the Tracks Area below existing tracks. GarageBand will automatically create a new track appropriate for that loop type (e.g., a Software Instrument track for a synth loop, an Audio track for a drum beat loop). You can also drag audio loops onto existing Audio tracks.

Arranging and Editing Your Music

Once you have some regions (MIDI or audio) on your tracks:

- **Arranging Regions:** Click and drag regions left or right in the Tracks Area to position them in time. Drag them up or down to move them between compatible tracks.

- **Looping Regions:** Hover your cursor over the top-right corner of a region. The cursor changes to a loop pointer (circle arrow). Click and drag to the right to repeat the region multiple times.

- **Splitting Regions:** Select a region, position the playhead where you want to cut, and press Command (⌘) + T (or Edit > Split Regions at Playhead).

- **Joining Regions:** Select multiple adjacent regions *on the same track* and press Command (⌘) + J (or Edit > Join Regions).

- **Editing MIDI (Piano Roll):** Double-click a Software Instrument MIDI region to open the Piano Roll editor. Here you can click notes to select them, drag them up/down to change pitch, drag left/right to change timing, drag edges to change duration. Use the Quantize menu to automatically align notes to the beat grid. Adjust Velocity (how hard the note was played) in the controller lane below.

- **Editing Audio:** Double-click an Audio region to open the Audio Editor. You can trim, split, and join audio regions similar to MIDI. Explore **Flex Time** (button looks like DNA helix) to manually adjust the timing of notes within the audio waveform without affecting pitch. Use **Pitch Correction** to subtly correct vocal pitch.

- **Mixing:** Use the **Volume slider** and **Pan knob** (left/right balance) in each track's header to balance the levels of your different instruments. Use the **Master Volume** slider in the Control Bar for the overall output level. Explore adding effects like Reverb and Delay using the Smart Controls or track plugins.

Sharing Your Creation

When your masterpiece is ready:

1. Go to the **Share** menu.

2. Choose your destination:

    - **Song to Music App:** Exports the mix directly into your Music app library.

    - **Song to SoundCloud:** Uploads directly to SoundCloud (requires account setup).

    - **Export Song to Disk...:** The most versatile option. Choose the format (AAC, MP3 for sharing; AIFF, WAV for higher quality), select quality settings, provide song info, choose the save location, and click **Export**.

GarageBand Feature	Description	Use Case
Tracks Area	Main workspace where musical regions are arranged over time.	Building the song structure.
Library	Browser for selecting Software Instrument sounds and presets.	Choosing the sound for virtual instruments.
Smart Controls	Easy knobs/buttons to tweak the selected track's sound.	Quickly adjusting instrument tone, effects (reverb, delay), amp settings.

Editors	Piano Roll (MIDI), Score (Notation), Audio Region (Waveform) editors.	Fine-tuning notes, timing, pitch, audio waveforms.
Loop Browser	Library of pre-made, royalty-free Apple Loops (beats, melodies, effects).	Quickly building song foundations, finding inspiration, adding texture.
Drummer Track	Virtual drummer providing realistic beats in various styles.	Easily adding professional-sounding drum parts without manual programming.
Musical Typing	Use your computer keyboard to play Software Instruments.	Playing melodies or chords without a dedicated MIDI keyboard.
Flex Time	Manually adjust the timing of notes within an audio recording.	Correcting rhythmic inaccuracies in recorded audio.

GarageBand is an incredibly deep application disguised in a user-friendly package. Don't be afraid to experiment with loops, try recording yourself, and explore the vast library of sounds – it's a fun way to get creative with audio on your Mac.

Leveraging the M4 Chip for Creative Tasks (GPU & Neural Engine Benefits)

While the creative applications we've discussed – Photos, iMovie, and GarageBand – are designed to run well on a range of Macs, the advanced **Apple M4 chip** inside your MacBook Air provides significant performance and efficiency advantages, making your creative process smoother, faster, and more capable than ever before on an Air. Let's break down how the M4's specific components benefit these workflows.

The Power of Apple Silicon: CPU, GPU, Neural Engine, Unified Memory

Apple Silicon chips like the M4 integrate several specialized processors onto a single piece of silicon, working together efficiently:

- **CPU (Central Processing Unit):** Handles general computing tasks. The M4 features a powerful 10-core CPU (with 4 high-performance cores for demanding tasks and 6 high-efficiency cores for background processes and saving battery life). This ensures overall responsiveness when running creative apps, managing files, and multitasking.

- **GPU (Graphics Processing Unit):** Specialized for handling graphics, visual effects, and parallel computations. The M4 comes with either an 8-core or a more powerful 10-core GPU.

- **Neural Engine (NPU):** Designed specifically to accelerate machine learning (often called AI) tasks. The M4 boasts a significantly faster 16-core Neural Engine compared to previous generations.

- **Media Engine:** Dedicated hardware for encoding and decoding video formats (like H.264, HEVC, and importantly, ProRes), dramatically speeding up video editing tasks while using very little power.

- **Unified Memory:** A high-bandwidth pool of memory directly accessible by the CPU, GPU, and Neural Engine, eliminating the need to copy data between separate memory pools, which boosts performance and efficiency. Your M4 Air starts with 16GB and can be configured up to 32GB.

How the M4's GPU Supercharges Visual Tasks

The enhanced GPU in the M4 chip directly benefits visually intensive creative work:

- **Faster Graphics Rendering:** This means smoother performance across the board. In **Photos**, applying complex adjustments or filters feels more instantaneous, and browsing through large libraries or zooming into high-resolution images is fluid. In **iMovie**, you'll experience smoother real-time playback, especially when adding effects, titles, or transitions – you see the results immediately without stuttering. Scrubbing through the timeline feels more responsive. Even in **GarageBand**, complex projects with many visual elements or plugins benefit from a faster GPU.

- **Hardware-Accelerated Ray Tracing:** While primarily a feature for high-end 3D graphics and gaming, the M4's support for hardware-accelerated ray tracing (a technique for creating incredibly realistic lighting and reflections) future-proofs your Mac for next-generation creative applications that might incorporate these advanced rendering techniques.

- **Efficient Video Handling (Media Engine):** This is a game-changer for video editing on a MacBook Air. The dedicated Media Engine in the M4 chip handles the heavy lifting of encoding (exporting) and decoding (playing back) common video codecs, including professional formats like ProRes.

  - **Result in iMovie:** Exporting your finished movies is significantly faster compared to older Intel Macs or even earlier M-series chips without equivalent Media Engines. Editing high-resolution footage, like 4K video shot on an iPhone, is remarkably smooth – playback doesn't drop frames as easily, and rendering times are drastically reduced. This makes the M4 Air a genuinely viable machine for editing substantial video projects, something that was often challenging on previous Air models.

How the M4's Neural Engine Powers Intelligent Features

The leap in performance of the M4's 16-core Neural Engine unlocks and accelerates a growing number of "smart" features within macOS and creative apps:

- **In the Photos App:**
  - *Faster Recognition:* Identifying people, faces, pets, and objects in your photos happens much faster and more accurately thanks to the NPU. This improves the automatic curation of the People & Pets albums and makes searching for photos by content (e.g., searching for "beach" or "dog") more effective.
  - *Intelligent Curation:* Features like Memories, which automatically create themed slideshows, rely on machine learning to select the best photos and video clips – the NPU speeds up this analysis.
  - *Subject Isolation:* The ability to easily lift the subject out of a photo background (in Photos, Preview, Safari, etc.) is powered by the Neural Engine's image analysis capabilities.

- **In Video Editing (iMovie & Professional Apps):**
  - While iMovie's basic features might not heavily tax the NPU *yet*, professional apps like Final Cut Pro and DaVinci Resolve increasingly use it for tasks like:
    0. *Smart Reframe:* Automatically reframing video for different aspect ratios (e.g., horizontal to vertical for social media).
    1. *Object Tracking:* Following moving objects in a scene for effects or color correction.
    2. *Scene Edit Detection:* Automatically finding cuts in existing video files.
    3. *Voice Isolation/Background Noise Removal:* Advanced audio cleanup powered by AI.
  - The M4's powerful NPU means these features run significantly faster and more efficiently on the MacBook Air compared to systems without a capable NPU.

- **In Audio Production (GarageBand & Professional Apps):**
  - Again, while basic GarageBand might not push the limits, professional DAWs like Logic Pro use the NPU for features such as:
    0. *Stem Separation:* Automatically separating a mixed audio track into its components (vocals, drums, bass, etc.).
    1. *Smart Tempo:* Automatically analyzing the tempo of imported audio or recordings.

- **Third-Party Creative Apps:** Many popular creative applications from Adobe (Photoshop, Lightroom, Premiere Pro), Blackmagic Design (DaVinci Resolve), Affinity, and others are optimized for Apple Silicon and leverage the Neural Engine for a wide array of AI-powered features like generative fill, AI denoising, intelligent upscaling, automatic transcription, and much more. The M4's NPU ensures these demanding features run smoothly and efficiently on your thin-and-light MacBook Air.

The Overall Impact: A Creative Powerhouse in an Air

What does all this mean for you as a creator using a MacBook Air M4?

- **Smoother Experience:** Editing photos, trimming videos, and even working with moderately complex GarageBand projects feels more fluid and responsive.

- **Faster Exports:** Significantly reduced waiting times when exporting videos from iMovie or rendering projects in other apps.

- **Better Battery Life:** The efficiency of Apple Silicon means you can perform these creative tasks for longer without needing to plug in compared to older Intel-based laptops.

- **Access to AI Features:** You can effectively use the growing number of intelligent, time-saving features built into macOS and third-party creative apps that rely on machine learning.

- **Viable Prosumer Workflows:** The M4 chip elevates the MacBook Air from being just a basic machine to one that can comfortably handle moderately complex photo editing, 4K video editing (especially with the Media Engine's help), and multi-track audio production, blurring the lines with the MacBook Pro for many users.

M4 Chip Component	Key Creative Benefit(s)	Examples in Apps
GPU (8/10-core)	Faster graphics rendering, smoother UI, real-time effects playback.	Fluid photo adjustments (Photos), smooth video timeline scrubbing/playback (iMovie), faster visual feedback in graphics apps.
Media Engine	Hardware acceleration for video encode/decode (H.264, HEVC, ProRes).	Dramatically faster video export times (iMovie, Final Cut Pro), smooth editing of high-resolution (4K+) footage, efficient video playback.

Neural Engine (16-core)	Accelerates machine learning / AI tasks.	Faster People/Object recognition (Photos), Subject Isolation, AI features in pro apps (denoise, upscaling, smart reframing, transcription).
CPU (10-core)	Fast general processing for application logic, file management, system responsiveness.	Quick app launching, responsive interface, handling complex calculations or project logic.
Unified Memory (16GB+)	High-bandwidth memory shared between CPU, GPU, NPU, reducing data copying bottlenecks.	Improved performance when working with large media files or multiple demanding creative apps simultaneously.

While professional users working on extremely demanding projects might still opt for a MacBook Pro with even more cores, active cooling, and higher memory ceilings, the MacBook Air M4 represents a remarkable leap, bringing serious creative potential to Apple's most portable laptop. Don't hesitate to push its boundaries and explore your creative ideas!

Security & Privacy Essentials

In our increasingly digital world, protecting your personal information and securing your devices is more important than ever. Your MacBook Air M4 and macOS Sequoia are equipped with powerful, built-in security and privacy features designed to safeguard your data without getting in your way. Understanding and utilizing these tools is key to using your Mac with confidence. In this chapter, we'll cover the convenience and security of Touch ID, explore modern ways to manage passwords and the even more secure Passkeys using iCloud Keychain, learn about encrypting your entire drive with FileVault, and dive into controlling which apps have access to your sensitive information through Privacy & Security settings. Let's make sure your Mac is as secure as it is powerful.

Setting Up and Using Touch ID for Secure Logins and Purchases

Remember that sleek, blank key in the top-right corner of your MacBook Air M4's keyboard? That's not just the power button; it's also the **Touch ID** sensor – your personal fingerprint reader. Touch ID provides a fantastic blend of security and convenience, allowing you to unlock your Mac, authorize purchases, and fill in passwords with just a simple touch of your finger, replacing the need to type your password in many situations.

Setting Up Your Fingerprint(s)

You likely had the option to set up Touch ID during the initial macOS Setup Assistant walkthrough when you first turned on your Mac (as mentioned in Chapter 1). If you skipped it then, or if you want to add more fingerprints (for other fingers, or perhaps for another trusted user who has an account on your Mac – though using separate user accounts is generally better for privacy and data separation), you can easily manage it anytime:

1. **Open System Settings:** Click the gear icon (⚙️□) in your Dock or go to the Apple menu (□) > System Settings...

2. **Navigate to Touch ID & Password:** Scroll down the sidebar and click on "Touch ID & Password." You'll need to enter your user account password to proceed, ensuring only authorized users can manage fingerprints.

3. **Add a Fingerprint:** Look for the "Fingerprints" section. You'll see visual representations of any fingerprints already added. Click the **"Add Fingerprint..."** button (often showing a plus '+' sign).

4. **Follow On-Screen Instructions:** A panel will appear, guiding you through the scanning process. It will instruct you to place a finger lightly on the Touch ID sensor (the power button).

   o **Lift and Rest:** The key is *not* to press down hard, but to gently rest your finger on the sensor. You'll be prompted to lift and rest your finger repeatedly. As you do this, the on-screen graphic of a fingerprint will gradually fill in with red lines, indicating that the sensor is capturing the unique ridges and valleys of your print from different angles.

- **Capture Edges:** Once the central part of your fingerprint is captured, the system will specifically ask you to adjust your grip and roll the *edges* of your fingertip onto the sensor. This step is crucial for ensuring Touch ID works reliably even if you don't place your finger perfectly centered each time. Continue lifting and resting until the on-screen graphic is completely filled in.

- **Success!** A confirmation message will appear stating that the fingerprint has been added successfully. Click **Done**.

5. **Add More (Optional):** You can register up to three fingerprints per user account on your Mac, with a maximum of five fingerprints total across all user accounts. Adding fingerprints from different fingers (like the index finger on both hands, or maybe a thumb) gives you more flexibility when unlocking. To add another, simply click the "Add Fingerprint..." button again and repeat the process with a different finger.

6. **Name Your Fingerprints (Optional but Recommended):** After adding a fingerprint, it's helpful to label it. Hover your cursor over the default name below the fingerprint icon (e.g., "Finger 1"). The text should become editable, or you might need to click it. Type a clear, descriptive name like "Right Index Finger" or "Left Thumb" and press Return. This makes it easy to identify which fingerprint is which if you ever need to delete one later (perhaps if recognition for a specific finger becomes unreliable).

7. **Choose How to Use Touch ID:** Below the fingerprint management area, you'll find several checkboxes that let you control exactly where Touch ID can be used as an alternative to typing your password. Review these options carefully:

- **Unlocking your Mac:** This is the most common use. Enabling this allows you to wake your Mac from sleep or unlock the screen after the screen saver activates with just a touch. Highly recommended for convenience.

- **Apple Pay:** If you set up Apple Pay on your Mac (for making secure purchases on supported websites in Safari), this allows you to authorize those payments with your fingerprint instead of entering card details or passwords.

- **iTunes Store, App Store & Apple Books:** Allows you to authorize downloads (even free ones) and purchases within Apple's digital content stores using your fingerprint. Much faster than typing your Apple ID password every time.

- **Password autofill:** When Safari or certain apps offer to fill in a password saved in your iCloud Keychain (covered in the next section), enabling this allows you to approve the autofill action with a quick touch, rather than typing your Mac login password.

- Fast user switching: If you share your Mac with family members who have their own user accounts, enabling this allows a registered user to quickly switch to their account from the login screen or the user menu in the Menu Bar simply by placing their finger on the sensor.

Make sure the boxes are checked for all the functions where you want the convenience and security of Touch ID authentication.

Using Touch ID in Daily Life

Integrating Touch ID into your routine is seamless:

- **Unlocking/Logging In:** When your Mac's screen is locked or asleep, gently rest a registered finger on the Touch ID sensor. Within a second or two, the screen should unlock, taking you right back to where you left off. It feels almost instantaneous. (Remember: For security, macOS requires you to type your password the very first time you log in after a full restart or shutdown; Touch ID works for subsequent unlocks).

- **Authorizing Purchases:** When completing a purchase using Apple Pay in Safari, or buying content from the App Store, iTunes Store, or Books Store, a prompt will appear on screen asking you to confirm with Touch ID. Simply rest your finger on the sensor when indicated.

- **Autofilling Passwords:** When logging into a website where you've saved credentials in Safari, or using certain apps that integrate with iCloud Keychain, you might click in the password field and see a prompt offering to autofill. Often, this prompt will include a Touch ID icon. A quick touch on the sensor confirms it's you and fills in the password securely.

- **System Approvals:** Occasionally, when installing new software or changing protected settings in System Settings, macOS will ask for administrator authorization. Instead of typing your password, you'll often see a prompt allowing you to use Touch ID instead.

Where Touch ID Can Be Used	Benefit
Unlocking Mac (from sleep/lock screen)	Fast, convenient access without typing password.
Logging In (after first boot login)	Quicker login after initial password entry.
Apple Pay (on supported websites)	Securely authorize online payments without entering card details.
App Store, iTunes, Apple Books Purchases	Quickly approve purchases of apps, music, movies, books.
Password Autofill (Safari & Apps)	Securely fill saved passwords with just a touch.
Unlocking System Settings Panes	Approve changes to sensitive settings without typing password repeatedly.

Unlocking Locked Notes	Quickly access notes you've secured in the Notes app.
Fast User Switching	Easily switch between user accounts on a shared Mac.
Third-Party App Logins/Authorizations	Some apps integrate Touch ID for their own secure actions.

How Secure is Touch ID?

Apple takes the security of your biometric data very seriously:

- **Secure Enclave:** Your fingerprint isn't stored as a picture file that could be stolen. Instead, the sensor captures detailed data about the ridges and patterns, creates a complex mathematical representation of it, encrypts this representation, and stores it exclusively within a dedicated, hardware-based secure processor called the **Secure Enclave**. This enclave is physically part of the M4 chip but isolated from the main operating system.

- **Data Isolation:** Critically, this encrypted fingerprint data *never* leaves the Secure Enclave. It's not sent to Apple's servers, it's not included in iCloud backups or Time Machine backups, and it cannot be accessed by macOS or any applications. It's designed to be tamper-resistant.

- **Matching Process:** When you place your finger on the sensor, the sensor reads the print and sends the data *directly* to the Secure Enclave. The Secure Enclave then compares this new data against the securely stored mathematical representations. If it finds a match, it sends a simple cryptographic "yes" token back to the operating system, authorizing the requested action (like unlocking or approving a purchase). The actual fingerprint data is never exposed.

Tips for Best Results

- **Keep it Clean:** Both the Touch ID sensor (the power button) and your fingers should be clean and dry for optimal performance. Occasionally wipe the sensor gently with a soft, lint-free cloth (like the one you might use for your screen or glasses).

- **Good Scan:** Ensure your fingers are free of excessive moisture, lotions, oils, or dirt when using Touch ID. These can sometimes interfere with the sensor's ability to get a clear reading.

- **Full Enrollment:** During setup, make sure you follow the prompts to capture the edges of your fingerprint thoroughly. This significantly improves recognition reliability when you touch the sensor from slightly different angles.

- **Troubleshooting:** If Touch ID consistently fails to recognize a particular finger, try deleting that fingerprint in System Settings > Touch ID & Password (hover over it, click the 'X', authenticate) and then re-adding it, carefully following the setup prompts. Adding a different finger is also a good option.

Touch ID on your MacBook Air M4 is a perfect marriage of robust security technology and everyday convenience, making interactions requiring authentication faster and more fluid.

Managing Passwords, Passkeys, and Safari Autofill with Keychain Access

In today's online world, we juggle countless accounts – email, banking, shopping, social media, streaming services, and more. Each requires a password, and security experts constantly advise using **strong, unique passwords** for every single site. Trying to remember dozens of complex, unique passwords is a recipe for frustration or, worse, resorting to weak or reused passwords, which puts all your accounts at risk if one site suffers a data breach. Thankfully, macOS provides a built-in, secure, and convenient solution called **iCloud Keychain**, along with support for the even more secure next-generation login technology: **Passkeys**.

iCloud Keychain: Your Secure Digital Vault

iCloud Keychain is Apple's integrated password management system. It securely stores your various login credentials and other sensitive information, encrypts it, and keeps it synchronized across all your Apple devices (Mac, iPhone, iPad) that are signed into the same iCloud account and have Keychain enabled.

1. **What iCloud Keychain Stores:**
   o Website usernames and passwords.
   o App-specific passwords.
   o **Passkeys** (the modern replacement for passwords).
   o Wi-Fi network names and passwords (so you don't have to re-enter them on all your devices).
   o Credit card numbers and expiry dates (it *never* stores the 3- or 4-digit CVV security code for added protection).
   o Internet account credentials (like those used for Mail, Contacts, Calendar if added via System Settings > Internet Accounts).
   o Secure Notes (though these are primarily managed via the separate Keychain Access utility, not the main Passwords settings).

2. **Top-Notch Security:** The data stored in iCloud Keychain is protected using strong **end-to-end encryption**. This means the information is encrypted on your device *before* it's sent to iCloud, and it can only be decrypted on your other trusted devices where you are logged in with your Apple ID. Apple itself cannot access or read your Keychain data, ensuring a high level of privacy and security.

3. **Enabling iCloud Keychain:** You were likely prompted to enable this when you first set up your Mac and signed into iCloud. To verify or enable it:

   - Open **System Settings**.
   - Click your **[Your Name] (Apple ID)** at the very top of the sidebar.
   - Click **iCloud**.
   - In the list of "Apps Using iCloud," click **Show All**.
   - Locate **Passwords and Keychain** in the list.
   - Ensure the toggle switch next to it is **On**. If it's off, toggle it on. You may need to enter your Apple ID password or your Mac's login password for verification. Note that **Two-Factor Authentication (2FA)** must be enabled for your Apple ID to use iCloud Keychain.

Managing Your Passwords the Easy Way

With iCloud Keychain enabled, managing traditional passwords becomes much simpler and more secure:

1. **Saving Passwords in Safari:** When you log into a website for the first time, or when you change your password on a site, Safari will usually display a prompt asking if you want to save or update the password in your Keychain. Simply click **"Save Password"** (or "Update Password"). It's securely stored and will be available on your other devices shortly.

2. **Generating Strong Passwords:** Stop trying to invent complex passwords yourself! When you encounter a "create new password" field on a website registration form, Safari will often automatically suggest a very strong, unique password (a long, random combination of characters). Click the **"Use Strong Password"** button offered by Safari. This password is automatically saved to your Keychain – you don't need to write it down or memorize it. This is the *best* way to ensure every site has a unique, hard-to-crack password.

3. **Autofilling Passwords:** When you return to a login page, click in the username or password field. Safari should recognize the site and offer to fill your saved credentials. You might see your username appear, or a key icon. Click the suggestion or the key icon. You will then typically need to authenticate using **Touch ID** or by typing your Mac's login password to approve the autofill. This prevents someone else using your unlocked Mac from automatically logging into your accounts.

4. **Viewing, Editing, and Deleting Saved Passwords:** Need to look up a password you saved? Or perhaps update one manually?

   - Go to **System Settings > Passwords**. (Alternatively, in Safari, go to Safari menu > Settings... > Passwords tab).
   - Authenticate using Touch ID or your Mac login password.
   - You'll see a list of all your saved website and app credentials in the sidebar, usually sorted alphabetically by website/app name. You can use the search field at the top to quickly find a specific entry.

- Click on an entry in the list.
- The details appear on the right: Username, Password (hidden by dots), Website address, and potentially any Notes you've added or the date saved.
- To **view the password**, hover your cursor over the dots representing the password, then click. You'll likely need to authenticate again with Touch ID/password. The password will be revealed temporarily.
- To **edit** the entry (e.g., if you changed the password directly on the website and Safari didn't prompt to update), click the **"Edit"** button in the top right. You can modify the username, password, and website fields. Click **"Save"** when done.
- To **delete** an entry completely (e.g., for an account you no longer use), click the **'i' (info) button** next to the entry, then click the **"Delete Password"** button and confirm.

5. **Security Recommendations – Your Password Health Check:** This is a vital feature within the Passwords settings. Click on **"Security Recommendations"** in the sidebar. macOS automatically analyzes your saved passwords and alerts you to potential risks:
   - **Reused Passwords:** Identifies passwords you've used across multiple websites. This is risky because if one site is breached, attackers can try that same password on your other accounts.
   - **Weak Passwords:** Flags passwords that are too simple or easy to guess.
   - Compromised Passwords: Checks your passwords against publicly known lists of credentials leaked in data breaches. If a match is found, it means that password is out in the wild and should be changed immediately.

For each recommendation, macOS usually provides a direct link to the website's password change page, making it easier to fix the issue. Regularly checking and addressing these recommendations significantly boosts your online security.

Introducing Passkeys: Simpler, Stronger Logins

While Keychain helps manage passwords, the industry is moving towards an even better solution: **Passkeys**. Supported by Apple, Google, Microsoft, and growing numbers of websites and apps, passkeys aim to replace passwords entirely.

- **The Concept (Simplified):** Instead of you creating a password, when you set up a passkey for a site, your device (MacBook Air) creates a unique pair of related cryptographic keys. The **public key** is sent to the website's server. The **private key** stays securely stored and encrypted within your iCloud Keychain, never leaving your devices.

- **The Login Process:** When you want to log in, the website sends a challenge to your device. Your Mac asks you to authenticate using **Touch ID** (or Face ID on an iPhone/iPad). If successful, your device uses the *private key* to mathematically "sign" the challenge and sends the signature back to the website. The website uses your *public key* to verify the signature. If it matches, you're logged in! Notice you never typed or transmitted a password.

- **Why Passkeys are Better:**
  - **Phishing-Proof:** Since you never type a password, fake websites designed to steal your credentials (phishing sites) simply won't work. The passkey mechanism is tied to the legitimate website's domain.

  - **Extremely Strong:** Each passkey is unique and based on strong cryptography, eliminating the problem of weak or reused passwords.

  - **Protects Against Server Breaches:** Even if a company's server is hacked and the public keys are stolen, they are useless to attackers without the corresponding private keys stored securely on your devices.

  - **Convenient:** Logging in is often faster – just a touch of the Touch ID sensor.

- **Creating and Using Passkeys:** Look for options like "Sign in with a passkey," "Create a passkey," or similar wording on website login/registration pages or in account security settings. The process usually involves naming the passkey (often defaults to your username) and then authenticating with Touch ID. The passkey is saved to your iCloud Keychain, automatically syncing to your other trusted Apple devices. To log in later, simply choose the passkey option and use Touch ID when prompted.

- **Managing Passkeys:** Saved passkeys appear right alongside your traditional passwords in **System Settings > Passwords**. They are often indicated by a special icon (like a key or fingerprint). You can view which sites use them and delete them if necessary.

Feature	Traditional Password (Managed by Keychain)	Passkey (Managed by Keychain)
What it is	A secret word/phrase you create (or Keychain generates).	A cryptographic key pair (public/private) generated by device.
How you login	Type password (or autofill via Keychain + Touch ID/Password).	Authenticate with Touch ID / Face ID on your device.
Security	Vulnerable to phishing, weak/reused passwords, server breaches.	Phishing-resistant, always strong, protects against server breaches.
Convenience	Requires remembering or managing many secrets.	Simpler login (often just Touch ID/Face ID).

Availability	Universal (all websites/apps).	Growing adoption by websites and apps.
Syncing	Yes (via iCloud Keychain).	Yes (via iCloud Keychain).

As passkey adoption grows, embrace it! It's a major step forward for online security and usability.

Safari Autofill: Contact Info and Credit Cards

Beyond logins, Safari's AutoFill, powered by Keychain and your Contacts, can save you typing time in online forms:

- **Contact Info:** Safari can automatically fill in your name, address, email, and phone number based on your "My Card" in the Contacts app. Manage this in **Safari > Settings... > AutoFill**. Ensure your contact card is selected and accurate.

- **Credit Cards:** Securely store card numbers and expiry dates (never the CVV) in **Safari > Settings... > AutoFill > Credit Cards** (or System Settings > Passwords). When checking out online, Safari offers to fill the details. You'll need to authorize with Touch ID/password and manually enter the CVV code each time for security.

The Keychain Access Utility

For most users, managing passwords and passkeys through **System Settings > Passwords** is the most straightforward approach. However, macOS also includes a more technical application called **Keychain Access** (found in the /Applications/Utilities folder). This tool gives you a much more detailed view of all the items stored in your various keychains (login, iCloud, System, etc.). You can manage passwords, passkeys, secure notes (text snippets stored encrypted in the keychain), digital certificates (used for secure communication), and cryptographic keys. While powerful, it's generally overkill for typical password management but good to know it exists for advanced troubleshooting or specific needs.

Using iCloud Keychain effectively—letting Safari generate and save strong, unique passwords, adopting passkeys when available, and regularly checking Security Recommendations—is one of the easiest and most impactful ways to bolster your online security while using your MacBook Air M4.

Encrypting Your Data with FileVault

Securing your online accounts with strong passwords and passkeys is vital, but what about the data physically stored on your MacBook Air's internal drive? What happens if your laptop is lost or stolen? To protect all your documents, photos, emails, applications, and system files from unauthorized physical access, macOS offers a crucial security feature called **FileVault**.

What is FileVault Full-Disk Encryption?

FileVault is a technology that encrypts the entire contents of your Mac's startup disk using the industry-standard **XTS-AES-128 encryption algorithm with a robust 256-bit key**. Essentially, it scrambles all the data on your drive, turning it into unreadable code. The only way to unscramble (decrypt) this data and make it usable is by providing the correct "key" when your Mac starts up. This key is intrinsically linked to your user account login password or a special recovery key you set up.

- **The Core Benefit: Data Protection at Rest:** With FileVault enabled, even if someone were to physically steal your MacBook Air, they wouldn't be able to simply boot it up and browse your files. Without the correct login password or recovery key, the encrypted data remains secure. Even advanced techniques like removing the internal SSD and connecting it to another computer would yield only encrypted gibberish. FileVault protects your data "at rest" – when the computer is turned off or locked.

- **How it Works (Simplified):** When you enable FileVault, it creates encryption keys tied to your user account(s). As your Mac runs, data is automatically encrypted just before it's written to the drive and automatically decrypted just before it's read into memory for you to use.

- **Transparency and Performance:** This encryption and decryption process happens constantly in the background. On modern Macs like your M4 Air, which have specialized encryption hardware built directly into the Apple Silicon chip (the Secure Enclave helps manage the keys), this process is incredibly efficient. You should not notice any slowdown in your Mac's performance during normal use due to FileVault being enabled. It's designed to be secure *and* transparent.

Enabling FileVault: A Step-by-Step Guide

Apple often prompts users to enable FileVault during the initial macOS setup process. If you enabled it then, great! If not, or if you want to verify its status, you can manage it easily:

1. **Open System Settings:** Click the Apple menu (☐) > System Settings...

2. **Go to Privacy & Security:** Scroll down the sidebar and select "Privacy & Security."

3. **Locate FileVault:** Scroll down the main pane to find the **FileVault** section (it's usually towards the bottom, under the "Security" heading).

4. **Check the Status:** The pane will clearly state "FileVault is turned on for the disk '[Your Disk Name]'" or "FileVault is turned off for the disk '[Your Disk Name]'."

5. **Turn FileVault On:** If it's currently off, click the **"Turn On..."** button.

6. **Authenticate:** You'll be prompted to enter your administrator password to authorize this change. Type it and click "Unlock" or "OK."

7. **CRITICAL STEP: Choose Your Recovery Method:** This is the most vital decision during FileVault setup. Because your data will be encrypted, you need a backup method to unlock your drive and access your data *if you ever forget your Mac login password*. Forgetting your password *without* a valid recovery method means your data could be lost forever. FileVault offers two recovery options:

   - **Option A: Allow my iCloud account to unlock my disk.**

     - **Explanation:** This method ties your FileVault recovery capability to your Apple ID account that's linked with iCloud on this Mac. If you forget your Mac login password, macOS can guide you through a password reset process that involves verifying your identity using your Apple ID password and potentially Two-Factor Authentication codes sent to your trusted devices or phone number.

     - **Pros:** Generally the most convenient option for many users. You don't need to safeguard a separate physical key. Recovery relies on the Apple ID you use for many other services.

     - **Cons:** You must be able to access your Apple ID account (remember the password, have access to trusted devices/numbers for 2FA). If you lose access to your Apple ID itself, recovering your FileVault-encrypted Mac might become impossible through this method. It relies on an online service for recovery.

   - **Option B: Create a recovery key and do not use my iCloud account.**

     - **Explanation:** If you choose this, macOS will generate a unique, long **Recovery Key** composed of letters and numbers, usually formatted with dashes (e.g., RKEY-ABCD-EFGH-IJKL-MNOP-QRST). This key becomes the *only* alternative way to unlock your encrypted disk if you forget all user login passwords.

     - **Pros:** Recovery is entirely offline and independent of Apple's servers or your iCloud account status. You possess the sole backup key. Preferred by some users who want maximum control or operate in environments where iCloud access might be restricted or distrusted.

     - **Cons: Extreme caution required.** You *must* write down this Recovery Key *exactly* as shown (it's case-sensitive). Store it securely in multiple safe places, completely separate from your Mac. Do *not* save it as a file on the encrypted Mac itself! If you lose this key and also forget your login password(s), **your data**

will be permanently inaccessible. Apple cannot help you recover a lost FileVault recovery key.

8. **Confirm and Proceed:** Select the recovery option that you understand and feel comfortable managing. Follow the on-screen prompts. If you chose the recovery key option, macOS will display the key and strongly advise you to write it down accurately before continuing. **Do not skip this step or rush it.** Double-check what you've written.

Encryption Process: Once you confirm your recovery method, click **Continue** or **Done**. FileVault will now start encrypting your entire startup disk. This process happens securely in the background while you continue to use your Mac. The initial encryption can take anywhere from minutes to several hours, depending on the size of your drive and how much data is on it. You can usually check the encryption progress in the FileVault settings pane. Your Mac might need to be plugged into power during the initial encryption. A restart might be required to finalize the process.

FileVault Recovery Option	How It Works	Pros	Cons	Recommendation
Use iCloud Account	Links recovery to Apple ID/Password.	Convenient, no separate key to manage.	Relies on iCloud access; potential Apple ID account recovery issues.	Good for most users comfortable with iCloud security.
Create Recovery Key	Generates a unique key stored only by the user.	Independent of iCloud; user holds key.	**CRITICAL:** Losing key = permanent data loss if password forgotten.	For users who prefer offline recovery / distrust cloud recovery, *if* they can guarantee key safety.

Using Your Mac with FileVault Enabled

The beauty of FileVault is its transparency after setup:

- **Login:** When you start up your Mac, you'll see the usual login screen. Enter your user password as normal. This password not only logs you into your account but also simultaneously decrypts the necessary parts of the disk to allow macOS to load. After this initial login, Touch ID (if enabled) can be used to unlock your Mac from sleep or the lock screen.

- **Performance:** As highlighted earlier, the M4 chip's dedicated encryption hardware ensures that the constant encryption/decryption process has virtually no noticeable impact on your Mac's speed or responsiveness during everyday use.
- **Security:** You have the significant added security layer knowing your files are protected against unauthorized physical access.

Turning FileVault Off

Disabling FileVault is possible but generally **not recommended** from a security standpoint, as it removes this crucial protection for your data at rest. If you have a specific need to turn it off (perhaps for advanced troubleshooting directed by support personnel):

1. Return to **System Settings > Privacy & Security > FileVault**.
2. Click the **"Turn Off..."** button.
3. Authenticate with your administrator password.
4. The decryption process will begin in the background. Similar to encryption, this can take some time, and you can continue using your Mac while it happens. Your data becomes progressively unencrypted during this period.

For the vast majority of users, especially with a portable device like a MacBook Air, leaving FileVault turned **On** is the recommended and responsible choice. It provides essential protection for your personal information with minimal impact on your daily workflow. Just be absolutely certain you have a reliable recovery method (either iCloud or a safely stored recovery key) in case you ever forget your login password.

Understanding and Configuring System Privacy Settings & App Permissions

In addition to securing your device and accounts, macOS provides extensive controls for managing your **privacy** – specifically, controlling which applications are allowed to access your personal information (like contacts, calendars, photos, location) and sensitive hardware components (like the microphone and camera). Giving apps appropriate access is often necessary for them to function, but granting unnecessary permissions can expose your data. macOS requires apps to ask for your permission first, and the **Privacy & Security** settings provide a central place to review and manage these permissions.

Navigating Privacy & Security Settings

1. Open **System Settings** (Gear icon in Dock or Apple menu □ > System Settings...).
2. Scroll down the sidebar and click on **Privacy & Security**.

3. The main pane lists various categories of data and hardware that require specific permissions for apps to access. Clicking on any category name (e.g., "Microphone," "Photos," "Location Services") will show you which apps have requested or been granted access to that specific item.

The Permission Model: Apps Must Ask First

macOS operates on an "ask first" principle for sensitive data. When an application attempts to access something like your contacts, location, camera, or microphone for the very first time, macOS will interrupt the app and display a standard dialog box directly asking for your consent. This prompt will typically say something like:

"[App Name]" would like to access your [Data Type, e.g., Contacts / Photos / Microphone].

You will usually have buttons like "Don't Allow" and "OK" or "Allow." Your choice is recorded, and you can change it later in the Privacy & Security settings. This ensures that apps can't silently access sensitive information without your explicit approval.

Understanding Key Privacy Categories and Why Apps Ask

Let's walk through some of the most important categories found under Privacy & Security:

1. **Location Services:** Controls whether apps and system services can determine your Mac's physical location (usually based on nearby Wi-Fi networks).
   - *Settings:* Toggle Location Services on/off globally. See a list of apps that have requested access; toggle permission for each. Click "Details..." next to System Services for fine-grained control over macOS features using location (Find My, Time Zone, Suggestions, etc.).
   - *Why apps ask:* Mapping apps (Maps) need it for directions and showing your current location. Weather apps need it for local forecasts. Photos can use it to geotag where pictures were taken (Places album). Some websites accessed via Safari might request location.

2. **Contacts, Calendars, Reminders:** These control access to the data stored within the respective standard macOS applications.
   - *Settings:* Simple toggle switches for each app that has requested access.
   - *Why apps ask:* Email clients (like Mail or third-party ones) might request Contacts access to autocomplete addresses. Third-party calendar apps need Calendar access to display/edit your events. Productivity or task management apps might want to integrate with Reminders. Communication apps might request Contacts to find friends.

3. **Photos:** Governs access to your entire photo library managed by the Photos app.

   o *Settings:* Toggle access for requesting apps. Sometimes, macOS offers more granular control, allowing an app access only to *specific photos* you select, rather than the whole library (look for this option when the app first asks).

   o *Why apps ask:* Photo editing software, video editors (like iMovie), social media apps for uploading pictures, presentation apps (Keynote, PowerPoint) for inserting images.

4. **Camera & Microphone:** These control direct access to your MacBook Air's built-in camera and microphone hardware.

   o *Settings:* Toggle switches for each requesting app.

   o **Indicator Lights:** Crucially, macOS provides hardware-linked visual indicators in the Menu Bar whenever these are active: an **orange dot (□)** means the microphone is currently in use by an application; a **green dot (□)** means the camera is currently in use (and if the camera is on, the microphone is usually also assumed to be potentially active). Pay attention to these dots! If they appear when you don't expect them to, open Control Center – it often lists which app recently used the mic/camera.

   o *Why apps ask:* Essential for video conferencing (FaceTime, Zoom, Teams, Webex), audio recording (GarageBand, Voice Memos, audio editors), dictation software, video creation tools (iMovie, QuickTime Player recording). Grant permission only to apps you trust and expect to use these features.

5. **Screen Recording & Input Monitoring:** These grant powerful capabilities and should be treated with extra caution.

   o *Screen Recording:* Allows an app to capture everything displayed on your screen, or specific windows.

   o *Input Monitoring:* Allows an app to observe keystrokes, mouse clicks, and trackpad input, even when you are working in other applications.

   o *Why apps ask:* Screen sharing apps (for remote support or presentations), remote desktop tools, some accessibility software, certain system utilities, potentially keylogging malware (which is why caution is needed!). Only grant these permissions to well-known, trusted applications where this functionality is clearly required and expected.

6. **Accessibility:** This permission allows apps to control your Mac using system accessibility features. It grants very broad capabilities, including simulating keyboard input and mouse actions, and reading screen content.

   o *Why apps ask:* Assistive technologies for users with disabilities, automation utilities (like Keyboard Maestro), text expansion software, some window management tools, specialized input device drivers.

   o *Caution:* Be extremely careful when granting Accessibility access. Only approve apps you absolutely trust and that require this level of control for their legitimate function. Malware might seek this permission to gain extensive control over your system.

7. **Files and Folders:** macOS protects specific user folders. Apps need explicit permission to access your Desktop, Documents, and Downloads folders, as well as external drives (Removable Volumes) and network storage (Network Volumes).

   o *Settings:* Toggle access for each app that requests it for these specific locations.

   o *Why apps ask:* Word processors need Documents access, web browsers or download managers need Downloads access, file sync utilities might need Desktop/Documents access, backup software or video editors might need access to Removable Volumes.

8. **Full Disk Access:** This is the highest level of file access permission. Apps granted Full Disk Access can read and write data almost anywhere on your Mac, including system areas and potentially sensitive user data like Mail databases, Messages history, Safari browsing data, Time Machine backups, and even files belonging to other users on the Mac.

   o *Settings:* Toggle access for requesting apps. You often need to manually add apps here using the '+' button after authenticating.

   o *Caution:* Grant Full Disk Access *extremely* sparingly. Only give it to highly trusted applications where it is absolutely essential for their core function (examples might include reputable system backup utilities, anti-malware software that needs deep scanning capabilities, or certain data recovery tools). Most everyday applications do not need Full Disk Access.

9. **Other Important Categories:**

   o *Analytics & Improvements:* Control whether anonymous diagnostic and usage data is shared with Apple and app developers.

   o *Advertising:* Options to limit ad tracking using Apple's advertising identifier.

   o *App Management:* Allows apps to update or delete other apps.

- *Focus, Bluetooth, HomeKit, Media & Apple Music:* Control app access related to these specific system features or data types.

Managing Permissions: Your Control Panel

Reviewing and adjusting permissions is easy:

1. Navigate to the relevant category in **System Settings > Privacy & Security**.

2. Look at the list of applications shown on the right.

3. Use the **toggle switch** next to each application's name to enable (On - blue/green) or disable (Off - gray) its permission for that specific category.

4. For some changes, especially in sensitive categories like Accessibility or Full Disk Access, you may need to click the lock icon at the bottom left (if present) and authenticate with your password or Touch ID before you can make modifications.

App Store Privacy Information

Remember the "App Privacy" section on Mac App Store pages? Before installing an app, review this section (often called "Privacy Nutrition Labels"). Developers self-report the types of data their app collects (like Contact Info, Location, Identifiers, Usage Data) and whether that data is linked to you or used for tracking purposes. This helps you make informed decisions *before* granting permissions later.

General Privacy Best Practices

- **Think Before Clicking Allow:** When an app requests permission, pause for a second. Does this app *really* need access to my location/contacts/microphone for what I want it to do? If unsure, deny permission initially; you can usually grant it later via System Settings if needed.

- **Least Privilege:** Grant the minimum level of permission necessary. If an app only needs access to specific photos, try to use the "Selected Photos" option instead of granting full library access if available.

- **Periodic Review:** Make it a habit (perhaps every few months) to quickly review the lists in Privacy & Security settings. Remove permissions for apps you no longer use. Ensure no unexpected apps have access to sensitive areas like Camera, Microphone, Accessibility, or Full Disk Access.

- **Heed the Dots:** Pay attention to the orange (mic) and green (camera) indicator dots in the Menu Bar. They are your real-time alert system for hardware usage.

By actively managing your Privacy & Security settings, you take control over how applications interact with your personal data and your Mac's hardware, ensuring your MacBook Air M4 remains a secure and trustworthy digital environment.

iCloud & Continuity: Seamless Apple Ecosystem Integration

One of the most compelling reasons people choose Apple devices is how well they work together. This seamless integration, often referred to as the Apple "ecosystem," is largely powered by **iCloud** and a suite of features collectively known as **Continuity**. When set up correctly, these technologies allow your MacBook Air M4, iPhone, iPad, and even Apple Watch to share information, sync data, and hand off tasks effortlessly, making your digital life significantly more convenient and efficient. In this chapter, we'll explore how iCloud Drive keeps your files accessible everywhere, how iCloud syncs data within core apps, how Handoff lets you start tasks on one device and finish on another, and how features like Universal Control and AirPlay further blur the lines between your devices.

Understanding iCloud Drive: Syncing Files Across Devices

We briefly introduced iCloud when discussing your Apple ID in Chapter 1, but let's focus specifically on **iCloud Drive**. Think of iCloud Drive as Apple's cloud storage service, similar in concept to Dropbox or Google Drive, but deeply integrated into macOS and iOS/iPadOS. It allows you to store files and folders securely in the cloud and access them from virtually anywhere – your Mac, iPhone, iPad, and even via a web browser on any computer.

How iCloud Drive Works

When you save files to iCloud Drive (or specific folders synced via iCloud Drive), those files are uploaded securely to Apple's servers. They are then automatically downloaded or made available (depending on settings) to all other devices where you are signed in with the same Apple ID and have iCloud Drive enabled. Any changes you make to a file on one device are automatically synced through the cloud and reflected on your other devices.

- **Storage:** Remember that iCloud Drive uses your iCloud storage allocation. Apple provides **5GB of free storage** to every Apple ID. If you plan to store many large files, photos (using iCloud Photos), or device backups in iCloud, you'll likely need to upgrade to a paid **iCloud+ plan** for more storage (options typically range from 50GB up to multiple terabytes). You manage storage in System Settings > [Your Name] > iCloud > Account Storage > Manage... or Change Storage Plan...

Enabling iCloud Drive on Your Mac

You likely enabled iCloud Drive during the initial Mac setup. To check or enable it:

1. Go to **System Settings > [Your Name] (Apple ID)** at the top of the sidebar.
2. Click **iCloud**.
3. In the list of "Apps Using iCloud," find **iCloud Drive**.

4. Ensure the toggle switch next to it is **On**.

5. Click the **"Options..."** button next to the iCloud Drive toggle for crucial settings (discussed below).

Key Feature: Syncing Desktop & Documents Folders

This is perhaps the most significant (and sometimes confusing for new users) feature within iCloud Drive's options.

1. In the iCloud Drive Options panel (from step 5 above), you'll see a section often labeled **"Folders"** or similar, with an option for **"Desktop & Documents Folders."**

2. **If you check this box:** The *entire contents* of your Mac's traditional Desktop and Documents folders are moved *into* your iCloud Drive. They will still *appear* to be on your Desktop and in your Documents folder via Finder's Favorites, but their actual storage location is now managed by iCloud Drive.

3. **The Benefit:** Any file you save to your Desktop or Documents folder on this Mac will automatically upload to iCloud Drive and become accessible in the corresponding Desktop and Documents folders within iCloud Drive on your other Macs, in the Files app on your iPhone/iPad, and via iCloud.com. It's incredibly convenient for keeping your primary work files synchronized without manually dragging them to a specific cloud folder.

4. **The Implication (Especially with Optimize Mac Storage):** Because these folders are now part of iCloud Drive, the files within them are subject to the "Optimize Mac Storage" setting (see below). This means if storage space gets low, files you haven't opened recently might be removed from your local Mac storage and kept only in iCloud, requiring an internet connection to re-download them when needed. Understand this before enabling the feature, especially if you frequently work offline or have limited internet bandwidth.

Syncing Desktop & Documents	Pros	Cons
Enabled	Seamless syncing of primary work folders across devices; easy access everywhere.	Uses iCloud storage; files subject to Optimize Mac Storage (might require download); changes sync everywhere.
Disabled	Desktop/Documents files stored locally only; doesn't use iCloud storage.	Files not automatically synced; requires manual copying/moving to iCloud Drive folder for syncing.

1. Many users find the convenience worth it, especially with larger iCloud+ storage plans. If you disable it later, your files will be moved from iCloud Drive back into a standard local Home folder structure.

Accessing Your iCloud Drive Files

Once enabled, accessing your synced files is easy:

- **Finder Sidebar (Mac):** Click **iCloud Drive** in the Favorites section. You'll see standard folders (like Keynote, Pages, Numbers, etc., for documents created in those apps) and any other folders or files you've saved directly to iCloud Drive. If you enabled Desktop & Documents syncing, those folders will also appear here (or might replace the standard local Desktop/Documents links in Favorites).

- **Files App (iPhone/iPad):** Open the built-in Files app. Tap "Browse," then select "iCloud Drive" under Locations. You'll see the same folder structure and files as on your Mac.

- **iCloud.com (Web Browser):** Go to www.icloud.com on any computer's web browser, sign in with your Apple ID, and click the iCloud Drive icon. You can view, download, upload, and organize files directly through the web interface. This is handy when accessing your files from a non-Apple computer.

Optimize Mac Storage: Saving Local Space

This setting, found in the **iCloud Drive Options** panel (System Settings > [Your Name] > iCloud > iCloud Drive > Options...), helps manage your Mac's local storage when using iCloud Drive (including synced Desktop & Documents).

- **How it Works:** When **Optimize Mac Storage** is checked (often the default), macOS intelligently manages which iCloud Drive files are stored fully on your Mac and which are stored primarily in iCloud. If your Mac starts running low on storage space, macOS will automatically remove the local copies of older, less frequently used files from your iCloud Drive folders (including Desktop/Documents if synced), leaving behind only a pointer or thumbnail. The full file remains safe in iCloud.

- **Identifying Online-Only Files:** Files stored only in iCloud will have a small **cloud icon with a downward arrow (☁□↓)** next to their name in Finder.

- **Accessing Online-Only Files:** When you double-click an online-only file (with the cloud icon), macOS automatically downloads the full version from iCloud Drive (requires an internet connection). Once downloaded, the cloud icon disappears, and the file is stored locally again (until macOS decides to optimize it away later if space is needed).

- **Forcing Local Copies:** If you want to ensure specific files or folders within iCloud Drive are always stored locally (e.g., for offline access), right-click the item in Finder and choose **"Download Now."**

- **Pros:** Automatically frees up local disk space, which can be crucial on laptops with limited SSD storage. You still see all your files in Finder.

- **Cons:** Requires an internet connection to access files that have been offloaded. Downloading large files can take time depending on your internet speed. Might be inconvenient if you frequently work offline and need access to older files unexpectedly.

If you have ample local storage and prefer having all your iCloud Drive files available offline instantly, you can *uncheck* "Optimize Mac Storage." Just be aware that your iCloud Drive contents will then consume more space on your Mac's internal drive.

Sharing Files and Folders from iCloud Drive

iCloud Drive makes collaboration easy:

1. In Finder, locate the file or folder *within your iCloud Drive* that you want to share.

2. Right-click (Control-click) the item.

3. Hover over the **Share...** submenu.

4. Choose how you want to share:

   o **Collaborate:** This is the most powerful option. It allows you to invite specific people (via Mail, Messages, or by copying a link) to view or *make changes* to the shared file or folder. Changes made by anyone are synced via iCloud. You can set permissions (who can access, view only vs. can make changes). Great for working on shared documents or projects.

   o **Send Copy:** This uses standard sharing methods (Mail, Messages, AirDrop) to send a *separate copy* of the file, rather than collaborating on the original.

iCloud Drive is a powerful tool for keeping your important files synchronized and accessible across your Apple ecosystem, with flexible options for managing storage and collaboration.

Syncing Photos, Contacts, Calendars, and More with iCloud

Beyond storing files in iCloud Drive, iCloud is the invisible engine that keeps the data *within* many of your core Apple applications perfectly synchronized across your MacBook Air M4, iPhone, iPad, and other Apple devices. This ensures consistency and convenience, meaning changes made on one device automatically reflect everywhere else.

Managing iCloud Sync Settings for Apps

The central place to control which apps use iCloud for syncing is:

1. Go to **System Settings > [Your Name] (Apple ID)** at the top of the sidebar.

2. Click **iCloud**.

3. You'll see a list of some primary apps using iCloud (like Photos, iCloud Drive, iCloud Mail, Passwords & Keychain).

4. Click the **"Show All"** button under the "Apps Using iCloud" heading to reveal a longer list of individual apps and system services that can sync data via iCloud.

5. For most apps in this list, you'll see a simple **On/Off toggle switch**. Turning the switch **On** enables iCloud syncing for that app's data. Turning it **Off** disables syncing for that app on *that specific Mac* (it doesn't delete the data from iCloud itself, just stops syncing it to/from that device).

Key Apps and Data Synced via iCloud

Let's look at some of the most important apps and the data they sync when their respective toggles are enabled in iCloud settings:

1. **Photos (Requires iCloud Photos toggle):**

   o Syncs your *entire* photo and video library, including albums, edits, keywords, People & Pets data, and Memories.

   o Changes made on one device (like editing a photo on your Mac) appear on your iPhone, and vice-versa.

   o **Important:** Uses significant iCloud storage. Ensure you have an adequate iCloud+ plan if your library is large. Offers an "Optimize Mac Storage" option similar to iCloud Drive to save local space by keeping full-resolution originals in iCloud.

2. **Contacts:**

   o Syncs all your contact cards, including names, phone numbers, email addresses, notes, photos, etc.

   o Add a contact on your iPhone, and it instantly appears in the Contacts app on your Mac.

3. **Calendars:**

   o Syncs all your calendars (Home, Work, custom ones created under your iCloud account) and all the events within them.

   o Add an appointment on your Mac, and it shows up on your iPad's calendar. Accept an invitation on your iPhone, and it reflects on your Mac.

4. **Reminders:**

   o Syncs all your reminder lists (including custom lists) and the individual reminder items within them (including due dates, notes, subtasks, tags).

   o Check off a reminder on your Apple Watch, and it marks as completed on your Mac.

5. **Notes:**
   - Syncs all your notes, including text, formatting, checklists, tables, attachments (images, scans, sketches), folders, tags, and locked note status.
   - Start jotting down ideas in Notes on your Mac, continue adding to it on your iPad later.

6. **Safari:**
   - Syncs your Bookmarks, Reading List, browsing History, open Tabs (via iCloud Tabs feature – see open tabs from other devices), Tab Groups, and Profiles across devices.
   - Bookmark a site on your Mac, and it's available in Safari on your iPhone.

7. **Keychain (Requires Passwords & Keychain toggle):**
   - Securely syncs your saved website/app passwords, passkeys, Wi-Fi passwords, credit card info (sans CVV), and internet account credentials using end-to-end encryption.
   - Save a password on your Mac, and Safari on your iPhone can autofill it (after authentication).

8. **Mail (Requires iCloud Mail toggle for @icloud.com address; other accounts sync via their own protocols like IMAP):**
   - Primarily syncs settings for your @icloud.com email account and mail rules you set up on your Mac. The emails themselves for an @icloud.com account are stored on iCloud's servers and accessed via the standard IMAP protocol, ensuring they appear consistent across Mail apps. Other email accounts (Gmail, Outlook) sync their emails via their respective servers (IMAP/Exchange).

9. **Messages (Requires Messages in iCloud toggle):**
   - Syncs your entire iMessage conversation history across all devices. When enabled, deleting a message or conversation on one device removes it from all others. If disabled, message history might be inconsistent between devices. Uses iCloud storage.

10. **Other Apps & Services:** Many other Apple apps and system services leverage iCloud for syncing preferences or data, including:
    - **Home:** Syncs your HomeKit smart home configuration.
    - **Siri:** Syncs Siri settings and learned information.
    - **Stocks & News:** Syncs your watchlists, followed topics, and reading history.
    - **Books:** Syncs library contents, reading/listening progress, notes, highlights, collections.
    - **Wallet:** Syncs passes and settings (though Apple Pay cards are added per device).

- o **Find My:** Uses iCloud to locate your devices and track shared items/people.
- o **Third-Party Apps:** Many apps from the App Store also offer iCloud syncing for their own data (check the app's settings).

App/Service	Key Data Synced via iCloud	Benefit
Photos	Entire library, edits, albums, people, places, keywords.	Consistent photo access & edits everywhere; saves local storage (optional).
Contacts	All contact cards and groups.	Up-to-date address book on all devices.
Calendars	All calendars and events (including shared/subscribed).	Consistent schedule across Mac, iPhone, iPad, Watch.
Reminders	All lists and reminder items (incl. details like dates, tags).	To-do lists stay in sync everywhere.
Notes	All notes, folders, tags, attachments, locked status, collaboration.	Access and edit notes seamlessly on any device.
Safari	Bookmarks, Reading List, History, iCloud Tabs, Tab Groups, Profiles.	Consistent browsing experience, continue browsing between devices.
Keychain	Passwords, Passkeys, Wi-Fi passwords, Credit Cards (end-to-end encrypted).	Secure login autofill, easy Wi-Fi connection across devices.
Messages	Full iMessage conversation history (optional).	See complete chat history on all devices; delete once, delete everywhere.
Books	Library, reading/listening progress, highlights, notes, collections.	Pick up reading/listening exactly where you left off on another device.
(iCloud Drive)	Files/folders in iCloud Drive, synced Desktop & Documents (optional).	Access files from any device; keeps primary folders synced (optional).

The Magic of Seamless Syncing

The primary benefit of iCloud syncing is **convenience and consistency**. You no longer need to manually transfer contacts, update calendar events on multiple devices, or email notes to yourself. Make a change once, and iCloud takes care of updating it everywhere else automatically and securely in the background. It makes using multiple Apple devices feel like using one unified system for your important information. Just ensure you have enough iCloud storage for the services you rely on most (especially Photos and iCloud Drive).

Handoff: Starting Tasks on One Device and Finishing on Another

Have you ever started writing an email on your Mac and then needed to rush out the door, wishing you could easily finish it on your iPhone? Or perhaps you found directions on your Mac but want to use your iPhone for navigation in the car? **Handoff**, a key feature of Apple's Continuity suite, makes these scenarios incredibly smooth. It allows you to seamlessly transfer your current activity in a supported application from one Apple device to another nearby device.

How Handoff Works

Handoff uses a combination of technologies:

- **Bluetooth Low Energy (BLE):** Your devices use Bluetooth to detect when they are near each other.

- **Wi-Fi:** The devices need to be on the same Wi-Fi network (though sometimes direct Wi-Fi can work).

- **iCloud:** Your devices must be signed into the same Apple ID via iCloud to verify they belong to you and to transfer the activity state.

Ensuring Handoff is Enabled

For Handoff to work, you need to make sure it's turned on for all participating devices:

- **On your MacBook Air M4:**
  - Go to **System Settings > General**.
  - Click on **AirDrop & Handoff**.
  - Ensure the toggle switch for **"Allow Handoff between this Mac and your iCloud devices"** is **On**.
- **On your iPhone or iPad:**
  - Go to **Settings > General**.
  - Tap on **AirDrop & Handoff**.
  - Ensure the **Handoff** toggle switch is **On**.

Additionally, make sure Bluetooth and Wi-Fi are enabled on all devices, they are relatively close to each other, and they are all signed into the same iCloud account with Two-Factor Authentication enabled.

Using Handoff: Passing the Baton

Using Handoff feels almost magical once you know where to look:

- **Handing Off from Mac to iPhone/iPad:**
  - Be actively using a Handoff-compatible application on your Mac (like Mail, Safari, Notes, Maps, Pages, Numbers, Keynote, etc.).
  - Unlock your nearby iPhone or iPad.
  - Open the **App Switcher** on your iPhone/iPad (swipe up from the bottom edge of the screen and pause briefly).
  - At the bottom of the App Switcher screen, you should see a banner appear showing the icon of the app you were using on your Mac and a description of the activity (e.g., "Safari from MacBook Air," "Mail Composing Message").
  - **Tap this banner.** The corresponding app will open on your iPhone/iPad, taking you directly to the webpage, email draft, note, or document you were working on, ready for you to continue. (On older iOS versions or the Lock Screen, the Handoff icon might appear differently).

- **Handing Off from iPhone/iPad to Mac:**
  - Be actively using a Handoff-compatible application on your iPhone or iPad.
  - Look at the **Dock** on your MacBook Air.
  - An **additional icon** representing the app you're using on your mobile device will appear on the **far left end of the Dock** (or the far right end if your Dock is positioned vertically). This icon might have a small device symbol (like a tiny iPhone) superimposed on it.
  - **Click this special Handoff icon** in the Dock.
  - The corresponding application will launch on your Mac (if not already running) and open directly to the content or task you were working on, allowing you to pick up right where you left off.

Handoff Direction	Where to Look on Destination Device	Action to Take
Mac → iPhone/iPad	App Switcher (banner at bottom) or sometimes Lock Screen.	Tap the Handoff banner/icon.
iPhone/iPad → Mac	Far left (or right) end of the Dock (extra app icon appears).	Click the special Handoff icon in the Dock.

Which Apps Support Handoff?

Handoff works with many of Apple's built-in applications, including:

- Mail (composing messages, viewing drafts)
- Safari (viewing webpages)
- Maps (viewing locations, routes)
- Notes (editing notes)
- Reminders (viewing lists)
- Calendar (creating/editing events)
- Contacts (viewing/editing cards)
- Pages, Numbers, Keynote (editing documents)
- Some system settings

Additionally, some third-party applications from the App Store also build in support for Handoff.

Handoff is designed for those moments when you need to switch devices mid-task. It eliminates the need to manually save, send the file to yourself, and reopen it on the other device, making transitions between your Mac, iPhone, and iPad incredibly fluid.

Universal Control, AirPlay, and Other Continuity Features

Handoff is just one piece of Apple's broader **Continuity** strategy, which encompasses several features designed to make your Apple devices work together more intelligently and seamlessly. Let's explore some other powerful Continuity features available on your MacBook Air M4: Universal Control, AirPlay to Mac, and a quick recap of others.

Universal Control: One Keyboard & Mouse for Multiple Devices

This feature feels truly futuristic. **Universal Control** allows you to use the keyboard and mouse (or trackpad) already connected to your Mac to *also* control one or two other nearby Macs or iPads that are signed into the same iCloud account. Your cursor moves effortlessly between the screens as if they were part of a single extended desktop, but each device continues running its own operating system (macOS or iPadOS).

- **The Magic:** Imagine your MacBook Air in the center, and your iPad sitting next to it. With Universal Control, you just move your Mac's cursor off the edge of the Mac screen towards the iPad, and it magically appears on the iPad's screen! Now, your Mac's keyboard and trackpad control the iPad. Move the cursor back towards the Mac screen, and it seamlessly returns control to your Mac. You can even drag and drop files between the devices this way!

- **Requirements:**
  - Compatible macOS (Monterey 12.3 or later) and iPadOS (15.4 or later) versions on all devices.

- Devices must be within Bluetooth/Wi-Fi range (approx. 10 meters / 30 feet).

- Bluetooth and Wi-Fi must be turned On for all devices.

- Handoff must be enabled on all devices.

- All devices must be signed into the **same Apple ID** using **Two-Factor Authentication**.

- The devices must not be using Internet Sharing (Personal Hotspot).

- **Setup/Enabling:** It's often enabled by default if requirements are met, but you can check/adjust settings:

  - On your Mac, go to **System Settings > Displays**.

  - Click the **"Advanced..."** button at the bottom.

  - Look for the "Link to Mac or iPad" section. Ensure these toggles are generally **On**:

    0. "Allow your pointer and keyboard to move between any nearby Mac or iPad."

    1. "Push through the edge of a display to connect a nearby Mac or iPad." (Lets you initiate the connection by moving the cursor).

    2. "Automatically reconnect to any nearby Mac or iPad." (Remembers previous connections).

  - On your iPad, check Settings > General > AirPlay & Handoff > "Cursor and Keyboard".

- **Using Universal Control:**

  - **Connecting:** Simply move your Mac's cursor past the left or right edge of its screen *towards* the physical location of your other Mac or iPad. You should see a small animation or border appear on the edge of the target device's screen as the cursor "pushes" through. Continue moving, and the cursor will appear on the other device.

  - **Controlling:** Once the cursor is on the other device's screen, your Mac's keyboard and trackpad/mouse now control that device. You can type, click, scroll, and use gestures just as if they were directly connected.

  - **Dragging Files:** You can click and drag a file (like an image or document) from one device's screen across the boundary to the other device's screen and drop it to copy the file over.

  - **Disconnecting:** Simply move the cursor back across the boundary to your primary device. The connection usually disconnects automatically after a period of inactivity or if the devices move too far apart.

- **Use Cases:** Perfect for using your comfortable Mac keyboard/trackpad to quickly type something on your iPad, easily dragging a sketch from Procreate on iPad to a document on your Mac, managing files across two Macs side-by-side without needing extra peripherals.

AirPlay to Mac: Turn Your Mac into an AirPlay Receiver

Typically, AirPlay is used to send content *from* your Mac/iPhone/iPad *to* an Apple TV or AirPlay-enabled speaker. But **AirPlay to Mac** reverses this, allowing your MacBook Air M4 to *receive* AirPlay streams from your other Apple devices.

- **The Concept:** You can wirelessly mirror the screen of your iPhone or iPad onto your Mac's display, or stream audio or video from an app on your mobile device directly to your Mac's speakers and screen.

- **Enabling AirPlay Receiver:**
  - On your MacBook Air, go to **System Settings > General > AirDrop & Handoff**.
  - Find the **AirPlay Receiver** toggle and turn it **On**.
  - Configure who is allowed to AirPlay to your Mac:
    0. **"Current User":** Only other devices signed into *your* Apple ID can AirPlay to this Mac. (Most secure).
    1. **"Anyone on the Same Network":** Any Apple device connected to the same Wi-Fi network can discover and AirPlay to your Mac.
    2. **"Everyone":** Any nearby Apple device can potentially AirPlay (use with caution, similar to AirDrop's "Everyone").
  - You can also optionally require a password for AirPlay connections.

- **Using AirPlay to Mac:**
  - On your sending device (iPhone, iPad, or another Mac):
    0. **Screen Mirroring:** Open Control Center, tap the Screen Mirroring button (two overlapping rectangles), and select your MacBook Air from the list of available devices.
    1. **App-Specific AirPlay:** In apps like Music, Photos, TV, or Safari, look for the **AirPlay icon** (triangle pointing into concentric circles or sometimes a screen icon). Tap it and select your MacBook Air as the playback destination.
  - The content will start streaming or mirroring onto your Mac's screen/speakers. A notification might appear on your Mac confirming the connection.

- **Use Cases:** Quickly showing photos from your iPhone on your Mac's larger display without transferring files, playing a podcast from your iPad through your Mac's speakers, mirroring an iOS app for a demo or presentation shown on your Mac screen.

Other Notable Continuity Features

These features further enhance the synergy between your Apple devices:

- **Continuity Camera:** Use the high-quality camera system on your nearby iPhone or iPad as the webcam and/or microphone for your Mac. When starting a video call or using a camera app on your Mac, your iPhone might automatically offer to be used, or you can select it from the camera/mic input options. This includes **Desk View**, which uses the iPhone's Ultra Wide camera to show both your face and an overhead view of your desk simultaneously. Manage in System Settings > General > AirDrop & Handoff > Continuity Camera.

- **Continuity Sketch & Markup:** Start creating a sketch or marking up a document/image on your Mac (e.g., in Notes, Pages, Preview's Markup tools), and you might see an option to "Insert from iPhone or iPad > Add Sketch". This lets you draw or write on your mobile device's touchscreen using your finger or Apple Pencil, and the result appears instantly back on your Mac.

- **Instant Hotspot:** If your Mac doesn't have an internet connection but your iPhone (with cellular data) is nearby and Personal Hotspot is enabled, your Mac can automatically see and connect to your iPhone's hotspot via the Wi-Fi menu without you needing to enter the password. Requires devices to be signed into the same iCloud account.

- **Auto Unlock with Apple Watch:** If you wear an Apple Watch that's authenticated and paired with your iPhone (which uses the same Apple ID as your Mac), you can set your Mac to automatically unlock when you wake it while wearing your watch nearby. No need for password or Touch ID! Enable in System Settings > Touch ID & Password > "Use your Apple Watch to unlock your applications and your Mac".

- **Universal Clipboard:** Copy text, an image, or a file on one Apple device (e.g., your iPhone), and then simply paste it on another nearby Apple device (e.g., your Mac) within a short time frame. It works automatically in the background if Handoff is enabled. Just Copy on one, then Paste (⌘+V) on the other!

Continuity Feature	Function	Key Requirement(s)
Handoff	Start task on one device, continue on another nearby device.	Same Apple ID, Bluetooth/Wi-Fi On, Handoff enabled, devices nearby.
Universal Control	Use one keyboard/mouse to	Same Apple ID (2FA), Bluetooth/Wi-Fi On,

	control multiple nearby Macs/iPads.	Handoff enabled, devices nearby, compatible OS.
AirPlay to Mac	Receive AirPlay stream (mirroring, video, audio) from other Apple devices.	Same Apple ID (optional, depending on setting), Wi-Fi On, AirPlay Receiver enabled.
Continuity Camera	Use iPhone/iPad camera/mic as Mac's webcam/mic wirelessly.	Same Apple ID, Bluetooth/Wi-Fi On, devices nearby, compatible OS.
Continuity Sketch/Markup	Draw/annotate on iPhone/iPad, insert result instantly onto Mac.	Same Apple ID, Bluetooth/Wi-Fi On, devices nearby.
Instant Hotspot	Mac easily connects to iPhone's Personal Hotspot without password.	Same Apple ID, Bluetooth/Wi-Fi On, Personal Hotspot enabled on iPhone.
Auto Unlock	Unlock Mac automatically when wearing authenticated Apple Watch nearby.	Same Apple ID, Bluetooth/Wi-Fi On, Watch paired & passcode enabled.
Universal Clipboard	Copy on one device, paste on another nearby device.	Same Apple ID, Bluetooth/Wi-Fi On, Handoff enabled, devices nearby.

The suite of iCloud syncing and Continuity features transforms your individual Apple devices into a powerful, interconnected system. By enabling and understanding these features, you can significantly streamline your workflow, save time, and enjoy a more fluid experience as you move between your MacBook Air M4 and your other Apple gear.

Connecting Accessories & Peripherals

Your MacBook Air M4 is a sleek and powerful machine on its own, but its versatility truly shines when you connect external accessories and peripherals. Whether you need more screen real estate for multitasking, extra storage space for large files, a more ergonomic keyboard and mouse for long work sessions, or simply need to connect older devices, understanding how to connect and manage these peripherals is key. In this chapter, we'll cover connecting external monitors (highlighting the M4 Air's enhanced capabilities), using various types of external storage, choosing and connecting input devices like keyboards and mice, and expanding your port options with USB-C hubs and Thunderbolt docks.

Connecting External Monitors (M4 Dual Display Capability)

While the MacBook Air's built-in Liquid Retina display is gorgeous, adding one or even two external monitors can dramatically increase your productivity and comfort. More screen space means less window juggling, easier comparison of documents, and the ability to dedicate screens to specific tasks (like communication on one, work on another).

The M4 Advantage: Native Dual External Display Support

This is a significant upgrade for the M4-powered MacBook Air compared to its predecessors with base M1, M2, or M3 chips. Previous base-chip Air models could only natively drive *one* external display. The **MacBook Air M4 natively supports connecting up to two external displays**, each with a resolution up to 6K at a 60Hz refresh rate, *all while keeping the built-in laptop display active as well*. This brings the Air much closer to the multi-monitor capabilities previously reserved for MacBook Pro models, making it a far more versatile machine for complex workflows.

Ports for Connection: Thunderbolt / USB 4

Your MacBook Air M4 features two high-performance **Thunderbolt / USB 4 ports** on the left side, identifiable by the USB-C connector shape and often a small lightning bolt (⚡) icon nearby. These ports are incredibly versatile and are your primary means for connecting external displays. They support:

- **Thunderbolt 4 (up to 40Gb/s):** Highest speed data transfer and display connectivity.

- **USB 4 (up to 40Gb/s):** The latest USB standard, incorporating Thunderbolt features.

- **DisplayPort:** The underlying video signal standard used to drive most high-resolution displays.

- **Charging:** Either port can be used to charge your MacBook Air.

- **USB 3.1 Gen 2 (up to 10Gb/s) and older USB standards.**

How to Connect Your Monitor(s)

The best way to connect depends on the ports available on your external monitor(s):

1. **Direct Connection (USB-C or Thunderbolt Monitor):** This is the simplest and often preferred method if your monitor supports it.

   - **Monitor Input:** Look for a USB-C or Thunderbolt 3 / 4 input port on your monitor.

   - **Cable:** Use a high-quality **Thunderbolt 3, Thunderbolt 4, or USB-C cable** that explicitly supports DisplayPort Alternate Mode (DP Alt Mode) and the required bandwidth (check cable specs for 4K/6K support). A Thunderbolt cable is usually the most reliable choice for high resolutions.

   - **Connection:** Connect one end of the cable to a Thunderbolt / USB 4 port on your MacBook Air and the other end to the USB-C/Thunderbolt input on the monitor.

   - **Benefits:** Often provides video, data, and even **Power Delivery (PD)** over a single cable, meaning the monitor can charge your MacBook Air while displaying video, reducing cable clutter.

   - **For Two Monitors:** Repeat the process using the second Thunderbolt / USB 4 port on your Mac and a second compatible monitor and cable.

2. **Using Adapters or Docks (HDMI or DisplayPort Monitors):** If your monitor only has older HDMI or DisplayPort inputs, you'll need an adapter or a dock/hub.

   - **Monitor Input:** Identify if your monitor uses HDMI or DisplayPort.

   - **Adapter/Cable:**

     - For **HDMI:** You'll need a **USB-C to HDMI adapter** or a USB-C hub/dock with an HDMI port. Ensure the adapter/dock explicitly supports the resolution and refresh rate you need (e.g., "4K @ 60Hz"). Cheaper adapters might only support 4K @ 30Hz, which results in noticeably choppy cursor movement. Use a standard HDMI cable between the adapter/dock and the monitor.

     - For **DisplayPort:** You'll need a **USB-C to DisplayPort adapter** or cable, or a dock/hub with a DisplayPort output. Again, verify support for your desired resolution/refresh rate. Use a standard DisplayPort cable if using an adapter.

   - **Connection:** Connect the adapter/dock to a Thunderbolt / USB 4 port on your Mac. Then connect the HDMI or DisplayPort cable from the adapter/dock to the corresponding input on your monitor.

   - **For Two Monitors:** You can use adapters/docks connected to both Thunderbolt ports on your Mac. A single Thunderbolt dock with multiple video outputs (e.g., dual HDMI or dual DisplayPort) can often drive both external monitors from one Mac port (check the dock's specifications carefully for Mac compatibility and dual display support specifics).

Configuring Your Display Arrangement

Once your external monitor(s) are connected and powered on, your Mac should automatically detect them. You can then customize how they work together:

1. Go to **System Settings > Displays**.

2. You should see icons representing your built-in display and each connected external display.

3. **Arrangement:** Click the **"Arrange..."** button (if available, or the displays might already be shown spatially). A schematic view appears. Drag the display icons around to match the physical placement of your monitors on your desk (e.g., external monitor to the left or right of your MacBook Air screen, or above it). This ensures your mouse cursor moves naturally between screens.

4. **Primary Display:** The display with the white **Menu Bar** shown on its icon in the arrangement view is the primary display (where new windows and notifications usually appear first). You can drag the white Menu Bar from one display icon to another to change the primary display.

5. **Mirroring vs. Extended Desktop:** By default, macOS uses **Extended Desktop** mode, where each display shows independent content, effectively giving you one large workspace. If you want all displays to show the exact same content (**Mirroring**), go back to the main Displays settings, click on the external monitor's icon, and use the "Use as" dropdown menu to select "Mirror for Built-in Retina Display" (or similar wording). Mirroring is useful for presentations but doesn't increase your workspace. Choose "Extended display" to go back.

6. **Resolution and Refresh Rate:** In the Displays settings, click on the icon for an external monitor. You can usually adjust its resolution ("Scaled" options often provide easy choices like "Larger Text" or "More Space") and sometimes the refresh rate (usually defaults to 60Hz, but higher might be available on gaming monitors). It's generally best to leave resolution at "Default for display" unless you have specific needs.

7. **Rotation:** You can also rotate the image on an external display if you physically pivot the monitor (e.g., for coding or long documents).

Choosing an External Monitor

If you're buying a new monitor for your M4 Air:

- **Resolution:** 4K (3840x2160) offers excellent sharpness and is widely available. 5K or 6K monitors (like Apple's Studio Display or Pro Display XDR) offer even more pixel density for incredibly crisp text and images, but are more expensive. QHD/1440p (2560x1440) is a good mid-range option.

- **Connectivity:** Monitors with **USB-C or Thunderbolt input** are highly recommended for easy single-cable connection and potential power delivery. Ensure it supports DisplayPort Alt Mode and sufficient Power Delivery wattage (e.g., 60W+) if you want single-cable charging.

- **Size:** Choose based on your desk space and viewing distance (27-inch and 32-inch are popular choices).

- **Panel Type:** IPS panels generally offer the best color accuracy and viewing angles, ideal for creative work and general use. VA panels offer better contrast, while TN panels offer faster response times (better for competitive gaming but worse colors/angles).

- **Refresh Rate:** 60Hz is standard for general use and video. Higher refresh rates (120Hz, 144Hz+) provide smoother motion, primarily beneficial for gaming.

- **HDR (High Dynamic Range):** If you watch HDR movies or do HDR creative work, look for monitors with good HDR support (e.g., DisplayHDR 600 or higher certification) for brighter highlights and deeper contrast.

Connection Method	Cable(s) Needed	Pros	Cons
Direct USB-C/Thunderbolt	Thunderbolt 3/4 or USB-C (DisplayPort Alt Mode) cable	Single cable for video, data, possibly power (PD); simplest setup.	Monitor must have USB-C/Thunderbolt input; quality cable needed.
USB-C to HDMI Adapter/Hub	USB-C to HDMI Adapter + HDMI Cable	Connects to common HDMI monitors.	Requires adapter; ensure adapter supports desired resolution/refresh rate (4K@60Hz+).
USB-C to DisplayPort Adapter/Cable	USB-C to DisplayPort Adapter/Cable + DP Cable (if adapter)	Connects to DisplayPort monitors; often better high-res support than HDMI adapters.	Requires adapter/specific cable; ensure compatibility.
Thunderbolt Dock	Thunderbolt Cable (Mac to Dock) + Monitor Cables (HDMI/DP/TB)	Connects multiple monitors & peripherals via one Mac port; charges Mac.	Most expensive option; requires external power for the dock.

Basic Troubleshooting

- **No Signal:** Check cables are securely plugged into both the Mac and monitor. Ensure the monitor is powered on and set to the correct input source (e.g., HDMI 1, DisplayPort, USB-C). Try a different cable or port. Restart your Mac.

- **Wrong Resolution/Flickering:** Check System Settings > Displays for resolution options. Ensure your cables/adapters support the desired resolution and refresh rate (especially 4K@60Hz). Try lowering the refresh rate if flickering occurs. Check for macOS updates or monitor firmware updates.

Adding external monitors, especially taking advantage of the M4 Air's dual-display capability, can transform your productivity and computing comfort.

Using External Storage: Hard Drives, SSDs, and USB Flash Drives

While your MacBook Air M4 comes with fast internal Solid-State Drive (SSD) storage, you might find yourself needing more space over time, especially for large photo or video libraries, extensive music collections, or crucial backups. External storage devices connect easily to your Mac via its Thunderbolt / USB 4 ports, providing a flexible and often cost-effective way to expand your storage capacity.

Why Use External Storage?

- **Backups:** Regularly backing up your Mac is critical. External drives are essential for use with macOS's built-in **Time Machine** backup software (covered in Chapter 12).

- **Large Media Libraries:** Storing extensive photo libraries (Photos app), video projects (iMovie/Final Cut Pro libraries), or music collections (Music app library) on an external drive can free up significant space on your internal SSD.

- **Archiving:** Storing older projects or less frequently accessed files externally.

- **Transferring Large Files:** Moving large amounts of data between computers, especially when cloud uploads are too slow or impractical.

- **Working Directly:** High-speed external SSDs allow you to edit videos or run virtual machines directly from the external drive.

Common Types of External Storage

1. **External Hard Disk Drives (HDDs):**
   - **Technology:** Use traditional spinning magnetic platters to store data.
   - **Pros:** Offer the largest storage capacities (multiple terabytes, e.g., 4TB, 8TB, 16TB+) for the lowest cost per gigabyte. Widely available.

- o **Cons:** Significantly slower read/write speeds compared to SSDs. More susceptible to damage from drops or bumps due to moving parts. Can be physically larger and sometimes require external power adapters (especially larger desktop models).

- o **Best Use Cases:** Time Machine backups, archiving large amounts of data where speed isn't the top priority, storing large media libraries for playback (not necessarily editing).

2. **External Solid-State Drives (SSDs):**
   - o **Technology:** Use flash memory chips (like the internal drive in your Mac) with no moving parts.

   - o **Pros:** Much, much faster read/write speeds than HDDs (ranging from ~500MB/s for basic SATA-based USB SSDs up to ~2800MB/s or more for high-end NVMe-based Thunderbolt SSDs). More durable and resistant to shock. Compact and often bus-powered (drawing power from the Mac via the USB-C cable). Silent operation.

   - o **Cons:** More expensive per gigabyte than HDDs. Highest capacities are typically smaller than the largest HDDs available (though multi-terabyte SSDs are common).

   - o **Best Use Cases:** Running operating systems or virtual machines, editing large photo or video libraries directly from the drive, fast Time Machine backups, frequently transferring large files, any task where speed is important.

3. **USB Flash Drives (Thumb Drives / Memory Sticks):**
   - o **Technology:** Also use flash memory, but typically optimized for portability and lower cost rather than maximum speed or endurance.

   - o **Pros:** Very small, portable, convenient, relatively inexpensive for smaller capacities (e.g., 32GB, 64GB, 128GB, 256GB).

   - o **Cons:** Generally much slower than external SSDs (speed varies wildly between models). Lower capacities compared to HDDs/SSDs. Less suitable for continuous read/write operations or running software from. Easier to lose!

   - o **Best Use Cases:** Quickly transferring documents or photos between computers, creating bootable macOS installers, carrying essential files.

Storage Type	Speed	Cost per GB	Durability	Capacity Range	Primary Use Cases
External HDD	Slower	Low	Lower	High (1TB-20TB+)	Backups (Time Machine), Archiving, Bulk Media Storage
External SSD	Much Faster	Higher	Higher	Medium (256GB-8TB+)	Fast Backups, Editing Media, Running VMs, Speed-Critical Tasks
USB Flash Drive	Varies (Often Slow)	Medium	Medium	Low (32GB-1TB+)	Quick File Transfer, Portability, Bootable Installers

Connecting Your External Drive

Your MacBook Air M4 uses **Thunderbolt / USB 4 ports** (with the USB-C connector).

- **Drives with USB-C:** If your external drive has a USB-C port, simply use the appropriate cable (USB-C to USB-C, or Thunderbolt if it's a Thunderbolt drive) to connect it directly to one of your Mac's ports.

- **Drives with USB-A:** Many older external drives use the traditional rectangular USB-A connector. To connect these, you'll need a **USB-C to USB-A adapter** or a **USB-C hub/dock** that has USB-A ports (see section 11.4).

Formatting External Drives with Disk Utility

New external drives sometimes come pre-formatted for Windows (NTFS or FAT32) or might need reformatting for optimal use with your Mac, especially for Time Machine backups or storing macOS libraries. **Warning: Formatting erases all data currently on the drive.**

1. **Connect the Drive:** Plug the external drive into your Mac.

2. **Open Disk Utility:** Go to Applications > Utilities folder and open **Disk Utility**.

3. **Select the Drive:** In Disk Utility's sidebar, you'll see internal and external drives. *Carefully* select the **external drive** you want to format. It's often best to choose **View > Show All Devices** first, then select the top-level drive device itself (e.g., "WD My Passport Media"), not just the volume indented underneath it.

4. **Click Erase:** With the correct external drive selected, click the **Erase** button in the Disk Utility toolbar.

5. **Choose Options:** A dialog box appears:
   - **Name:** Enter a descriptive name for the drive (e.g., "Time Machine Backup," "Photo Library External").
   - **Format:** This is the crucial choice:
     - **APFS (Apple File System):** The modern standard for macOS, optimized for SSDs but also works fine on HDDs. Offers features like space sharing, snapshots, and strong encryption. **Recommended format for drives used exclusively with modern Macs (macOS High Sierra 10.13 and later), especially SSDs and Time Machine drives on recent macOS versions.** Several APFS options exist (Case-sensitive, Encrypted) – standard APFS is usually fine unless you need encryption (APFS Encrypted) or case-sensitivity (rarely needed).
     - **Mac OS Extended (Journaled) (HFS+):** The older standard Mac format. Still widely compatible with all Macs. A good choice for HDDs or if you need compatibility with older macOS versions (pre-High Sierra). Also offers encrypted and case-sensitive variants.
     - **ExFAT:** Designed for cross-platform compatibility between macOS and Windows. Good choice if you need to regularly plug the drive into both operating systems. Doesn't support all macOS features like Time Machine backups (usually).
     - **MS-DOS (FAT) (FAT32):** Very old format with significant limitations (e.g., 4GB maximum file size). Generally only use for compatibility with very old devices or systems if ExFAT isn't supported.
   - **Scheme:** Almost always choose **GUID Partition Map**. This is the standard for modern Macs and required for bootable drives.
6. **Confirm Erase:** Double-check you've selected the correct drive and chosen the right format. Click **Erase**. The process usually only takes a few moments. Click **Done** when finished.

Using Your External Drive

- **Accessing:** Once connected and formatted, the drive should appear automatically:
  - In the **Finder Sidebar** under the "Locations" section.
  - On your Desktop (if enabled in Finder > Settings... > General > Show these items on the desktop: External disks).
- Click its icon to open it and browse its contents just like any other folder.
- **Transferring Files:** Drag and drop files or folders between the external drive and your Mac's internal drive (e.g., Desktop, Documents).

- **Ejecting Safely (Very Important!):** Before physically unplugging an external drive (especially HDDs, but also good practice for SSDs/flash drives), you *must* eject it properly to prevent data corruption. Do one of the following:

   o Drag the drive's icon from the Desktop or Finder Sidebar to the **Trash** icon in the Dock (it will change to an Eject symbol ⏏☐).

   o Right-click (Control-click) the drive's icon and choose **Eject "[Drive Name]"**.

   o In a Finder window sidebar, click the small Eject icon that appears next to the drive name when you hover over it.

Wait until the drive's icon disappears from the Desktop/Sidebar before unplugging the cable.

External storage is an indispensable tool for backups, managing large files, and expanding the utility of your MacBook Air M4. Choose the type and format that best suits your needs.

Choosing and Connecting Keyboards, Mice, and Trackpads

While the MacBook Air M4 boasts Apple's excellent Magic Keyboard and a best-in-class Force Touch trackpad, you might want to use external input devices, especially when using your laptop in a "clamshell" mode connected to an external monitor, or simply due to personal ergonomic preferences. You have many choices, connecting either wirelessly via Bluetooth or wired via USB.

Connection Methods

1. **Bluetooth (Wireless):** This is the most common method for wireless peripherals, offering a cable-free setup.

   o **Pairing:** As detailed in section 6.2, you'll need to put the keyboard, mouse, or trackpad into pairing mode and then connect to it via **System Settings > Bluetooth** on your Mac.

   o **Apple Options:** Apple's own **Magic Keyboard** (available in different layouts, with or without numeric keypad, with or without Touch ID), **Magic Mouse** (multi-touch surface for scrolling/gestures), and **Magic Trackpad** (large glass surface with Force Touch and full gesture support) are popular choices designed specifically for Mac. Newer versions charge via USB-C, older ones via Lightning.

   o **Third-Party Options:** Many excellent Bluetooth keyboards (Logitech MX Keys, Keychron mechanical keyboards), mice (Logitech MX Master series, ergonomic mice), and even some trackpads are available from other manufacturers. Ensure they are Mac-compatible (look for specific Mac layouts or software support).

   o **Battery Life:** Wireless devices need charging (via USB) or replaceable batteries. Check battery levels in Bluetooth settings or the Menu Bar icon.

2. **Wired (USB):** A simple, reliable connection, especially for desktop setups where cable management isn't a major concern.

   o **Connection:** Most wired keyboards/mice use a USB-A connector. Since your M4 Air has USB-C ports, you'll need a **USB-C to USB-A adapter** or a **USB-C hub/dock** with USB-A ports (see section 11.4). Some newer peripherals might come with a USB-C cable for direct connection.

   o **Plug and Play:** Generally, wired USB keyboards and mice work instantly when plugged in, requiring no setup beyond physical connection.

3. **Dedicated Wireless Dongle (USB):** Some wireless mice and keyboards (especially gaming or budget models) don't use Bluetooth but instead come with their own small USB-A wireless receiver (dongle) that plugs into the computer.

   o **Connection:** You'll need a **USB-C to USB-A adapter** or hub to plug the dongle into your M4 Air.

   o **Pairing:** Usually pre-paired to the dongle, offering a simple plug-and-play wireless experience without needing Bluetooth setup, but it does occupy a USB port (via the adapter/hub).

Choosing Your Input Devices

Consider these factors when selecting external peripherals:

- **Keyboards:**

  o *Layout & Size:* Compact (like the built-in Air keyboard), tenkeyless (no number pad), or full-size (with number pad)? Mac layout (Command/Option keys) preferred?

  o *Key Feel (Switch Type):* Standard laptop keyboards often use scissor switches or low-profile mechanisms. External keyboards offer variety: membrane (mushy feel), mechanical (various switch types - clicky, tactile, linear - offering distinct feel and sound, popular for typing/gaming), scissor-switch (like Apple's Magic Keyboard). Try different types if possible.

  o *Features:* Backlighting? Ergonomic split/curved design? Programmable keys? Wireless multi-device switching?

- **Mice:**

  o *Ergonomics:* Crucial for comfort during long use. Shapes vary greatly (standard, vertical, trackball). Consider your hand size and grip style.

  o *Sensor:* Optical or laser, DPI (dots per inch - higher DPI means faster cursor movement). Most modern mice are accurate enough for general use.

- *Buttons & Scroll Wheel:* Standard two buttons + wheel, or extra programmable buttons for shortcuts? Smooth scrolling vs. notched/clicky wheel? Tilt wheel for horizontal scrolling?
- *Apple Magic Mouse:* Unique multi-touch surface allows scrolling and gestures similar to a trackpad, but ergonomics are divisive. Charges via Lightning (older) or USB-C (newer) on the bottom (can't be used while charging on older models).

- **Trackpads:**
  - *Apple Magic Trackpad:* Widely considered the best external trackpad, offering a large glass surface, Force Touch pressure sensitivity, and support for all macOS multi-touch gestures. Charges via USB-C (newer) or Lightning (older). Essential if you rely heavily on gestures.
  - *Third-Party:* Fewer options available, and often don't replicate the full macOS gesture experience as well as Apple's.

Customizing Your Devices in System Settings

macOS provides extensive options to tailor how your external (and built-in) input devices behave:

- **System Settings > Keyboard:**
  - *Keyboard Tab:* Adjust Key Repeat rate and Delay Until Repeat.
  - *Text Input Tab:* Manage Input Sources (keyboard layouts for different languages), set text replacements/substitutions.
  - *Keyboard Shortcuts Tab:* View and customize shortcuts for system functions, apps, accessibility features, Spotlight, etc. You can even create your own app-specific shortcuts.
  - *Dictation Tab:* Configure voice dictation settings.
  - *Modifier Keys... Button:* Remap special keys like Caps Lock, Control, Option, Command (useful if using a non-Mac keyboard).

- **System Settings > Mouse:** (Options vary depending on connected mouse)
  - *Tracking speed:* Adjust how fast the pointer moves relative to mouse movement.
  - *Scrolling speed:* Adjust how fast content scrolls.
  - *Natural scrolling:* Checkbox to determine scroll direction (checked = content moves with fingers, like on iOS; unchecked = scroll bar moves with fingers, traditional).
  - *Secondary click:* Configure right-click behavior (Click on right side, Click on left side, or disabled).
  - *Smart zoom:* Configure double-tap gesture (Magic Mouse).

- *Other Gestures (Magic Mouse):* Configure swiping between pages/full-screen apps.

- **System Settings > Trackpad:** (Applies to built-in and Magic Trackpad)
  - *Point & Click Tab:* Configure Tap to click (allow tapping instead of physically clicking), Secondary click (two-finger tap/click), Look up & data detectors (Force Click with one finger), Three finger drag.
  - *Scroll & Zoom Tab:* Configure Natural scrolling, Pinch to zoom, Smart zoom (double-tap with two fingers), Rotate gesture.
  - *More Gestures Tab:* Configure crucial navigation gestures: Swipe between pages (two fingers left/right), Swipe between full-screen apps (three/four fingers left/right), Notification Center (swipe left from right edge with two fingers), Mission Control (swipe up with three/four fingers), App Exposé (swipe down with three/four fingers), Launchpad (pinch with thumb and three fingers), Show Desktop (spread with thumb and three fingers). **Learning these trackpad gestures is highly recommended for efficient Mac use.**

Settings Location	Key Customizations Available
System Settings > Keyboard	Key repeat, Modifier key remapping, Keyboard shortcuts, Input sources, Dictation.
System Settings > Mouse	Tracking/Scrolling speed, Natural scrolling, Secondary click, Gestures (Magic Mouse).
System Settings > Trackpad	Tap to click, Secondary click, Natural scrolling, Zoom/Rotate gestures, Multi-finger swipes (Mission Control, Spaces, Exposé, Launchpad, etc.).

Investing time in choosing comfortable external input devices and customizing their settings can significantly improve your ergonomics and productivity when working on your MacBook Air M4.

Expanding Ports with USB-C Hubs and Docks

The MacBook Air M4 embraces the modern standard of **Thunderbolt / USB 4 ports** using the versatile **USB-C connector**. While powerful, the Air only includes two of these ports (plus the MagSafe 3 charging port and a headphone jack). If you need to connect multiple peripherals simultaneously – like an external monitor, a storage drive, a wired keyboard, an SD card, and power – you'll quickly find yourself needing more ports. This is where **USB-C hubs** and **Thunderbolt / USB 4 docks** come in.

Why You Might Need a Hub or Dock

- **Connecting Multiple Devices:** The most obvious reason – turning one port on your Mac into many different types of ports.

- **Using Older Peripherals:** Connecting devices that use the traditional rectangular USB-A connector (external drives, keyboards, mice, printers, flash drives).

- **Connecting External Displays:** Providing HDMI or DisplayPort outputs if your monitor doesn't have a USB-C input. Driving multiple displays (especially with the M4 Air's dual display support).

- **Adding Functionality:** Gaining ports not built into the Air, such as an SD card reader or a wired Ethernet port for faster/more reliable internet.

- **Single-Cable Desktop Setup ("Docking"):** Using a powered dock allows you to connect all your desktop peripherals (monitor(s), keyboard, mouse, storage, network, etc.) to the dock, and then connect the dock to your MacBook Air with just a *single* Thunderbolt/USB 4 cable that also charges your laptop. This makes it incredibly easy to "dock" and "undock" your laptop.

Understanding the Difference: Hubs vs. Docks

While the terms are sometimes used interchangeably, there's generally a distinction based on capability, power, and cost:

1. **USB-C Hubs:**

   o **Characteristics:** Typically smaller, more portable, and often **bus-powered** (meaning they draw power directly from the Mac's USB-C port they're plugged into). They connect to the Mac via an integrated or separate USB-C cable.

   o **Common Ports:** Usually offer a few **USB-A ports** (often USB 3.0, 5Gbps), an **HDMI port** (critical to check supported resolution/refresh rate – many cheaper hubs only do 4K@30Hz), **SD and/or microSD card readers**, and sometimes a USB-C port for data or **Power Delivery (PD) passthrough**.

   o **PD Passthrough:** If a hub has PD passthrough, it means you can plug your Mac's USB-C power adapter into the hub's designated USB-C PD input port, and the hub will then pass power through to charge your Mac while also powering the hub's other ports. Note: The hub itself consumes some power, so the wattage delivered to the Mac will be slightly less than the power adapter's rating.

- **Limitations:** Being bus-powered (unless using PD passthrough), they might struggle to power multiple high-draw devices simultaneously. Video output capabilities (resolution/refresh rate, number of displays) are often limited by the USB-C standard's bandwidth constraints (non-Thunderbolt). Data speeds on USB ports might be slower than on docks.

- **Best Use Cases:** Travel, adding a few essential ports like USB-A and SD card reader on the go, connecting a single 1080p or basic 4K monitor temporarily.

2. **Thunderbolt / USB 4 Docks:**

- **Characteristics:** Generally larger desktop units that require their own **external power adapter** plugged into the wall. They connect to your Mac using a high-speed **Thunderbolt 3, Thunderbolt 4, or USB 4 cable** (these look like USB-C cables but support much higher bandwidth – 40Gbps).

- **Common Ports:** Offer a much wider array and higher performance:

    - Multiple **Thunderbolt / USB 4 downstream ports:** Allow connecting other high-speed Thunderbolt devices (like fast SSDs or even another display) in a daisy chain.

    - Multiple high-speed **USB-A and USB-C data ports** (often 10Gbps USB 3.1 Gen 2 or faster).

    - Dedicated **DisplayPort and/or HDMI ports:** Often capable of driving **dual 4K@60Hz displays** or single higher-resolution displays (like 5K, 6K, or even 8K) – check dock specs carefully for Mac compatibility.

    - **Gigabit Ethernet** (or faster 2.5Gb/5Gb/10Gb Ethernet) port for wired networking.

    - **SD/microSD card readers** (often faster UHS-II speeds).

    - **Audio input/output jacks** (headphone/microphone).

- **Power Delivery:** Provide substantial power (typically 60W to 100W or more) back to the connected MacBook Air through the single Thunderbolt cable, easily charging it even under heavy load.

- **Benefits:** Highest performance for data transfer and display output, ability to connect many demanding peripherals simultaneously, single-cable connection for power and all peripherals (true docking solution).

- **Limitations:** Significantly more expensive than USB-C hubs, less portable due to size and external power brick.

o **Best Use Cases:** Creating a powerful desktop workstation setup, connecting multiple high-resolution monitors, using high-speed external SSDs or other Thunderbolt peripherals, needing a reliable wired Ethernet connection.

Feature	USB-C Hub	Thunderbolt / USB 4 Dock
Connection	USB-C	Thunderbolt 3 / 4 or USB 4 (via USB-C connector)
Power	Often Bus-Powered (may have PD Passthrough)	Requires External Power Adapter
Port Variety	Fewer ports, typically USB-A, HDMI (often limited), SD	More ports, diverse types (TB/USB4, DP/HDMI, Eth, Audio)
Performance	Lower bandwidth (USB speeds), limited video output	High bandwidth (40Gbps), high-res/multi-display support
Power Delivery	Passthrough only (if available), lower wattage	High wattage (60W-100W+) provided to Mac
Portability	High (small, no power brick usually)	Low (larger, requires power brick)
Cost	Lower	Higher
Best For	Travel, basic port expansion, single basic display	Desktop setups, multiple/high-res displays, high-speed peripherals, single-cable docking

Choosing the Right Hub or Dock for Your M4 Air

Consider these factors:

1. **Identify Your Needs:** Make a list of *all* the devices you want to connect simultaneously (monitors, storage, keyboard, mouse, SD cards, Ethernet, etc.).

2. **Monitor Requirements:** This is often the deciding factor. How many external monitors? What resolution and refresh rate? Ensure the hub/dock explicitly supports your desired configuration *for Mac* (especially dual displays for the M4 Air). Thunderbolt docks generally offer better multi-monitor support. Check if DisplayPort or HDMI is needed.

3. **Power Delivery:** Do you want the hub/dock to charge your MacBook Air? If so, ensure it provides sufficient wattage (at least matching your Apple power adapter, e.g., 30W, or higher like 60W-90W for headroom). This usually requires a powered dock rather than a bus-powered hub.

4. **Data Speed:** Do you need to connect high-speed external SSDs? Look for docks/hubs with USB 10Gbps ports (USB 3.1 Gen 2 / USB 3.2 Gen 2) or Thunderbolt ports.

5. **Specific Ports:** Do you absolutely need an Ethernet port? An SD card reader? Specific audio jacks? Make sure the model you choose has them.

6. **Budget:** USB-C hubs are much cheaper but offer less capability. Thunderbolt docks provide the most features and performance but come at a premium price.

7. **Brand Reputation:** Stick with reputable brands known for quality, reliability, and good Mac compatibility. Examples include CalDigit (especially popular for Thunderbolt docks), OWC, Belkin, Anker, Satechi, Kensington, Brydge. Read reviews focusing on Mac usage.

Connecting and Using Hubs/Docks

- **Plug and Play:** In most cases, hubs and docks are plug-and-play. Connect the hub/dock to one of your MacBook Air's Thunderbolt / USB 4 ports using the appropriate cable (often built-in for hubs, a separate Thunderbolt cable for docks). If it's a powered dock, plug in its power adapter.

- **Connect Peripherals:** Plug your monitors, storage drives, keyboard, mouse, etc., into the corresponding ports on the hub/dock.

- **Drivers:** The vast majority of standard peripherals connected through a hub/dock won't require extra drivers on macOS. Very specialized equipment might occasionally need a driver provided by the manufacturer.

Using a well-chosen USB-C hub or Thunderbolt dock can transform your highly portable MacBook Air M4 into the heart of a versatile and powerful workstation, bridging the gap between portability and extensive connectivity.

System Maintenance, Updates & Backups

Your MacBook Air M4 is a sophisticated piece of technology, and like any advanced tool, a little regular maintenance goes a long way toward keeping it performing at its best and ensuring your data remains safe. Thankfully, macOS Sequoia includes excellent built-in tools to handle the most important aspects: keeping the operating system and applications up-to-date, creating reliable backups of your precious files, managing your storage space effectively, and monitoring system activity if things seem sluggish. This chapter focuses on these crucial housekeeping tasks that will help ensure a long, healthy life for your Mac and protect you from data loss.

Keeping macOS Sequoia Up-to-Date via Software Update

One of the most important things you can do for the security, stability, and feature set of your Mac is to keep its operating system (macOS Sequoia) and your applications updated. Apple regularly releases updates that patch security vulnerabilities, fix bugs discovered after release, improve performance, ensure compatibility with new hardware or services, and sometimes introduce entirely new features.

Why Updating is Crucial

- **Security:** This is paramount. Hackers and malware creators constantly look for weaknesses in software. Software updates frequently include patches to close these security holes, protecting your Mac and your personal data from threats. Running outdated software is one of the biggest security risks.

- **Bug Fixes:** No software is perfect. Updates address bugs and glitches that might cause crashes, unexpected behavior, or compatibility issues.

- **Performance & Stability:** Updates can include optimizations that make macOS and apps run faster or more reliably.

- **New Features:** Major macOS upgrades (usually released annually) and sometimes even minor updates introduce new capabilities and refinements to the operating system and built-in apps.

- **Compatibility:** Updates ensure continued compatibility with new Apple services, hardware (like printers or accessories), and third-party applications that are also being updated.

Checking for and Installing macOS Updates

macOS makes checking for updates simple:

1. **Open System Settings:** Click the Apple menu (□) in the top-left corner > System Settings...

2. **Navigate to General:** Click "General" in the sidebar.

3. **Click Software Update:** In the main pane, click on "Software Update."

4. **Checking:** Your Mac will automatically check Apple's servers for available updates. You'll see a message like "Checking for updates..."

5. **Results:**
   o **Up to Date:** If no updates are currently available, it will display "Your Mac is up to date - macOS Sequoia [current version number]."
   o **Update Available:** If an update is found, it will display information about the update (e.g., "macOS Sequoia 15.x.x Update") often with a brief description of what's included (click "More Info..." for details). You'll see buttons like "Update Now" or "Upgrade Now" (for major new versions).

Understanding Different Types of Updates

- **Major macOS Upgrades:** These are significant new versions of macOS, typically released once a year in the fall (e.g., upgrading from macOS Sequoia version 15 to macOS version 16). They usually introduce major new features, design changes, and significant under-the-hood improvements. These are large downloads and installations that take longer. The button might say "Upgrade Now."

- **Minor macOS Updates (Point Releases):** These update the version number after the first decimal point (e.g., updating from macOS Sequoia 15.3 to 15.4). They primarily focus on bug fixes, security patches, and minor feature refinements within the current major macOS version. The button usually says "Update Now."

- **Supplemental Updates & Rapid Security Responses (RSRs):** These are smaller, often more frequent updates pushed out between minor updates to address critical security vulnerabilities or specific urgent bugs. Rapid Security Responses are particularly important as they deliver crucial security fixes quickly without requiring a full OS update and restart (though sometimes a restart is still needed).

Automatic Updates: Convenience vs. Control

macOS offers options to handle updates automatically, which is generally recommended for security. In the **Software Update** settings pane, click the **small 'i' info button (ⓘ)** next to "Automatic updates":

Automatic Update Option	What it Does	Recommendation
Check for updates	Automatically checks Apple's servers for new updates in the background.	**Strongly Recommended (Keep On).** Ensures you're notified promptly.
Download new updates when available	Downloads the update file automatically in the background once detected, saving you time later.	**Recommended (Keep On).** The update won't install until you approve it (unless auto-install is also on), but it's ready to go.

Install macOS updates	Automatically installs downloaded minor macOS updates (like 15.3 to 15.4). Might require restarts overnight.	**Consider Carefully.** Convenient, but installs happen automatically. Some users prefer manual control to install at a convenient time.
Install application updates from the App Store	Automatically installs updates for apps you downloaded from the Mac App Store.	**Generally Recommended (Keep On).** Keeps App Store apps up-to-date easily.
Install Security Responses and system files	Automatically installs critical security fixes (RSRs) and other essential system data files. Often requires no restart or a very quick one.	**Strongly Recommended (Keep On).** This is crucial for staying protected against the latest threats.

- **Our Recommendation:** For most users, keeping **all** these options turned **On** provides the best balance of security and convenience. At a minimum, ensure "Check for updates," "Download new updates," and especially **"Install Security Responses and system files"** are enabled. If you prefer manual control over *when* macOS point updates restart your machine, you might disable "Install macOS updates" and just click "Update Now" in the main Software Update pane when you are ready. Major macOS upgrades (like going to version 16) usually always require manual initiation via the "Upgrade Now" button.

The Update Process: What to Expect

When you click "Update Now" or "Upgrade Now," or if an automatic installation begins:

1. **Download (if not already done):** The update file is downloaded. Progress is shown.

2. **Preparation:** macOS prepares the update for installation. This can take some time.

3. **Restart Prompt:** You will almost always be prompted to restart your Mac to complete the installation. **Save all your work in open applications before restarting!**

4. **Installation:** Your Mac restarts. You might see the Apple logo with a progress bar for several minutes (sometimes 15-30 minutes or more for major upgrades). Do not interrupt this process or turn off your Mac.

5. **Login:** Once complete, your Mac boots back up to the login screen. Log in as usual.

6. **Finishing Up:** Sometimes, macOS does some final optimization after the first login post-update. Things might feel slightly sluggish for a few minutes but should return to normal quickly.

Updating Your Applications

- **App Store Apps:** If you enabled automatic app updates, apps downloaded from the Mac App Store will update in the background. To check manually or see update history, open the **App Store** application (from Dock or Applications folder) and click **Updates** in the sidebar. You can click "Update" next to individual apps or "Update All."

- **Apps from Other Sources:** Applications installed from websites or other sources (not the App Store) usually have their own update mechanisms. Look for a "Check for Updates..." option in the application's main menu (e.g., under the "Safari" or "Word" menu) or sometimes in its Preferences/Settings window. Some apps prompt you automatically when a new version is available. It's good practice to check for updates for these apps periodically as well.

Staying diligent about software updates is a simple yet powerful way to keep your MacBook Air M4 secure, stable, and equipped with the latest features Apple has to offer. Make checking Software Update a regular part of your routine if you opt out of full automatic installation.

Setting Up and Using Time Machine for Reliable Backups

This is arguably the most important section in this chapter. Hardware fails, accidents happen, files get accidentally deleted, malware can strike, laptops get lost or stolen. Without a reliable backup, your precious photos, important documents, creative projects, and years of accumulated data could be lost forever. Fortunately, macOS includes an excellent, easy-to-use, automatic backup solution called **Time Machine**. Taking the time to set it up is not just recommended; it's essential.

What is Time Machine?

Time Machine creates incremental backups of your entire Mac system – including macOS itself, applications, settings, user accounts, emails, photos, music, and all your personal files – to an external storage drive.

- **Incremental Backups:** After the initial full backup, Time Machine works quietly in the background, automatically backing up only the files that have *changed* since the last backup. This makes subsequent backups much faster and more space-efficient.

- **Versioning:** It keeps multiple versions of your files, allowing you to "go back in time" to restore a file as it existed yesterday, last week, or even months ago (depending on how long you've been backing up and the size of your backup drive). It keeps:
    - Hourly backups for the past 24 hours.
    - Daily backups for the past month.
    - Weekly backups for all previous months.

- **Automatic Deletion:** When your backup drive eventually starts to fill up, Time Machine automatically removes the *oldest* weekly backup sets to make space for new ones, ensuring your backups continue without interruption.

What You Need: An External Drive

Time Machine requires an **external storage drive** connected to your Mac.

- **Type:** You can use either an external Hard Disk Drive (HDD) or an external Solid-State Drive (SSD).
  - **HDDs** are more cost-effective for large capacities, making them a popular choice for backups where speed isn't the absolute top priority.
  - **SSDs** are much faster (making backups and restores quicker), more durable, and silent, but cost more per gigabyte. An external SSD is an excellent choice if your budget allows.

- **Capacity:** The backup drive should ideally be **at least two to three times the size** of the data you intend to back up (i.e., the used space on your Mac's internal drive, plus any other drives you might include). For example, if your M4 Air has a 512GB internal drive and you're using about 300GB, a 1TB external drive is a minimum, but a 2TB drive would be better to allow for longer backup history.

- **Connection:** Connect the drive using one of your Mac's Thunderbolt / USB 4 ports (using an adapter if the drive has a USB-A connector).

- **Recommendation:** It's strongly recommended to use a drive **dedicated solely to Time Machine backups**. Don't store other frequently accessed files on the same drive, as Time Machine needs reliable access and will eventually fill the available space.

Setting Up Time Machine: Step-by-Step

Setting up Time Machine is surprisingly simple:

1. **Connect Your External Drive:** Plug your chosen external drive into one of your MacBook Air's Thunderbolt / USB 4 ports.

2. **Initial Prompt (Maybe):** If the drive is new or hasn't been used with Time Machine before, macOS might display a dialog box asking if you want to use this drive to back up with Time Machine. If this happens, you can proceed directly – make sure to check the "Encrypt Backup Disk" option if presented, set a password, and click "Use as Backup Disk."

3. **Manual Setup (If No Prompt):** If you don't get the prompt, or want to change settings:
   - Go to **System Settings > General > Time Machine**.
   - Click the **"Add Backup Disk..."** button (or the '+' button if a disk is already listed and you want to add another).

- A list of connected, suitable external drives will appear. Select the drive you want to use for backups.

- **CRUCIAL STEP: Encryption:** Before clicking "Set Up Disk," look for an **"Encrypt Backup Disk" checkbox**. **Check this box.** This is *highly recommended*. Encrypting your backup means that if your external backup drive is ever lost or stolen, no one can access the backed-up data without the password you set.

- Click the **"Set Up Disk..."** button.

- **Set Encryption Password:** If you checked "Encrypt Backup Disk," you will be prompted to create and verify a password specifically for this backup disk. **Choose a strong password that you will remember, and store it safely somewhere separate from your Mac and the backup drive.** Losing this password means you won't be able to restore from the backup. You can add a password hint. Click **"Done."**

- **Erase Disk (If Necessary):** If the drive isn't formatted correctly (Time Machine prefers APFS or Mac OS Extended Journaled, and APFS Encrypted if you chose encryption), Time Machine will offer to **erase** the drive for you. **Warning:** This will delete *all* data currently on that external drive. Make sure you've selected the correct drive and that it doesn't contain other important files before clicking **"Erase."**

4. **Backup Starts:** Time Machine will now automatically prepare the disk and begin the initial full backup. This first backup copies everything and can take a significant amount of time (from an hour to many hours, depending on the amount of data and the speed of your drives). You can continue using your Mac normally while it runs in the background.

How Time Machine Backs Up Automatically

Once set up, Time Machine works automatically whenever the backup drive is connected:

- It performs backups roughly every hour.

- It only copies files that have changed since the last backup.

- You don't need to manually start it (unless you want to force an immediate backup via the Menu Bar icon).

Restoring Files from a Time Machine Backup

The real magic of Time Machine is how easy it makes retrieving lost files:

1. **Enter Time Machine:**

   - **Menu Bar:** If you've added the Time Machine icon to your Menu Bar (via System Settings > Control Center > Time Machine > Show in Menu Bar), click it and choose **"Browse Time Machine Backups."**

   - **System Settings:** Go to System Settings > General > Time Machine, and click the button to enter Time Machine (wording might vary).

- Applications Folder: Launch the Time Machine application from the Utilities folder.

2. **Navigate Through Time:** Your screen will change to the Time Machine interface, often showing stacked windows receding into the distance or a "star field" background. You'll see a Finder-like window showing your files *as they existed at the time of the selected backup.*

   - Use the **Timeline** along the right edge of the screen. Click on dates (past days, weeks, months) or use the up/down arrows to travel back to the specific date and time just before your file was deleted or changed. The Finder window in the center updates to show the state of your files at that point in time.

3. **Find Your File(s):** Navigate through the folders in the Time Machine Finder window just like you would in a normal Finder window until you locate the specific file or folder you want to restore. You can even use Quick Look (Spacebar) within Time Machine to preview files!

4. **Select and Restore:** Click once to select the file(s) or folder(s) you want to recover. Then, click the **"Restore"** button at the bottom right of the screen.

5. **Choose Destination (If Needed):** Time Machine will copy the selected item(s) back to their original location on your Mac. If the original location no longer exists, or if a file with the same name currently exists there, Time Machine might ask you if you want to replace the current item, keep both (renaming the restored one), or choose a different location to restore to.

Restoring Your Entire System

If the worst happens (e.g., your internal drive fails completely, or you get a new Mac), you can use **Migration Assistant** (available during macOS setup on a new Mac, or run later from the Utilities folder) to restore your entire system – applications, settings, user accounts, and files – directly from your Time Machine backup drive. It makes setting up a replacement Mac much easier.

Time Machine Options & Exclusions

In **System Settings > General > Time Machine**, click the **"Options..."** button after setting up a disk:

- **Backup Frequency:** While Time Machine backs up automatically hourly when connected, you can see status here.

- **Exclude items from backups:** Click the '+' button to add specific folders or even entire external drives that you *do not* want Time Machine to back up. This can save space on your backup drive if you have large items (like virtual machine files or temporary scratch disks) that you don't need backed up. Be careful not to exclude important user data!

- **Backup while on battery power:** By default, Time Machine might pause backups when on battery to conserve power. You can choose to allow backups even when not plugged in.

- **Notify when old backups are deleted:** Get an alert when Time Machine starts deleting the oldest backup sets to make space.

Time Machine Setup Step	Action	Key Consideration
1. Connect Drive	Plug in a suitable external HDD or SSD.	Drive should be 2-3x the size of data to back up; ideally dedicated.
2. Add Backup Disk	Go to System Settings > General > Time Machine > Add Backup Disk... Select the drive.	macOS might prompt automatically upon connection.
3. Enable Encryption	Check the "Encrypt Backup Disk" box during setup.	**Highly Recommended.** Requires setting a secure password for the backup.
4. Set Encryption Password	Create and verify a strong, unique password for the encrypted backup.	**Store this password safely and separately!** Losing it means losing access to the backup.
5. Erase Disk (If Needed)	Allow Time Machine to reformat the drive if prompted (usually to APFS Encrypted or HFS+ Encrypted).	**Warning: Erases all existing data on the drive.** Ensure you selected the correct drive.
6. Initial Backup	Allow the first full backup to complete (can take hours).	Mac can be used normally during backup.
7. Automatic Backups	Keep drive connected for automatic hourly incremental backups.	Regular backups are key to effective data protection.

Time Machine Best Practices

- **Back Up Regularly:** Keep your Time Machine drive connected as often as possible so backups run automatically. At least daily is recommended.

- **Encrypt Your Backup:** Always choose the "Encrypt Backup Disk" option during setup for security.

- **Use a Dedicated Drive:** Avoid using your Time Machine drive for other storage.

- **Check Status:** Occasionally glance at the Time Machine Menu Bar icon or settings pane to ensure backups are completing successfully.

- **Consider Multiple Backups:** For maximum safety, experts recommend the 3-2-1 backup strategy: 3 copies of your data, on 2 different types of media, with 1 copy stored offsite. Time Machine handles one local backup excellently. Consider adding a cloud backup service or a second Time Machine drive stored at a different location (like work or a relative's house) for offsite protection against disasters like fire or theft.

Time Machine is your safety net. Setting it up takes only a few minutes but can save you from potentially devastating data loss. **Make setting up Time Machine a top priority.**

Managing Storage Space Effectively

Your MacBook Air M4 comes with a super-fast internal Solid-State Drive (SSD). While speeds are great, SSD storage capacity can fill up over time with applications, documents, photos, videos, system files, and more. Keeping an eye on your storage usage and managing it effectively is important for a couple of reasons:

1. **Performance:** SSDs tend to slow down slightly when they become almost completely full. Keeping some free space (ideally 10-15% or more) helps maintain optimal performance.

2. **Space for Updates & New Files:** You need enough free space to download and install macOS updates, application updates, and to save new documents, photos, and other files you create or download.

Checking Your Storage Usage

macOS provides an easy way to see what's taking up space:

1. Go to **System Settings > General > Storage**.

2. Your Mac will take a few moments to calculate and analyze your storage usage.

3. You'll see a **colored bar** visually representing how your storage is allocated across different categories. Hovering over a color segment shows the category name and space used. Common categories include:

   - **Applications:** Space used by installed apps.

   - **Documents:** Files within your Home folder, excluding other specific categories like Photos/Music/etc. Can include large downloads or user-created files.

   - **Photos:** Space used by your Photos library.

   - **Music Creation:** GarageBand/Logic Pro projects and sound libraries.

   - **iCloud Drive:** Space used by locally downloaded iCloud Drive files (including Desktop/Documents if synced and not optimized).

   - **Mail:** Locally stored emails and attachments.

   - **Messages:** Locally stored message history and attachments.

- **System Data:** This catch-all category includes system caches, temporary files, fonts, plugins, virtual memory swap files, local Time Machine snapshots, and other system-related files. Its size can fluctuate.

- **macOS:** Space occupied by the operating system itself.

4. Below the bar, you'll see the amount of **Available** (free) space.

Built-in Storage Management Recommendations

macOS offers several intelligent recommendations right within the Storage settings window to help you optimize space automatically or easily find things to clean up:

1. **Store in iCloud:** This prominently suggests using iCloud Photos and iCloud Drive (with Desktop & Documents sync) combined with the **"Optimize Mac Storage"** feature (discussed in Chapters 10.1 and 8.1). When enabled, less frequently used photos (full resolution) and files are kept primarily in iCloud, freeing up local space. This is one of the most effective ways to manage storage if you have a good internet connection and sufficient iCloud+ storage. Click the button here to easily enable these features.

2. **Optimize Storage (TV App):** If you download purchased movies and TV shows from the Apple TV app, this option allows the system to automatically remove items you've already watched, keeping them available to re-download from your purchase history.

3. **Empty Trash Automatically:** A simple but effective option. Enabling this will automatically delete items that have been sitting in your Mac's Trash for more than 30 days.

4. **Reduce Clutter (Review Files):** Clicking the "Review Files" button (or similar wording) launches a special interface that helps you identify:

   - **Large Files:** Lists files on your Mac sorted by size, making it easy to find space hogs.

   - **Downloads:** Shows the contents of your Downloads folder.

   - **Unsupported Apps:** Lists older 32-bit applications that no longer run on modern macOS versions.

   - Containers & File Browser: More advanced views for specific app data or browsing your entire drive.

You can select files directly in this interface and click a "Delete" button (which usually moves them to the Trash).

Manual Cleanup Strategies: Taking Control

Beyond the automated recommendations, here are practical steps you can take:

1. **Tackle the Downloads Folder:** This is often a major culprit for accumulated clutter. Open your Downloads folder in Finder (Option + Command + L is a shortcut). Sort the contents by **Size** (View > Arrange By > Size, or click the Size column header in List view) or **Date Added**. Delete installers (.dmg files) for apps you've already installed, old documents, large ZIP archives you no longer need, etc. Drag unwanted items to the Trash.

2. **Empty the Trash Regularly:** Remember that dragging items to the Trash doesn't free up space until you empty it. Right-click (Control-click) the Trash icon in your Dock and choose **"Empty Trash"**. Confirm the action.

3. **Uninstall Unused Applications:** Apps can take up considerable space. Review your Applications folder.

   o **App Store Apps:** Open **Launchpad** (rocket icon in Dock or F4 key). Click and hold on any app icon until they start to jiggle. Apps downloaded from the App Store will show a small 'X' in their corner. Click the 'X' to uninstall.

   o **Other Apps:** For apps installed from websites, usually dragging the application from the Applications folder to the Trash is sufficient. However, some complex apps come with their own dedicated uninstaller utility (check the developer's website or look for an Uninstaller app within the app's original download or folder). Using the official uninstaller is often better as it removes associated preference files and system components. **Never** just randomly delete files from System or Library folders trying to uninstall an app manually unless you are absolutely sure what you are doing.

4. **Identify and Manage Large Files:**

   o Use the **Reduce Clutter / Review Files** tool mentioned above (System Settings > General > Storage).

   o Use **Finder Search:** Open Finder, press Command (⌘) + F. Click the '+' button below the search bar. Change the first dropdown from "Kind" to "File Size," the second to "is greater than," and enter a size (e.g., 100 MB, 500 MB, 1 GB). This will list all files larger than your specified size across your Mac (or the current folder if you change the search scope). Review these large files – are they old videos, backups, disk images, or projects you no longer need? Delete them or move them to an external drive.

   o Check common locations for large media: Your Movies, Music, and Pictures folders within your Home folder. Libraries for apps like iMovie, Final Cut Pro, Logic Pro, or virtual machine files can become enormous.

5. **Manage Photo/Video Libraries:** If your Photos library is huge and you *don't* use iCloud Photos with Optimization, consider moving the entire library file (Photos Library.photoslibrary, usually found in your Pictures folder) to a fast external SSD. **Important:** Quit the Photos app first, then drag the library file to the external drive. Once copied, hold down the **Option (⌥)** key while launching the Photos app, click "Choose Library...", and select the library file in its new location on the external drive. Ensure this external drive is included in your backups!

6. **Clear Caches (Use Caution):** macOS and applications store temporary data (caches) to speed things up. Sometimes these caches can grow large or become corrupted. While manually deleting cache files (~/Library/Caches, /Library/Caches) can sometimes free up space or fix issues, it's generally **not recommended for average users** as deleting the wrong files can cause instability. Often, simply **restarting your Mac** clears out many temporary caches safely. Specialized Mac cleaning utilities exist, but use them with extreme caution and choose reputable ones, as overly aggressive cleaning can cause problems.

7. **Manage iOS/iPadOS Backups:** If you back up your iPhone or iPad to your Mac using Finder (instead of iCloud), these backups can consume significant space. Connect your iPhone/iPad, open Finder, select the device in the Sidebar, go to the General tab, and click **"Manage Backups..."**. Select old backups you no longer need and click "Delete Backup."

Understanding "System Data"

This category in the Storage display can sometimes seem mysteriously large. It includes:

- System caches and logs.

- Fonts, plugins, extensions.

- Spotlight index.

- Virtual memory swap files (used when physical RAM is full).

- **Local Time Machine Snapshots:** If you use Time Machine, macOS often keeps local "snapshots" on your internal drive for recent backups, allowing some level of file recovery even when your main Time Machine drive isn't connected. These are designed to be automatically deleted when space is needed by other operations, but can temporarily inflate System Data size.

- Other temporary files and system resources.

You generally don't need to (and shouldn't try to) manually manage System Data directly. macOS handles most of it automatically. If the size seems excessive and doesn't decrease after a restart or waiting, it might indicate other underlying issues, but often it fluctuates based on system activity and local snapshots.

Storage Management Area	Key Actions / Tips
System Settings > Storage	Check overall usage, enable Optimize Storage recommendations (iCloud, TV, Trash), use Reduce Clutter tool.
Downloads Folder	Regularly review and delete old installers (.dmg), large archives (.zip), unneeded downloaded files. Sort by Size or Date Added.
Trash	Empty frequently (right-click Dock icon > Empty Trash).
Applications Folder	Uninstall apps you no longer use (use Launchpad 'X' for App Store apps, drag others to Trash, or use official uninstallers).
Large Files	Use Storage settings 'Review Files' or Finder search (by size) to locate and delete/move large media, projects, archives.
Media Libraries (Photos, etc.)	Consider moving large libraries to external SSDs if not using iCloud Optimization (ensure backups!).
iOS/iPadOS Backups (Finder)	Delete old device backups made to the Mac if no longer needed.
Caches	Generally leave alone; restart Mac to clear some temporary caches safely. Use cleaning utilities with extreme caution.

By periodically checking your storage usage and proactively managing your files and applications, you can ensure your MacBook Air M4 has the space it needs to operate smoothly and efficiently for years to come.

Monitoring System Health with Activity Monitor

Most of the time, your MacBook Air M4 with its efficient Apple Silicon chip will feel fast and responsive. However, occasionally, you might encounter situations where things seem sluggish, the fans (though the Air is often fanless or runs them silently) spin up unexpectedly, or your battery drains faster than usual. When this happens, **Activity Monitor** is your go-to diagnostic tool. It provides a detailed, real-time look at all the processes running on your Mac and how they are using system resources like the CPU, memory (RAM), energy, disk, and network.

Launching Activity Monitor

Activity Monitor isn't typically in the Dock by default. You can find it here:

1. Open **Finder**.

2. Go to the **Applications** folder.

3. Open the **Utilities** folder inside Applications.

4. Double-click Activity Monitor.

(Alternatively, just press Command (⌘) + Spacebar to open Spotlight, type "Activity Monitor," and press Return).

Understanding the Activity Monitor Tabs

The Activity Monitor window has five main tabs, each focusing on a different system resource:

- **CPU (Central Processing Unit):**
  - **What it Shows:** Lists all currently running processes (applications, background system tasks) and how much of the processor's power they are using, displayed as a percentage (% CPU). It also shows CPU time, number of threads, idle wake ups, etc.
  - **Why Check Here:** If your Mac feels slow or the fans are running high, sorting this tab by **% CPU** (click the column header) will quickly reveal if a specific application or background process is consuming excessive processor resources. Sometimes, a malfunctioning app or webpage can get stuck using close to 100% CPU, causing slowdowns and heat.
  - **Key Metrics:**
    0. **% CPU:** The percentage of total CPU capacity currently being used by that process.
    1. **CPU Time:** Total processor time used by the process since it started.
    2. **% System / % User / % Idle (Bottom):** Overall CPU usage breakdown. High idle means the CPU has spare capacity.

- **Memory:**
  - **What it Shows:** Details how your Mac's physical RAM (Random Access Memory) is being utilized by different processes. Lists processes by Memory usage.
  - **Why Check Here:** If your Mac feels sluggish, especially when switching between apps or opening new ones, it might be running low on available RAM. This tab helps identify which apps are using the most memory.
  - **Key Metrics:**
    0. **Memory Used:** Total physical RAM currently in use by apps and system processes.
    1. **App Memory:** RAM directly used by applications.
    2. **Wired Memory:** RAM that cannot be compressed or swapped to disk (essential system functions).

3. **Compressed:** macOS compresses inactive memory to make more RAM available; this shows the amount of compressed memory.

4. **Memory Pressure Graph (Bottom):** This is a crucial indicator!

   ▪ **Green:** Plenty of RAM available. Your Mac is running efficiently.

   ▪ **Yellow:** Memory is becoming constrained; macOS is actively compressing memory. Performance might start to degrade slightly under heavy load.

   ▪ **Red:** Significant memory pressure; macOS is heavily relying on compression and possibly using the slower internal SSD for virtual memory "swap." Performance will likely be noticeably sluggish. Consistent red pressure indicates you might benefit from closing demanding apps or potentially needing more physical RAM for your typical workload (though RAM is not upgradeable on the MacBook Air after purchase).

- **Energy:**

  o **What it Shows:** Estimates the relative energy impact of each running process. Helpful for identifying apps that might be draining your battery quickly.

  o **Why Check Here:** If your battery life seems shorter than expected, check this tab to see if a particular app (or even a specific browser tab listed under the browser process) has a high "Energy Impact" or "Avg Energy Impact" value. It also shows if an app is utilizing "App Nap" (a macOS feature that pauses inactive background apps to save power).

  o **Key Metrics:**

     0. **Energy Impact:** Current estimated power consumption.

     1. **Avg Energy Impact:** Average impact over the last several hours. Helps identify persistently power-hungry apps.

     2. **App Nap:** Indicates if the process is currently "napping" to conserve energy.

- **Disk:**

  o **What it Shows:** Displays the amount of data each process is reading from and writing to your Mac's internal storage drive (SSD). Measured in bytes read/written.

  o **Why Check Here:** If your Mac feels slow and you hear excessive disk activity (less common with silent SSDs, but can still indicate heavy load), this tab can show if a specific process is constantly reading or writing large amounts of data. This could be Time Machine running a backup, Spotlight indexing files, a large file download/copy in progress, or potentially a malfunctioning application.

- Key Metrics:
    - 0. **Bytes Written / Bytes Read:** Total data transferred by the process since it started or since the Mac booted. Look for rapidly increasing numbers.
    - 1. **Writes Out / Reads In (I/O):** Number of separate read/write operations. Frequent small operations can also impact performance.

- **Network:**
    - **What it Shows:** Lists processes and the amount of data they are sending and receiving over your network (Wi-Fi or Ethernet). Measured in bytes sent/received.
    - **Why Check Here:** Useful for identifying which applications are using your internet bandwidth. If your internet connection feels slow, check here to see if a background process (like cloud syncing, software updates, or a large download) is consuming bandwidth. You can also spot unexpected network activity.
    - **Key Metrics:**
        - 0. **Sent Bytes / Rcvd Bytes:** Total data transferred by the process.
        - 1. **Data Sent/sec / Data Rcvd/sec (Bottom):** Overall current network traffic across all processes.

Using Activity Monitor for Troubleshooting

Activity Monitor is most useful when you suspect a performance problem:

1. **Identify the Culprit:** Open Activity Monitor and go to the relevant tab (CPU for slowness/fans, Memory for sluggishness/beach balls, Energy for battery drain, Disk/Network for related activity). Click the column header (like **% CPU** or **Memory**) to sort the list and bring the highest consumers to the top. Look for application names you recognize or system processes using unexpectedly high resources.

2. **Get More Info:** Select the suspicious process by clicking on its name in the list. You can then:

    - Press Command (⌘) + I (or click the 'i' button in the toolbar) to open an Inspector window with more detailed information about the process (memory breakdown, open files, network ports, etc.).

    - See basic information in the pane at the bottom of the main Activity Monitor window.

3. **Quit or Force Quit a Problem Process (Use Caution!):** If you identify an application that is clearly malfunctioning (e.g., using 100% CPU and marked "(Not Responding)" in red text), you can try to close it directly from Activity Monitor.

    - Select the unresponsive process.

- Click the **'X' button** in the Activity Monitor toolbar (it looks like an octagon stop sign).

- A dialog box appears asking if you're sure. You'll have two main options:
    - **Quit:** This sends the standard "quit" command to the application, asking it to close gracefully (allowing it to potentially save data if possible). Try this first.
    - **Force Quit:** This immediately terminates the process without giving it a chance to save data. Use this if "Quit" doesn't work or the app is completely frozen. Be aware you will likely lose any unsaved work in that application.

- **WARNING:** Be very careful about Force Quitting processes, especially ones you don't recognize by name. Many background processes listed are essential parts of macOS. Force quitting critical system processes could lead to instability or require a restart. Generally, only Quit or Force Quit applications you launched yourself unless you are following specific troubleshooting instructions.

4. **Monitor Memory Pressure:** Keep an eye on the Memory Pressure graph under the Memory tab during demanding tasks. If it frequently stays in the yellow or red, it's a sign that your current workload might be exceeding your available RAM, suggesting you may need to close some applications or browser tabs.

Activity Monitor Tab	Primary Information Shown	Useful For Diagnosing...
CPU	% Processor usage per process	Slowness, high fan speed, heat, unresponsive apps.
Memory	RAM usage per process, Memory Pressure graph	Sluggishness, app switching delays, frequent beach balls.
Energy	Estimated power consumption per process	Unexpectedly fast battery drain.
Disk	Data read/written to storage per process	Slowness potentially related to heavy disk I/O.
Network	Data sent/received over network per process	Slow internet connection, identifying bandwidth-hungry apps.

You don't need to keep Activity Monitor open all the time. Think of it as a diagnostic tool, like looking under the hood of your car when something doesn't feel right. It provides valuable insights into what your MacBook Air M4 is doing behind the scenes and helps you pinpoint the cause of performance issues when they arise.

Advanced Customization & Accessibility

By now, you're comfortable with the core applications and workflows on your MacBook Air M4. But the Mac experience is also about making the system truly *yours*. macOS Sequoia offers a wealth of options for personalizing the look and feel, streamlining actions with keyboard shortcuts and gestures, and providing powerful tools to accommodate diverse user needs through its Accessibility features. This chapter encourages you to explore beyond the defaults, diving deep into System Settings, mastering shortcuts and gestures, and discovering the often-overlooked power of Accessibility options that can benefit everyone.

Deep Dive into System Settings for Personalization

We've visited **System Settings** (Apple menu □ > System Settings...) multiple times throughout this guide to configure specific features like Wi-Fi, Bluetooth, Touch ID, FileVault, Time Machine, and more. Now, let's take a broader look at it as the central command center for personalizing almost every aspect of your Mac's appearance and behavior. Don't be afraid to explore – most settings can be easily changed back if you don't like the result.

Understanding the System Settings Layout

The System Settings window, redesigned in recent macOS versions to resemble the Settings app on iPhone and iPad, uses a clear sidebar-based navigation:

- **Sidebar (Left):** Contains categories grouping related settings. At the top is your Apple ID profile. Below that are sections roughly organized by function:
    - *Network/Connectivity:* Wi-Fi, Bluetooth, Network, VPN.
    - *Notifications & Focus:* Notifications, Sound, Focus.
    - *General Look & Feel:* Appearance, Accessibility, Control Center, Siri & Spotlight, Desktop & Dock, Displays, Wallpaper, Screen Saver.
    - *User Management & System:* Users & Groups, General (Software Update, Storage, Time Machine, Startup Disk, Language & Region, Date & Time, Sharing, etc.), Privacy & Security.
    - *Hardware Input:* Keyboard, Trackpad, Mouse, Game Controllers.
    - *App-Specific Settings:* Sometimes third-party apps add their own preference panes here.
- **Main Pane (Right):** Displays the specific settings and options for the category selected in the sidebar.
- **Search Bar (Top Left):** If you know what setting you're looking for but not where it lives, just type a keyword (e.g., "dark mode," "scroll," "shortcut," "firewall") into the search bar. System Settings will highlight relevant sections in the sidebar.

Key Areas for Personalization

Let's highlight some key areas (beyond those covered in detail elsewhere) where you can really tailor your Mac experience:

1. **Appearance:**

   o *Light/Dark/Auto Mode:* Choose the overall theme for windows, menus, and the Dock. Auto switches between Light and Dark based on the time of day.

   o *Accent Color:* Changes the color used for buttons, menu selections, and other interface highlights (e.g., blue, purple, green, graphite).

   o *Highlight Color:* Sets the color used to highlight selected text.

   o *Sidebar Icon Size:* Choose small, medium, or large icons for the Finder and System Settings sidebars.

   o *Scroll Bar Behavior:* Control when scroll bars appear (Automatically, When scrolling, Always) and whether clicking the scroll bar jumps to the spot clicked or the next page.

2. **Desktop & Dock:** (Revisiting with focus on extras)

   o *Dock Customization:* We covered size, magnification, position, hiding, and recent apps. Experiment to find what feels best for your screen size and workflow.

   o *Stage Manager Settings:* If you use Stage Manager, click "Customize..." here to fine-tune its behavior (Show Recent Apps, Show Desktop Items, Window handling).

   o *Widgets:* Control whether widgets appear on the Desktop or only in Notification Center. Choose widget style.

   o *Windows & Apps Section:* Configure default tab behavior, window closing/minimizing actions.

   o **Hot Corners:** This is a powerful, often underused feature. Click the "Hot Corners..." button. For each of the four corners of your screen, you can assign an action that triggers when you move your mouse pointer firmly into that corner (e.g., Mission Control, Notification Center, Launchpad, Quick Note, Start Screen Saver, Put Display to Sleep, Lock Screen). It's a very fast way to invoke common actions without clicking or using keyboard shortcuts.

3. **Displays:**

   o Beyond arrangement and resolution, explore:

   o **Night Shift:** Automatically shifts the colors of your display to the warmer end of the spectrum after sunset or during scheduled hours. This can reduce blue light exposure and potentially make viewing easier on the eyes in the evening. Configure the schedule and color temperature warmth.

   o **True Tone:** (If your display supports it) Automatically adjusts the color and intensity of your display to match the ambient lighting conditions, making images appear more natural across different environments.

4. **Sound:**

   o *Output/Input:* Select your default speakers/headphones and microphone. Adjust balance and input volume.

   o *Sound Effects:* Choose the alert sound played for system notifications, set its volume, and decide whether user interface sound effects (like moving files to the Trash) should play. Choose the output device specifically for sound effects.

5. **Notifications & Focus:**

   o *Notifications:* Beyond per-app settings, configure options like preview style and whether notifications appear on the Lock Screen.

   o *Focus:* Dive deeper into creating custom Focus modes beyond the defaults (Do Not Disturb, Work, Sleep). You can define specific schedules, allow notifications only from certain people or apps during that Focus, link a Focus to a specific Lock Screen/Desktop background, and have it automatically activate based on time, location, or app usage. This is incredibly powerful for managing distractions.

6. **General:**

   o *Language & Region:* Add preferred languages for macOS and apps. Set your region format (important for dates, times, numbers, and currency – e.g., ensuring CHF and proper date formats for Switzerland). Manage keyboard input sources for different languages.

   o *Date & Time:* Set automatically (recommended), choose time zone, customize clock appearance in Menu Bar (digital/analog, show date/day).

   o *Sharing:* Set your computer's network name (how it appears to other devices). Enable specific sharing services *with caution* if needed (Screen Sharing, File Sharing, Media Sharing, Remote Login/SSH – understand the security implications before enabling these).

- *Login Items:* See which applications are set to open automatically every time you log in. You can add apps here using the '+' button or remove unnecessary ones using the '-' button to potentially speed up your Mac's startup time.

7. **Users & Groups:**
   - Manage your user account password, profile picture. Add other Standard or Administrator user accounts for family members (generally recommended over sharing one account). Set up Parental Controls if needed. Configure Login Options like showing the password hint, enabling Fast User Switching (shows user list in Menu Bar or Control Center), and showing the Sleep/Restart/Shut Down buttons on the login window.

8. **Control Center (Revisited):** Go back here to fine-tune which status icons appear directly in your Menu Bar for instant access versus being tucked inside the Control Center panel.

System Settings Area	Key Personalization Options
Appearance	Light/Dark/Auto Mode, Accent & Highlight Colors, Sidebar Icon Size, Scroll Bar Behavior.
Desktop & Dock	Dock Size/Position/Hiding/Magnification, Stage Manager, Desktop Widgets, **Hot Corners**.
Displays	Arrangement, Resolution, Refresh Rate, **Night Shift**, True Tone.
Sound	Output/Input Devices, Alert Sounds & Effects.
Notifications	Per-App Alert Styles & Previews, Notification Grouping.
Focus	Creating Custom Focus Modes, Schedules, Allowed Apps/People, Linking to Lock Screens.
General	Language & Region Formats, Date & Time Display, Computer Name, Login Items.
Users & Groups	User Accounts, Passwords, Login Options, Fast User Switching.
Control Center	Customizing which status icons appear directly in the Menu Bar.
Keyboard/Trackpad/Mouse	Modifier Keys, Shortcuts, Tracking Speed, Scrolling Behavior, **Gestures**.

Don't hesitate to click around in System Settings. Most changes are easily reversible, and discovering options like Hot Corners or fine-tuning Focus modes can significantly improve your personal workflow and make your Mac feel perfectly attuned to your habits.

Mastering Essential Keyboard Shortcuts and Creating Custom Ones

While the trackpad and mouse are great for visual interaction, becoming proficient with **keyboard shortcuts** is arguably the single biggest step you can take towards using your MacBook Air M4 faster and more efficiently. Nearly every common action, from copying text to switching apps to taking screenshots, has a corresponding keyboard shortcut. Learning even a few key combinations can save you countless clicks and mouse movements every day.

Understanding the Modifier Keys

Mac keyboard shortcuts rely heavily on special "modifier" keys, pressed *in combination* with standard letter, number, or function keys. Get familiar with these:

- **Command (⌘):** Sometimes called the "Apple key," this is the most frequently used modifier key in Mac shortcuts, often analogous to the Control key on Windows for actions like Copy/Paste/Save. It's located on either side of the Spacebar.

- **Option (⌥):** Also labeled "Alt" on some keyboards. This key often modifies the behavior of other commands (e.g., ⌘+W closes a window, Option+⌘+W closes *all* windows of that app) or is used for typing special characters. Located next to the Command keys.

- **Control (^):** Often used for shortcuts related to text navigation, right-clicking (Control-click), or system functions like Mission Control/Spaces switching. Located towards the bottom left.

- **Shift (⇧):** Used for capitalizing letters, typing symbols above number keys, and often modifying other shortcuts (e.g., ⌘+Z is Undo, Shift+⌘+Z is Redo). Located on both left and right sides.

- **Function (Fn):** Usually in the bottom-left corner. Used to access the special functions printed on the top row of keys (F1-F12, brightness, volume, media controls, Mission Control key). Depending on your settings (System Settings > Keyboard > Keyboard Shortcuts... > Function Keys), you might need to hold Fn to use the F1-F12 keys as standard function keys, or vice-versa. Also used in some specific shortcuts (like Fn+Delete for forward delete).

- **Caps Lock:** Locks letter input to uppercase.

Essential System-Wide Shortcuts to Learn

These shortcuts work almost everywhere across macOS and are fundamental to efficient use:

Shortcut	Action	Notes
⌘ + C	Copy selected item/text	Puts a copy on the Clipboard.
⌘ + X	Cut selected item/text	Removes the item and places it on the Clipboard (works mainly with text/files).
⌘ + V	Paste item/text from Clipboard	Inserts the Clipboard contents.
Option + Shift + ⌘ + V	Paste and Match Style	Pastes text using the formatting of the surrounding text, not the original.
⌘ + Z	Undo last action	Your best friend! Reverses the previous command.
Shift + ⌘ + Z	Redo last undone action	Reverses the Undo command.
⌘ + A	Select All	Selects all text in a document, or all files in a folder.
⌘ + F	Find	Opens a Find bar/window within the current app to search for text.
⌘ + G	Find Next	Jumps to the next occurrence of the found text.
Shift + ⌘ + G	Find Previous	Jumps to the previous occurrence of the found text.
⌘ + S	Save current document	Saves changes to the currently open file.
Shift + ⌘ + S	Save As / Duplicate	Opens a dialog to save the current file with a new name or location.
⌘ + P	Print	Opens the Print dialog box.
⌘ + N	New Window / Document / Tab (App Dependent)	Creates a new item relevant to the current app.
⌘ + T	New Tab (in apps that support tabs)	Opens a new tab (e.g., Safari, Finder).

⌘ + O	Open	Opens a dialog to choose a file to open.
⌘ + W	Close Window / Tab	Closes the frontmost window or tab.
Option + ⌘ + W	Close All Windows (of current app)	Closes every open window for the active application.
⌘ + Q	Quit Application	Closes the application completely (prompts to save unsaved work).
⌘ + H	Hide Application	Hides all windows of the current app.
Option + ⌘ + H	Hide Others	Hides all apps *except* the current one. Great for focus!
⌘ + M	Minimize Window	Minimizes the frontmost window to the Dock.
⌘ + Spacebar	Spotlight Search	Opens the system-wide Spotlight search bar.
⌘ + Tab	Switch Applications (Forward)	Opens the App Switcher; tap Tab to cycle forward.
⌘ + ~	Switch Windows (Within App, Forward)	Cycles through open windows of the *same* application.
Option + ⌘ + Esc	Force Quit Applications	Opens the Force Quit window to close unresponsive apps.
Shift + ⌘ + 3	Screenshot (Full Screen)	Saves an image of the entire screen to the Desktop.
Shift + ⌘ + 4	Screenshot (Selection)	Cursor becomes crosshairs; drag to select area, save image to Desktop.
Shift + ⌘ + 5	Screenshot & Screen Recording Options	Opens a panel with options for capturing screen, window, selection, or recording video.
Control + ⌘ + Spacebar	Character Viewer (Emoji & Symbols)	Opens the panel for inserting special characters and emoji.
Fn + Delete	Forward Delete	Deletes character to the right of the cursor (like standard Delete on Windows).

Control + Up Arrow (or F3)	Mission Control	Shows all open windows and Spaces.
Control + Down Arrow	App Exposé	Shows all open windows of the *current* app.
Control + Left/Right Arrow	Switch Between Spaces	Moves to the adjacent Desktop Space.

This list covers many essentials, but it's just the beginning!

Finding More Shortcuts

- **Explore Application Menus:** The best way to learn shortcuts specific to an application you use often (like Pages, Mail, Photos, or even third-party apps) is to simply look at its menus in the Menu Bar (File, Edit, View, etc.). If a menu command has a keyboard shortcut assigned, it will be displayed directly to the right of the command name. Make a mental note of shortcuts for actions you perform frequently.

- **Cheat Sheets:** Search online for "macOS keyboard shortcuts cheat sheet" or "[App Name] keyboard shortcuts" for comprehensive lists.

Creating Your Own Custom Keyboard Shortcuts

What if a menu command you use constantly doesn't have a shortcut, or you dislike the default one? You can create your own!

1. Go to **System Settings > Keyboard**.
2. Click the **"Keyboard Shortcuts..."** button.
3. In the window that appears, select **"App Shortcuts"** from the sidebar list.
4. Click the **plus (+) button** below the right pane to add a new shortcut.
5. A dialog sheet appears:
   - **Application:** Choose the specific application you want the shortcut to work in from the dropdown list (e.g., Safari, Pages). You can also choose "All Applications" if the menu command exists in many apps (like perhaps a specific "Export" format), but be careful not to override standard shortcuts.
   - **Menu Title:** This is the **most critical step**. You must type the **exact name** of the menu command as it appears in the application's menu bar, including capitalization, punctuation, and ellipses (... - type three periods or use the Option+; shortcut for the actual ellipsis character). For example, if a command is "Make Plain Text" under the Format menu, you type Make Plain Text. If it's "Save As...", you type Save As....

o **Keyboard Shortcut:** Click in this field, then press the actual key combination you want to assign (e.g., Control + Option + S). Choose a combination that isn't already used for a standard function you need.

6. Click **Done**.

7. Your custom shortcut is now active! Test it in the application. To edit or delete a custom shortcut, select it in the App Shortcuts list and use the '-' button or double-click to modify.

8. **Example:** Let's say you frequently use the "Paste and Match Style" command in Pages (which has the default Option+Shift+⌘+V) but find that awkward. You could potentially create a custom App Shortcut for Pages, enter "Paste and Match Style" as the Menu Title, and assign a simpler shortcut like Control+⌘+V (if that isn't already critical for something else in Pages).

Tips for Learning and Using Shortcuts

- **Start Small:** Don't try to learn dozens at once. Pick 3-5 essential shortcuts for actions you do repeatedly (like Copy, Paste, Save, Switch Apps, Close Window) and focus on using them consistently.

- **Look Before You Click:** Before clicking a menu item, glance to see if it has a shortcut listed. Try using the shortcut next time.

- **Muscle Memory:** Practice is key. The more you use shortcuts, the more they become automatic reflexes, saving you significant time and effort.

- **Consistency:** Many shortcuts (like ⌘+C, ⌘+V, ⌘+S, ⌘+P, ⌘+Q) are consistent across most Mac applications, making them easier to learn and apply universally.

Investing a little time in learning and customizing keyboard shortcuts pays huge dividends in productivity and makes using your powerful MacBook Air M4 feel even faster and more fluid.

Advanced Trackpad and Mouse Gesture Customization

We've touched upon the excellent built-in trackpad on your MacBook Air M4 and mentioned external input devices. macOS is renowned for its fluid and intuitive **multi-touch gestures**, primarily performed on the trackpad (either built-in or an external Magic Trackpad), but also with some capabilities on the Magic Mouse. Mastering these gestures, and customizing them to your liking, is another key way to navigate and control your Mac with speed and grace.

Deep Dive into Trackpad Settings

Let's revisit **System Settings > Trackpad** and explore the options on each tab in more detail. Apple often includes helpful video previews demonstrating each gesture right in the settings pane – pay attention to these!

- **Point & Click Tab:**
  - **Look up & data detectors:** Usually set to "Force Click with one finger." This means pressing down firmly on the trackpad (you'll feel a second 'click' – that's the Force Touch haptic feedback) on a word can look up its definition, or on an address can show it in Maps, or on a date can create a calendar event. Can be changed to "Tap with three fingers" or turned off.
  - **Secondary click:** Configures your right-click. Options are "Click or tap with two fingers" (most common), "Click in bottom right corner," or "Click in bottom left corner."
  - **Tap to click:** Enable this to perform a standard click by simply tapping lightly with one finger, instead of needing to physically press the trackpad down. Many users find this faster and quieter.
  - **Click pressure:** Adjust the amount of force needed for a physical click (Light, Medium, Firm).
  - **Tracking speed:** Adjusts how fast the pointer moves across the screen relative to your finger movement on the trackpad. Find a speed that feels responsive but controllable.
  - **Silent clicking:** Makes the physical click feedback quieter (relies more on haptics).
  - **Force Click and haptic feedback:** Toggles the deeper Force Click functionality and the subtle vibrations you feel for certain actions.

- **Scroll & Zoom Tab:**
  - **Natural scrolling:** This is usually enabled by default. Scrolling *up* with two fingers moves the content *up* (like pushing paper up), and scrolling *down* moves content *down*. Unchecking this reverses the direction to match traditional scroll wheel behavior (scrolling down moves the scroll bar down, content moves up). Choose whichever feels more intuitive to you.
  - **Zoom in or out:** Enable the standard "Pinch with two fingers" gesture.
  - **Smart zoom:** Enable "Double-tap with two fingers" to intelligently zoom in on content (like a column of text or an image) and double-tap again to zoom out.
  - **Rotate:** Enable "Rotate with two fingers" to rotate items like photos in supported applications.

- **More Gestures Tab:** This tab contains the powerful multi-finger navigation and system control gestures:
  - **Swipe between pages:** Choose "Scroll left or right with two fingers" (works like browser back/forward), "Swipe with three fingers," or "Swipe with two or three fingers." Two fingers is common for back/forward navigation within apps.
  - **Swipe between full-screen applications:** Choose "Swipe left or right with three fingers" or "Swipe left or right with four fingers." This is how you move between your different **Spaces** (multiple desktops) and full-screen apps. Pick the finger count you prefer and practice this one – it's essential for multi-Space workflows.
  - **Notification Center:** Enable "Swipe left from right edge with two fingers" to quickly slide open the Notification Center.
  - **Mission Control:** Choose "Swipe up with three fingers" or "Swipe up with four fingers" to activate Mission Control (the bird's-eye view of windows/Spaces). Practice this along with the Spaces swipe.
  - **App Exposé:** Choose "Swipe down with three fingers" or "Swipe down with four fingers" to show all windows of the currently active application. The opposite of the Mission Control gesture.
  - **Launchpad:** Enable "Pinch with thumb and three fingers" (bring fingers together) to open Launchpad (grid of all apps).
  - **Show Desktop:** Enable "Spread with thumb and three fingers" (move fingers apart) to instantly hide all windows and reveal your Desktop. Useful for quickly grabbing a file from the Desktop.

Trackpad Gesture (Common Setting)	Action Performed	Tab in Settings
Tap with one finger	Click (if Tap to click enabled)	Point & Click
Click/Tap with two fingers	Secondary click (Right-click)	Point & Click
Force Click with one finger	Look up & data detectors	Point & Click
Scroll with two fingers	Scroll content vertically/horizontally	Scroll & Zoom
Pinch with two fingers	Zoom in or out	Scroll & Zoom
Double-tap with two fingers	Smart zoom	Scroll & Zoom
Rotate with two fingers	Rotate items (e.g., photos)	Scroll & Zoom

Swipe left/right with two fingers	Go back/forward (e.g., in Safari, Finder history)	More Gestures
Swipe left/right with 3/4 fingers	Switch between full-screen apps and Desktops (Spaces)	More Gestures
Swipe up with 3/4 fingers	Enter Mission Control	More Gestures
Swipe down with 3/4 fingers	App Exposé (show windows of current app)	More Gestures
Pinch (thumb + 3 fingers)	Show Launchpad	More Gestures
Spread (thumb + 3 fingers)	Show Desktop	More Gestures
Swipe left from right edge (2 fingers)	Show Notification Center	More Gestures

Take time to enable and practice these gestures, especially the multi-finger swipes for Mission Control and Spaces. They become incredibly fast ways to navigate macOS once you build the muscle memory.

Customizing Mouse Gestures (Magic Mouse)

If you use Apple's Magic Mouse, you also have gesture options available in **System Settings > Mouse**:

- **Natural scrolling:** Same concept as the trackpad.
- **Secondary click:** Configure right-click (Click on right or left side).
- **Smart zoom:** Configure "Double-tap with one finger" to zoom.
- **Swipe between pages:** Choose "Scroll left or right with one finger" or "Swipe left or right with two fingers" for back/forward navigation.
- **Swipe between full-screen apps:** Enable "Swipe left or right with two fingers" to switch Spaces (note this might conflict with the page swipe setting depending on your choice).
- **Mission Control:** Enable "Double-tap with two fingers" to activate Mission Control.

While the Magic Mouse offers some gesture capability on its multi-touch surface, it's generally less extensive and ergonomic for complex gestures compared to the Magic Trackpad.

Third-Party Customization Tools (For Power Users)

For users who want ultimate control beyond Apple's built-in settings, powerful third-party applications exist like **BetterTouchTool** or **Karabiner-Elements**. These tools allow extremely granular customization of trackpad gestures, mouse buttons, keyboard shortcuts, creating complex macros, and much more. They have a steeper learning curve and are generally aimed at power users, but offer unparalleled flexibility if you need it. Use these tools with care, as misconfiguration could potentially interfere with normal system behavior.

Whether you stick with the defaults or customize extensively, understanding and utilizing gestures is key to unlocking the fluid, efficient navigation that macOS is known for, especially on the excellent trackpad of your MacBook Air M4.

Exploring Accessibility Features (VoiceOver, Zoom, Display Options, Voice Control)

Apple has long been a leader in building powerful **Accessibility** features into its operating systems. While primarily designed to assist users with disabilities (vision, hearing, motor, cognitive), many of these features can actually be beneficial for *all* users by offering alternative ways to interact with the Mac, reduce eye strain, or automate tasks. Exploring these options in **System Settings > Accessibility** might reveal tools that enhance your own experience.

Navigating Accessibility Settings

Open **System Settings** and click **Accessibility** in the sidebar. The settings are logically grouped into categories:

- **Vision:** Features for users who are blind or have low vision.
- **Hearing:** Features for users who are deaf or hard of hearing.
- **Motor:** Features for users with physical or motor limitations.
- **General:** System-wide accessibility settings like Siri and the Accessibility Shortcut.

Let's highlight some key features within these categories:

Vision Features

1. **VoiceOver:** This is Apple's powerful built-in screen reader. When enabled, VoiceOver speaks descriptions of everything happening on the screen – text, buttons, interface elements – and provides detailed auditory feedback, allowing users who are blind or have significant vision impairment to navigate and interact with macOS using keyboard commands and gestures.

   - *Enabling:* Can be toggled with Command (⌘) + F5 (or Fn + Command + F5). A tutorial usually starts upon first activation.
   - *Usage:* Requires learning specific VoiceOver keyboard commands (using the VO keys, typically Control+Option) for navigation (e.g., VO +

Right Arrow to move to the next item, VO + Spacebar to activate an item).

- o *Audience:* Primarily for blind/low vision users, but exploring its capabilities offers insight into non-visual interface interaction.

2. **Zoom:** This feature magnifies the screen content.

- o *How it Works:* Offers different zoom styles: **Full screen** (magnifies the entire display), **Split screen** (magnifies one section while leaving the rest normal), or **Picture-in-picture** (shows a magnified lens that follows your cursor).

- o *Activation:* Can be toggled using keyboard shortcuts (e.g., Option + Command + = to zoom in, Option + Command + - to zoom out, Option + Command + 8 to toggle zoom). Trackpad gestures (like double-tap with three fingers or scroll with three fingers while holding Option) can also be configured.

- o *Hover Text:* A specific zoom feature where holding a modifier key (like Command) and hovering the cursor over text displays a large-type version of that text in a dedicated window.

- o *Benefits for All:* Even users with good vision might use Zoom occasionally to get a closer look at fine details in images or read very small text. Hover Text is great for quickly enlarging text without zooming the whole screen.

3. **Display:** This section contains numerous options to adjust visual appearance for comfort and clarity:

- o *Invert colors:* Reverses screen colors (light becomes dark, etc.).

- o *Reduce motion:* Minimizes animations like zooming windows or sliding Spaces, which can be uncomfortable for some users.

- o *Increase contrast:* Makes interface elements like borders and backgrounds more distinct.

- o *Reduce transparency:* Makes elements like the Menu Bar and Dock more opaque for better readability against busy backgrounds.

- o *Color filters:* Apply filters to help users with various types of color blindness differentiate colors.

- o *Pointer size and color:* Increase the size and change the outline/fill color of the mouse pointer to make it easier to see.

- o *Many users* without vision impairments find options like Reduce Motion or Reduce Transparency helpful for reducing visual "noise" or potential motion sickness. Increasing contrast can sometimes improve readability.

Hearing Features

- **Audio:**
  - *Play stereo audio as mono:* Combines left and right audio channels into one, useful if you have hearing loss primarily in one ear or use only one earbud.
  - *Flash the screen when an alert sound occurs:* Provides a visual cue for system alerts in addition to the sound.
  - *Background sounds:* Play calming background noises (like rain, ocean, white noise) directly from your Mac to help mask distracting environmental sounds or promote focus/relaxation.

- **RTT (Real-Time Text):** Allows text communication over phone calls for users who are deaf, hard of hearing, or speech-impaired, using compatible TTY devices or software RTT. Requires setup and carrier support.

- **Live Captions:** This powerful feature provides **system-wide, real-time captions** for *any* audio content playing on your Mac – FaceTime calls, videos in Safari, podcasts in the Podcasts app, audio from practically any application.
  - *Enabling:* Turn it on in Accessibility > Live Captions. It might download language data first.
  - *How it Works:* A floating window appears on screen, displaying automatically generated captions for whatever audio is currently playing. Works entirely on-device for privacy using the M4's Neural Engine.
  - *Customization:* You can change the caption window's position, font size, and appearance.
  - *Benefits for All:* Fantastic not only for users who are hard of hearing but also for anyone in a noisy environment, watching videos with unclear audio, or learning a new language.

Motor Features

- **Voice Control:** Allows you to control your entire Mac using only your voice. This is a comprehensive feature distinct from Siri's conversational commands.
  - *Enabling:* Turn it on in Accessibility > Voice Control. Requires an initial download of language files. A microphone icon appears on screen.
  - *How it Works:* Uses numbered grids/overlays and voice commands to click buttons, select menus, dictate text, navigate windows, etc. You speak commands like "Open Mail," "Click Done," "Scroll down," "Show numbers" (to overlay numbers on clickable items), "Click 14."
  - *Learning Curve:* Requires learning the specific commands but offers complete hands-free operation.
  - *Benefits for All:* While essential for users with physical limitations, it can also be useful for hands-busy situations or exploring alternative input methods.

- **Keyboard:**

    - *Sticky Keys:* Allows you to press modifier keys (Shift, Command, Option, Control) *sequentially* instead of having to hold them down simultaneously. Press Shift, then press 'A' to get a capital A. Helpful for one-handed typing or users who find chorded shortcuts difficult.

    - *Slow Keys:* Introduces a delay between when a key is pressed and when it's registered, helping prevent accidental key presses.

    - *Accessibility Keyboard:* An on-screen virtual keyboard that can be controlled with a mouse, trackpad, head-tracking, or switch control. Includes typing suggestions and dwell control (hovering performs a click).

- **Pointer Control:**

    - *Alternate Control Methods:* Options to control the pointer using head movements (via the camera), accessibility switches, or facial expressions.

    - *Dwell Control:* Allows performing mouse actions (click, drag, scroll) by simply hovering (dwelling) the pointer over an item for a set time, useful for users who cannot physically click.

    - *Other Options:* Adjust double-click speed, spring-loading delays (when dragging files over folders).

General Accessibility Settings

- **Siri:** Configure Type to Siri (interact via keyboard instead of voice), voice feedback options.

- **Accessibility Shortcut:** This is incredibly useful! Go here to choose which accessibility features you want to be able to toggle quickly on or off by **triple-pressing the Touch ID button** (or pressing Option + Command + F5). You could set this up to quickly toggle Zoom, VoiceOver, Color Filters, Sticky Keys, or the Accessibility Keyboard, for example.

Accessibility Feature	Category	Primary Function / Benefit	Potential Benefit for All Users?
VoiceOver	Vision	Complete screen reader for blind/low vision users.	Insight into non-visual UI.
Zoom	Vision	Magnifies screen content (full, split, picture-in-picture, hover text).	Examining details, reading small print.

Display Options	Vision	Invert colors, reduce motion/transparency, increase contrast, color filters, pointer size.	Reducing eye strain, improving clarity, personal preference.
Live Captions	Hearing	Real-time captions for any system audio.	Noisy environments, unclear audio, language learning.
Background Sounds	Hearing	Plays calming ambient sounds (rain, ocean, etc.).	Masking distractions, promoting focus/relaxation.
Voice Control	Motor	Control the entire Mac using voice commands.	Hands-free operation scenarios.
Sticky Keys	Motor	Press modifier keys sequentially instead of holding them down.	Easier shortcut entry for some users.
Accessibility Keyboard	Motor	On-screen keyboard controlled via mouse, dwell, head tracking, etc.	Alternative input method.
Accessibility Shortcut	General	Triple-press Touch ID (or Opt+Cmd+F5) to quickly toggle selected features on/off.	Fast access to occasionally needed accessibility tools (like Zoom).

Don't think of Accessibility settings as only being for users with specific disabilities. Explore the options – you might find features like Zoom, Display adjustments, Live Captions, Background Sounds, or the Accessibility Shortcut genuinely enhance your own comfort, focus, or efficiency while using your powerful and versatile MacBook Air M4. Apple's commitment here provides tools that can make the Mac experience better for everyone.

Maximizing M4, Apple Intelligence & Troubleshooting

Congratulations on making it through this guide! You've journeyed from unboxing your MacBook Air M4 to mastering its interface, applications, connectivity, security, and maintenance. In this final chapter, we'll focus on truly maximizing your experience. We'll recap the specific advantages the powerful M4 chip brings, peek into the future with Apple Intelligence features integrated into macOS Sequoia, share practical tips for keeping your Mac running at peak performance and extending its battery life, and provide a structured approach to troubleshooting common problems should they arise. Let's ensure you get the absolute most out of your incredible machine.

Understanding the M4 Advantage: Performance and Efficiency

At the very core of your MacBook Air lies the Apple M4 chip – a marvel of engineering that represents a significant leap in performance and power efficiency compared to previous generations, especially older Intel-based Macs and even earlier M-series Apple Silicon chips (M1, M2, M3). Understanding what makes the M4 special helps you appreciate the capabilities of your thin-and-light machine.

Recap: The Power Within (Building on Chapter 8.4)

The M4 chip isn't just one processor; it's a System on a Chip (SoC) integrating several specialized components designed to work together seamlessly:

- **CPU (Central Processing Unit):** The M4 features a 10-core CPU, built with both high-performance cores (for demanding tasks like video editing, compiling code, complex calculations) and high-efficiency cores (for handling background tasks, email, web browsing, consuming very little power). This hybrid design delivers both speed when you need it and excellent battery life during everyday use.

  - *Real-World Benefit:* Apps launch faster, switching between multiple open applications feels smoother, tasks like exporting documents or processing data in spreadsheets complete quicker. Even demanding "prosumer" tasks feel remarkably responsive on the Air.

- **GPU (Graphics Processing Unit):** With its 8-core or 10-core GPU options, the M4 delivers a substantial boost in graphics performance.

  - *Real-World Benefit:* Editing photos with complex filters in the Photos app is fluid, scrolling through graphically rich websites or documents is smooth, casual gaming performance is improved (with support for features like MetalFX Upscaling in compatible games), and importantly, it enables the M4 Air's native support for **dual external displays** (up to 6K each) with the lid open – a major productivity enhancement over previous Air models.

- **Neural Engine (NPU):** The M4 boasts a significantly faster 16-core Neural Engine, specifically designed to accelerate machine learning (ML) or Artificial Intelligence (AI) tasks.
  - *Real-World Benefit:* Features that rely on ML run much faster and more efficiently. This includes things like faster and more accurate face/object recognition in Photos, improved voice dictation accuracy and speed, quicker analysis for features like subject isolation ("Lift subject from background"), enabling the new suite of **Apple Intelligence** features (see next section), and accelerating AI-powered tools within many third-party creative and productivity apps.

- **Media Engine:** This dedicated hardware block is optimized for handling video.
  - *Real-World Benefit:* It dramatically speeds up the encoding (exporting) and decoding (playback) of common video formats like H.264 and HEVC, as well as professional codecs like ProRes. This makes editing 4K video in iMovie (or even Final Cut Pro) incredibly smooth and exporting times remarkably short for a laptop this thin and light – a task that often crippled older Air models.

- **Unified Memory Architecture (UMA):** Instead of separate pools of memory for the CPU and GPU, Apple Silicon uses a unified pool of high-bandwidth memory (16GB standard on the M4 Air, configurable up to 32GB) accessible directly by all components on the chip.
  - *Real-World Benefit:* Eliminates the performance bottleneck of copying large amounts of data between CPU and GPU memory, leading to significant speedups in graphics-intensive tasks, video editing, and when working with very large files or datasets. It makes the installed RAM highly efficient.

The Efficiency Equation: Power Without the Penalty

Perhaps the most remarkable aspect of the M4 (and Apple Silicon in general) is that it delivers this impressive performance while consuming significantly less power than the Intel processors used in older Macs.

- **Exceptional Battery Life:** This efficiency directly translates into the outstanding battery life the MacBook Air is famous for. You can work, browse, and watch videos for many hours without needing to reach for the power adapter (Apple typically quotes up to 15 hours of wireless web or 18 hours of video playback).

- **Cool and Quiet Operation:** Because the M4 chip generates less heat for a given task, the MacBook Air can often operate completely silently (many models are fanless or rarely need to spin up their fans). Even under sustained load, it remains cooler and quieter than many comparable laptops.

Putting the M4 Air in Context

The M4 chip effectively elevates the MacBook Air beyond just an "entry-level" laptop. It delivers performance that rivals or exceeds many older MacBook Pro models and handles tasks that were previously unthinkable on an Air. For the vast majority of users – including students, professionals, writers, photographers, and even those doing moderately heavy video editing or development – the M4 MacBook Air offers an incredible combination of power, portability, battery life, and value.

M4 Chip Component	Key Advantage(s)	Real-World Impact on MacBook Air M4
CPU (10-core Perf/Eff)	Fast general processing, efficient multitasking.	Snappy app launches, smooth switching between many apps, quick processing.
GPU (8/10-core)	Improved graphics rendering, hardware ray tracing support.	Smooth UI animations, better casual gaming, **native dual external display support**, faster photo/basic video edits.
Neural Engine (16-core)	Greatly accelerated machine learning / AI tasks.	Faster Siri/Dictation, quick Photos analysis (People/Objects/Memories), enables Apple Intelligence, speeds up AI features in apps.
Media Engine	Hardware acceleration for video encode/decode (H.264, HEVC, ProRes).	Dramatically faster video exports, smooth 4K+ video editing and playback, power-efficient video tasks.
Unified Memory (16GB+)	High-bandwidth shared memory pool, eliminates data copying bottlenecks.	Efficient handling of large files, smooth performance when RAM is heavily utilized by multiple apps or complex tasks.
Overall Efficiency	High performance per watt, low power consumption.	Exceptional battery life, cool and quiet operation (often fanless).

Understanding the power packed into the M4 chip helps you appreciate why your MacBook Air feels so capable and efficient across such a wide range of tasks.

Exploring Apple Intelligence Features in macOS Sequoia

One of the most exciting aspects of macOS Sequoia, especially when paired with the powerful Neural Engine in your M4 chip, is the introduction of **Apple Intelligence**. This isn't just a single feature, but rather a suite of intelligent capabilities woven throughout the operating system and core applications, designed to help you write better, communicate more effectively, manage tasks more easily, and express yourself creatively – all while maintaining Apple's strong focus on user privacy.

(Note: As of April 15, 2025, the specific final feature set and rollout details of Apple Intelligence in macOS Sequoia might still be evolving based on Apple's announcements. The following describes the generally expected capabilities and direction based on available information and industry trends.)

Apple's Approach: Personal Intelligence & Privacy

Apple emphasizes that its approach to AI is deeply personal and privacy-focused.

- **On-Device Processing:** Whenever possible, Apple Intelligence tasks are processed directly *on your MacBook Air M4* using the Neural Engine. This means your personal data (emails, notes, photos) doesn't need to leave your device for many intelligent features to work, significantly enhancing privacy.

- **Private Cloud Compute:** For more complex requests that require larger models or server-side processing, Apple has developed "Private Cloud Compute." This involves sending only the necessary data (encrypted) to special servers running on Apple Silicon. This data is used solely to fulfill your request, is *not* stored, and is cryptographically verified to be inaccessible even to Apple, ensuring your privacy is maintained even when leveraging cloud power.

- **Contextual Awareness:** Apple Intelligence aims to understand your personal context – your contacts, calendar, files, etc. (with your permission) – to provide more relevant and helpful assistance.

Key Areas Where Apple Intelligence Shines (Examples)

Expect to see Apple Intelligence enhancing your experience in numerous ways:

1. **Writing Tools (System-Wide):** Imagine having an intelligent writing assistant available anywhere you type text (Mail, Notes, Pages, Messages, even third-party apps).

   - **Proofreading:** Go beyond basic spell-check with advanced grammar correction, word choice suggestions, and structural improvements.

   - **Rewriting:** Select text you've written and ask Apple Intelligence to rewrite it in a different tone (e.g., more professional, more friendly, more concise) or to adjust its complexity.

   - **Summarization:** Select a long email, article, or note and instantly get a concise summary of the key points. Incredibly useful for quickly grasping the gist of lengthy content.

2. **Image Generation (Image Playground):** Unleash your creativity by generating unique images simply by describing them.

   o **How it Works:** You might find an "Image Playground" option within apps like Messages, Notes, Keynote, or Pages. You type a description (e.g., "a dog wearing sunglasses riding a skateboard in cartoon style"), choose a visual style (like Animation, Sketch, Illustration), and Apple Intelligence creates the image on-device.

   o **Use Cases:** Creating fun custom emoji-like images (Genmoji) for messages, illustrating notes or presentations, quickly visualizing ideas.

3. **Siri Gets Smarter:** Siri is expected to become significantly more capable and conversational.

   o **Improved Natural Language:** Understands more complex requests, remembers context from previous interactions, handles pauses and corrections better ("umms" and "ahhs").

   o **On-Screen Awareness:** Understands what's currently displayed on your screen, allowing you to ask questions or take actions related to the content without explicitly naming it (e.g., "Add this person to my contacts" while viewing contact info).

   o **Taking Actions Within Apps:** Potentially able to perform multi-step actions within and across apps based on your voice commands (e.g., "Find photos from my trip to Zurich last summer and share the best ones with Anna").

4. **Photos App Intelligence:** Building on existing ML features:

   o **Enhanced Search:** Find photos using more natural language descriptions or by searching for objects or actions within the photos themselves.

   o **Intelligent Editing Tools:** Features like the "Clean Up" tool (mentioned in the original book description) might use AI to easily remove distracting objects or people from the background of your photos.

   o **Smarter Memories:** Even better automatic curation of Memories movies based on semantic understanding of your photo library content.

5. **Mail and Messages Enhancements:**

   o **Priority Inbox / Notifications:** AI helps identify and surface your most important emails or messages, potentially summarizing less critical ones.

   o **Smart Replies:** Suggest relevant, context-aware replies to emails and messages.

- o **Email Summarization:** Get quick summaries of long email threads directly within Mail.

6. **Notes and Other Apps:** Expect AI features to appear contextually – perhaps summarizing meeting notes, automatically organizing information, or suggesting relevant actions based on note content.

Accessing Apple Intelligence Features

7. These features likely won't reside in a single "AI app." Instead, they'll be integrated contextually:

8. Look for new icons or menu options appearing when you select text (for Writing Tools).

9. Use Siri as you normally would, but try more complex or contextual requests.

10. Explore new options within the Photos, Mail, Messages, and Notes apps.

11. Image Playground might be accessible via a dedicated button or menu item within relevant apps.

Availability Considerations

- **Hardware:** Apple Intelligence features rely heavily on the Neural Engine, so they require Apple Silicon chips (your M4 is well-equipped).

- **Software:** Requires macOS Sequoia (or the corresponding iOS/iPadOS versions).

- **Language & Region:** Often, advanced AI features roll out initially in specific languages (like US English) and regions, with broader support added over time. Check Apple's documentation for current availability.

Apple Intelligence Category	Potential Features / Examples	Where You Might See It
Writing Tools	Proofreading, Rewriting (tone/conciseness), Summarization.	System-wide (Mail, Notes, Pages, Messages, third-party apps).
Image Generation	Creating images from text descriptions (Image Playground), custom emoji (Genmoji).	Messages, Notes, Keynote, Pages, Freeform.
Smarter Siri	Improved natural language understanding, contextual awareness, taking actions within/across apps.	Activated via "Hey Siri" or button press.

Photos Intelligence	Enhanced search, intelligent object removal ("Clean Up"), smarter Memories curation.	Photos app.
Mail / Messages	Priority Inbox/Notifications, Smart Replies, Email Summarization.	Mail app, Messages app, Notifications.
Other Apps	AI-powered summarization, organization, task suggestions.	Notes, potentially Calendar, Reminders, etc.

Apple Intelligence promises to make your interactions with your MacBook Air M4 more helpful, personal, and efficient, leveraging the power of the M4 chip while prioritizing your privacy through on-device processing and Private Cloud Compute. Keep an eye out for these features as you explore macOS Sequoia!

Tips for Optimizing Performance and Extending Battery Life

Your MacBook Air M4 is designed for excellent performance and industry-leading battery life right out of the box, thanks to the efficiency of Apple Silicon. However, there are still habits and settings you can adopt to ensure it consistently runs at its peak and that you squeeze every possible minute out of the battery when needed.

Tips for Maintaining Optimal Performance

While the M4 is fast, keeping things tidy helps ensure sustained speed:

1. **Keep macOS and Apps Updated:** As discussed in section 12.1, updates often include performance optimizations and bug fixes. Regularly check System Settings > General > Software Update and the App Store > Updates.

2. **Manage Login Items:** Prevent unnecessary applications from launching automatically every time you log in, as they consume resources in the background. Go to **System Settings > General > Login Items**. Review the "Open at Login" list. Select apps you don't need immediately upon startup and click the '-' button to remove them. Also check the "Allow in the Background" section for items you might not recognize or need.

3. **Quit Unused Applications:** Get in the habit of fully quitting applications (Command + Q) when you're finished using them, rather than just closing their windows (Command + W). Apps running in the background still consume RAM and occasionally CPU cycles.

4. **Tame Your Browser Tabs:** Having dozens (or hundreds!) of browser tabs open simultaneously can consume significant memory and CPU resources, especially if those tabs contain complex web apps, streaming video, or auto-refreshing content. Use Safari's **Tab Groups** to organize tabs you need for specific projects but don't need open *right now*. Use the **Reading List** for articles you want to save for later. Close tabs you're truly finished with.

5. **Monitor with Activity Monitor (When Needed):** If your Mac feels unusually sluggish or fans spin up, launch Activity Monitor (Applications > Utilities). Check the **CPU** and **Memory** tabs, sorting by % CPU or Memory usage to identify any runaway processes or apps consuming excessive resources (see section 12.4). Quit or Force Quit problematic apps if necessary (use caution).

6. **Restart Occasionally:** While macOS is generally stable, a simple restart (Apple menu □ > Restart...) once a week or so can clear out temporary files, reset system processes, and resolve minor glitches that might impact performance over time.

7. **Maintain Free Storage Space:** As covered in section 12.3, keep at least 10-15% of your internal SSD storage free. Performance can degrade when the drive is almost completely full. Regularly clean out downloads, empty the Trash, uninstall unused apps, and consider using "Optimize Mac Storage" with iCloud.

Tips for Extending Battery Life

Maximize your time away from the power adapter:

1. **Dim the Screen Brightness:** The display is one of the largest power consumers. Lower the brightness to the lowest comfortable level using the **F1** key or the slider in Control Center/Displays settings. Avoid using maximum brightness unless necessary.

2. **Adjust Keyboard Backlight:** If you don't need the keyboard backlight (e.g., in a well-lit room), dim it or turn it off completely using the **F5** key or Control Center. Set it to turn off automatically after inactivity in System Settings > Keyboard > Keyboard Brightness.

3. **Enable Low Power Mode:** Go to **System Settings > Battery**. Select **Low Power Mode** from the dropdown menu (options might be Never, Always, On Battery Only). This reduces energy consumption by slightly lowering screen brightness, reducing system clock speed, and pausing some background activities. It's a great option when you need to maximize remaining battery life.

4. **Optimize Battery Charging:** Also in System Settings > Battery > Battery Health, ensure **"Optimized Battery Charging"** is enabled. This helps reduce battery aging by learning your charging routine and delaying charging past 80% until closer to when you typically unplug.

5. **Quit Power-Hungry Apps:** Use **Activity Monitor > Energy** tab to identify applications with a high "Avg Energy Impact." Quit these apps if you aren't actively using them, especially demanding creative apps, games, or video conferencing tools. Even specific websites open in Safari can sometimes consume significant energy – check the disclosure triangle next to Safari in Activity Monitor.

6. **Disconnect Unused Peripherals:** External hard drives, hubs, some adapters, and other accessories draw power through the USB-C/Thunderbolt ports. Unplug them when not needed while on battery power.

7. **Turn Off Wi-Fi and Bluetooth (If Not Needed):** If you're working offline for an extended period (e.g., writing on a plane), turning off Wi-Fi and Bluetooth via Control Center can save a small amount of power.

8. **Minimize Background Activity:** Reduce the number of apps running simultaneously. Pause large downloads or file syncs until you can plug in. Adjust Mail's fetch frequency if needed (Mail > Settings > General > Check for new messages).

9. **Manage Video Playback:** Watching high-resolution streaming video consumes significant power. Consider downloading videos for offline viewing (via the TV app or other services) if possible. Lowering playback resolution might also help slightly. Ensure "Optimize video streaming while on battery" is checked in Battery settings.

10. **Avoid Extreme Temperatures:** Both very hot and very cold conditions can negatively impact battery performance and long-term health. Try to use and store your MacBook Air within reasonable ambient temperatures. Don't leave it in direct sunlight or a hot car.

Performance Tip	How To Do It	Why It Helps
Keep Software Updated	System Settings > General > Software Update; App Store > Updates.	Includes optimizations, bug fixes.
Manage Login Items	System Settings > General > Login Items. Remove unneeded apps.	Reduces background resource usage upon startup.
Quit Unused Apps	Command + Q apps you're finished with.	Frees up RAM and CPU cycles.
Manage Browser Tabs	Use Tab Groups, Reading List, close unneeded tabs.	Reduces memory and CPU load from background tabs.
Monitor Resource Hogs (If Needed)	Activity Monitor (Utilities folder). Check CPU/Memory tabs.	Identify and quit malfunctioning or overly demanding processes.
Restart Occasionally	Apple menu □ > Restart...	Clears temporary files, resets processes, resolves minor glitches.
Maintain Free Storage Space	System Settings > General > Storage. Keep 10-15%+ free.	Prevents SSD slowdown when drive is nearly full.

Battery Saving Tip	How To Do It	Why It Helps
Lower Screen Brightness	F1 key / Control Center / Displays settings.	Display is a major power draw.
Dim/Turn Off Keyboard Backlight	F5 key / Control Center / Keyboard settings.	Backlight consumes power when not needed.
Use Low Power Mode	System Settings > Battery > Low Power Mode.	Reduces clock speed, brightness, background activity to conserve power.
Enable Optimized Battery Charging	System Settings > Battery > Battery Health.	Reduces battery aging by managing charge cycles.
Quit Power-Hungry Apps	Check Activity Monitor > Energy tab; Command + Q demanding apps.	Reduces CPU/GPU load and energy consumption.
Disconnect Unused Peripherals	Unplug external drives, hubs, etc., when on battery.	Peripherals draw power via USB-C/Thunderbolt.
Turn Off Wi-Fi/Bluetooth (If Off)	Control Center toggles.	Radios consume power when searching/connected (use only if truly offline).
Minimize Background Activity	Pause large downloads/syncs, adjust Mail fetch frequency.	Reduces network and processing activity.
Optimize Video Streaming	System Settings > Battery > Optimize video streaming... Download videos if possible.	Video decoding/streaming is power-intensive.
Avoid Extreme Temperatures	Use/store Mac in moderate temperatures.	Extreme heat/cold negatively impacts battery performance and health.

By being mindful of these performance and battery optimization tips, you can ensure your MacBook Air M4 remains a fast, responsive, and long-lasting companion for all your tasks.

Troubleshooting Common Issues and Knowing Where to Get Help

Even with a reliable machine like the MacBook Air M4 and the stable macOS Sequoia operating system, occasional glitches or problems can occur. Knowing some basic troubleshooting steps and where to turn for help can save you time and frustration when things don't go as expected.

Basic Troubleshooting Steps: The First Things to Try

Before diving into complex solutions, always start with these fundamental steps, which resolve a surprising number of common issues:

1. **Restart Your Mac:** This is the golden rule. A simple restart (Apple menu □ > Restart...) clears temporary memory, resets system processes, and often resolves minor software glitches, unresponsiveness, or weird behavior. Try this first for almost any problem.

2. **Check Connections:** If the issue involves an external device (monitor, drive, printer, network), double-check that all cables (power, data) are securely plugged in at both ends. Try a different port on your Mac or hub/dock. Ensure peripherals have power. Check Wi-Fi/Ethernet connections.

3. **Update Software:** Ensure both macOS and the specific application you're having trouble with are fully updated (System Settings > General > Software Update; App Store > Updates; App's internal updater). Compatibility issues or bugs might have been fixed in a recent update.

4. **Isolate the Problem:** Try to determine the scope of the issue:

   o Does the problem occur in only *one specific application*, or does it affect the entire system? (If one app, focus troubleshooting there – force quit, check for updates, reset preferences, reinstall).

   o Does it happen with only *one specific document* or file? (The file itself might be corrupted).

   o Does it only happen when a *specific external device* is connected? (The device or its cable/driver might be the issue).

   o Does it happen only when connected to a *specific network*?

5. **Check Apple's System Status:** If you're having trouble with iCloud services, the App Store, FaceTime, or other Apple online services, check Apple's official System Status page online (www.apple.com/support/systemstatus/) to see if there's a known outage affecting those services.

Common Issues and Potential Solutions

Here are some frequent problems and common approaches:

1. **Application Freezes or Becomes Unresponsive ("Beach Ball"):**

   o Try waiting a moment, especially if the Mac is performing a demanding task.

   o Try switching to another app (⌘+Tab) and back.

   o **Force Quit:** If it remains stuck, press Option + Command (⌘) + Esc to open the "Force Quit Applications" window. Select the unresponsive app (it will likely say "Not Responding") and click "Force Quit." Alternatively, use Activity Monitor (Utilities folder) to force quit the process (see 12.4). Remember you might lose unsaved work in that app.

   o Check for updates for the specific app.

   o Restart your Mac.

   o If it happens repeatedly with one app, consider resetting its preferences (requires finding preference files in ~/Library/Preferences) or reinstalling the app.

2. **Mac Running Slowly:**

   o **Check Activity Monitor:** Use Activity Monitor (Utilities folder) to check CPU and Memory usage. Identify any processes consuming excessive resources (see 12.4). Quit unnecessary apps/processes. Check Memory Pressure – if constantly yellow/red, you're exceeding available RAM.

   o **Manage Login Items:** Too many apps launching at startup can slow things down (System Settings > General > Login Items).

   o **Check Storage Space:** Ensure you have adequate free space on your SSD (System Settings > General > Storage).

   o **Restart:** A simple restart often helps.

   o **Check for Malware:** While less common on Macs than Windows, malware exists. If you suspect an infection (unusual pop-ups, extreme slowness, strange behavior), run a scan with a reputable anti-malware application designed for Mac (e.g., Malwarebytes for Mac).

   o **Check Power Adapter:** Is performance slow only when on battery? Check Battery settings for Low Power Mode. Ensure you're using the correct wattage power adapter.

3. **Wi-Fi or Bluetooth Connectivity Problems:**

   o **Toggle Off/On:** Turn Wi-Fi/Bluetooth off and on again in Control Center or System Settings.

   o **Restart Devices:** Restart your Mac *and* your router (for Wi-Fi) or the Bluetooth peripheral.

   o **Forget and Reconnect:** Forget the Wi-Fi network (System Settings > Wi-Fi > Known Networks > ...) or Bluetooth device (System Settings > Bluetooth > 'i' icon > Forget This Device...) and then reconnect/re-pair it.

   o **Check Range & Interference:** Ensure devices are close enough and minimize potential sources of wireless interference (microwaves, other devices).

   o **Check Router (Wi-Fi):** Ensure your router firmware is up-to-date. Try connecting other devices to the same Wi-Fi network to see if the issue is specific to your Mac.

   o **Run Wireless Diagnostics (Wi-Fi):** Option-click the Wi-Fi Menu Bar icon > Open Wireless Diagnostics...

4. **External Device Not Working (Drive, Monitor, etc.):**

   o **Check Connections:** Reseat cables firmly. Try a different port on the Mac/hub. Try a different cable if possible. Ensure the device has power if required.

   o **Restart Mac:** Sometimes needed for the Mac to recognize a new device properly.

   o **Check System Information:** Go to Apple menu ☐ > About This Mac > More Info... > System Report... Check under relevant sections (e.g., USB, Thunderbolt, Storage, Graphics/Displays) to see if the Mac even detects the hardware.

   o **Check Disk Utility (for Drives):** Open Disk Utility (Utilities folder). Does the drive appear in the sidebar? Does it need formatting? Can you run "First Aid" on the volume?

   o **Check Drivers (Rare):** Most standard peripherals don't need drivers, but very specialized equipment might. Check the manufacturer's website for Mac compatibility and drivers for macOS Sequoia.

   o **Check Adapter/Hub:** If using one, the adapter or hub itself could be faulty or incompatible. Try connecting the device directly if possible, or try a different adapter.

5. **Mac Won't Start Up Properly:**

   o **Check Power:** Ensure MagSafe or USB-C power adapter is connected securely and has power.

   o **Safe Mode:** Shut down the Mac. Then, press and hold the **Power button (Touch ID sensor)** until you see "Loading startup options..." appear. Release the button. Select your startup disk (usually Macintosh HD). Now, press and hold the **Shift (⇧)** key, then click **"Continue in Safe Mode."** Release Shift when the login window appears (it might say "Safe Boot" in the Menu Bar). Safe Mode performs disk checks and loads only essential system extensions. If your Mac starts up in Safe Mode but not normally, it suggests a problem with a login item, system extension, or possibly corrupted caches. Restart normally after testing in Safe Mode.

   o **Disk Utility First Aid (Recovery Mode):** Shut down the Mac. Press and hold the Power button until startup options load. Click **Options**, then **Continue**. This loads macOS Recovery. Select **Disk Utility**. Select your startup volume (e.g., Macintosh HD) and click **First Aid**. Run it to check for and repair disk errors.

   o **Reinstall macOS (Recovery Mode):** From the macOS Recovery screen (accessed as above), you can choose **Reinstall macOS Sequoia**. This reinstalls the operating system *without* erasing your personal files and user accounts (though having a backup is still crucial!). It downloads the latest version and installs it over the current system, often fixing corrupted OS files. Requires an internet connection.

Knowing Where to Get Help

If you're stuck, don't despair! There are many resources available:

1. **Built-in Help:** Most applications have a **Help** menu in the Menu Bar. Use the search field there to find information about specific features or functions within that app.

2. Apple Support Website (support.apple.com/mac): This is your primary online resource. It contains:

   o **Knowledge Base Articles:** Detailed articles covering troubleshooting steps, how-to guides, and explanations for countless topics. Search using specific keywords related to your issue.

   o **Manuals:** Digital versions of user guides for your Mac model and macOS.

   o **Community Forums:** Ask questions and find answers from other Mac users and sometimes Apple specialists. Search the forums first, as your question may already be answered.

3. **Apple Support App (on iPhone/iPad):** A convenient app for accessing support articles, checking your warranty status, and initiating contact with Apple Support.

4. **Contacting Apple Support:** If self-help resources don't solve the problem:
   - **Online Chat/Phone:** Often initiated via the Support website or app. You can chat with a support advisor or request a phone call.
   - **Genius Bar Appointment:** Schedule an appointment at a physical Apple Store (check availability in Switzerland). Trained technicians ("Geniuses") can diagnose hardware and software issues in person. It's helpful to have a Time Machine backup before going, just in case.
   - Have your Mac's **Serial Number** ready (Apple menu □ > About This Mac).

5. **Reputable Third-Party Mac Websites/Forums:** Many excellent websites and forums are dedicated to Mac users, offering news, tips, tutorials, and troubleshooting advice (e.g., MacRumors Forums, 9to5Mac, iMore).

Issue Type	First Steps	Where to Get Help
App Freezing/Crashing	Wait, Force Quit (Opt+Cmd+Esc), Check for App Updates, Restart Mac.	App's Help Menu, Developer Website, Apple Support Website/Forums.
Mac Running Slow	Check Activity Monitor (CPU/Memory), Manage Login Items, Check Storage Space, Restart Mac, Check for Malware.	Activity Monitor, System Settings (Login Items, Storage), Apple Support Website.
Wi-Fi/Bluetooth Issues	Toggle Off/On, Restart Mac & Router/Device, Forget & Reconnect, Check Range/Interference, Wireless Diagnostics.	System Settings (Wi-Fi, Bluetooth), Router Manual, Apple Support Website.
External Device Issues	Check Connections/Power, Try Different Port/Cable, Restart Mac, Check System Information/Disk Utility, Eject Properly.	Device Manual, Manufacturer Website (Drivers), System Info, Disk Utility, Apple Support.
Startup Problems	Check Power, Boot in Safe Mode (Hold Shift after selecting disk in	Apple Support Website (Startup Issues), Contact

	startup options), Disk Utility First Aid (Recovery), Reinstall macOS (Recovery).	Apple Support / Genius Bar.

The Ultimate Safety Net: Your Backup!

Finally, always remember the importance of your **Time Machine backup** (section 12.2). While troubleshooting can resolve many issues, having a recent backup ensures that even if a serious problem occurs (like drive failure or needing to erase the drive), you can recover your valuable data and settings.

By approaching troubleshooting methodically and knowing where to find reliable help, you can tackle most common Mac issues confidently and keep your MacBook Air M4 experience positive.

Tips, Tricks & Secrets

You've learned the fundamentals, explored the core applications, and understand the key features of your MacBook Air M4 and macOS Sequoia. Now, let's unlock the next level! This chapter gathers a collection of practical tips for efficiency, clever tricks using built-in features you might have overlooked, and delves into some "secrets" – often just less obvious settings or deeper functionalities – to help you work faster, smarter, and get even more enjoyment out of your Mac.

Essential Tips for Everyday Efficiency

These are reminders and consolidations of good habits and useful settings, building on what we've learned. Consistently applying these tips makes a real difference.

1. Master File Organization Habits:

- **Consistent Naming:** Adopt a clear, consistent naming convention for your files and folders (e.g., ProjectName_DocumentType_Date_Version, like AlpineReport_Draft_2025-04-15_v2). This makes searching and sorting much easier.

- **Leverage Folders:** Don't let your Desktop or Documents folder become a chaotic dumping ground. Create logical folder hierarchies (as discussed in Chapter 3.2) for projects, subjects, or date ranges.

- **Embrace Tags:** Use Finder Tags (Chapter 3.2) for cross-category organization. Tag files by status (Urgent, Review Needed, Final), project, or context, regardless of which folder they reside in. Remember you can customize tag names and colors in Finder > Settings > Tags.

- **Utilize Stacks on Desktop:** Keep your Desktop tidy automatically by enabling Stacks (Right-click Desktop > Use Stacks). Group them by Kind, Date, or Tags to quickly find recent downloads, screenshots, or specific file types without manual filing (Chapter 3.2 / 2.1).

- **Smart Folders are Your Friends:** Set up Smart Folders (Chapter 3.2) for frequently needed dynamic searches (e.g., "PDFs Modified This Week," "Files Tagged 'Invoice'"). Add them to your Finder Sidebar for instant access.

2. Optimize Your Workspace Interaction:

- **Customize the Dock:** Pin your most frequently used apps, remove clutter, and add useful folders (like Applications or specific project folders) to the right side. Adjust size, magnification, and position (System Settings > Desktop & Dock) to fit your screen and workflow (Chapter 2.2). Hiding the Dock (Option+⌘+D or via settings) maximizes screen real estate.

- **Tailor the Menu Bar & Control Center:** Add frequently used controls (Bluetooth, Sound, Focus modes, Battery percentage) directly to the Menu Bar via System Settings > Control Center for one-click access. Remove icons you never use (Chapter 2.1 / 2.3).

- **Learn Trackpad Gestures:** Practice the multi-finger swipes for Mission Control, switching Spaces/full-screen apps, App Exposé, Launchpad, and Show Desktop (System Settings > Trackpad > More Gestures). They are significantly faster than clicking through menus or icons once you build muscle memory (Chapter 13.3).

- **Configure Hot Corners:** Set up actions (like Mission Control, Lock Screen, Quick Note) to trigger when you move your pointer to a screen corner (System Settings > Desktop & Dock > Hot Corners...). It's incredibly fast (Chapter 13.1).

3. Become a Keyboard Shortcut Ninja:

- **Memorize the Essentials:** Focus on mastering the fundamental system-wide shortcuts listed in Chapter 13.2 (⌘+C, ⌘+V, ⌘+Z, ⌘+S, ⌘+W, ⌘+Q, ⌘+Tab, ⌘+Spacebar, ⌘+H, etc.). Using these consistently saves enormous amounts of time.

- **Explore App Menus:** Pay attention to the shortcuts listed next to commands in the menus of apps you use regularly.

- **Create Custom Shortcuts:** Don't hesitate to create your own shortcuts (System Settings > Keyboard > Keyboard Shortcuts... > App Shortcuts) for menu commands you use often that don't have one, or if you prefer a different combination (Chapter 13.2).

4. Harness the Power of Spotlight:

- **Launch Everything:** Use ⌘+Spacebar as your primary way to launch applications – it's usually faster than finding them in the Dock or Applications folder.

- **Quick Info:** Use it for quick calculations, unit/currency conversions (150 CHF in EUR), definitions (define ubiquitous), weather, and stock quotes without opening separate apps (Chapter 3.4).

- **Find Anything:** Remember it searches file contents, emails, contacts, calendar events, and more. Use keywords (kind:, date:, tag:) to refine searches.

5. Prioritize Maintenance & Security:

- **Update Regularly:** Keep macOS and all applications up-to-date for security patches, bug fixes, and new features (Chapter 12.1). Enable automatic installation of Security Responses.

- **Back Up Religiously:** Set up Time Machine with an encrypted external drive and ensure it runs regularly. Your data is invaluable (Chapter 12.2).

- **Manage Storage:** Keep an eye on free space (System Settings > General > Storage). Use "Optimize Mac Storage" with iCloud if appropriate, clean out Downloads, empty Trash, uninstall unused apps (Chapter 12.3).

- **Enable FileVault:** Encrypt your startup disk for crucial data protection if your Mac is lost or stolen (Chapter 9.3). Ensure you have your recovery method (iCloud or Recovery Key) secured.

- **Use Strong Passwords & Passkeys:** Let Safari generate strong, unique passwords and save them to iCloud Keychain. Adopt Passkeys wherever available. Regularly check Security Recommendations (System Settings > Passwords) (Chapter 9.2).

- **Review Privacy Settings:** Periodically check System Settings > Privacy & Security to ensure apps only have the permissions they truly need (Chapter 9.4).

6. Maximize Battery Life (Recap):

- Lower screen brightness.

- Dim or disable keyboard backlight.

- Use Low Power Mode when needed (System Settings > Battery).

- Quit demanding apps when not in use (check Activity Monitor > Energy).

- Disconnect power-drawing peripherals.

- Manage background activity and downloads.

Clever Tricks and Lesser-Known Features

Now let's explore some specific functionalities and techniques that might not be immediately obvious but can significantly enhance your productivity or capabilities.

1. Advanced Screenshot & Screen Recording:

- **Beyond Basic Capture:** While Shift+⌘+3 (full screen) and Shift+⌘+4 (selection) are essential, Shift+⌘+5 is the power user's tool. It brings up an on-screen control panel with options to:
  - Capture Entire Screen.
  - Capture Selected Window (hover over a window, click – captures just that window, often with a nice shadow).
  - Capture Selected Portion (same as Shift+⌘+4).
  - Record Entire Screen (creates a video).
  - Record Selected Portion (drag to define recording area).
  - **Options Menu:** Click "Options" here to set a timer before capture, choose where to save the screenshot/recording (Desktop, Documents, Clipboard, Mail, Messages, Preview), show/hide the mouse pointer, remember last selection.

- **Capture Window without Shadow:** Use Shift+⌘+4, press Spacebar (cursor turns into a camera), then hold down the **Option (⌥) key** while clicking the window you want to capture. This saves the window image without the default drop shadow effect.

- **Adjust Selection:** After dragging a selection with Shift+⌘+4, you can hold **Spacebar** *before releasing the mouse button* to reposition the entire selection rectangle. Hold **Shift** to constrain the selection to horizontal or vertical movement while dragging.

2. Finder Power Moves:

- **Quick Look Markup:** Press Spacebar on an image or PDF, then click the **Markup button (pencil tip)** in the Quick Look window to instantly add annotations, shapes, text, or signatures without opening Preview (Chapter 3.3).

- **Batch Renaming:** Select multiple files in Finder. Right-click (Control-click) on the selected group and choose **Rename....** A panel appears allowing you to:
  - *Replace Text:* Find specific text in the filenames and replace it with something else.
  - *Add Text:* Add text before or after the current filename.
  - *Format:* Rename files with a custom format including a name, index number, counter, or date, with options for where the number appears. Incredibly useful for organizing batches of photos or documents.

- **Show Path Bar & Status Bar:** Enable these via the Finder's **View** menu. Path Bar shows the folder hierarchy at the bottom of the window; Status Bar shows item count and available disk space. Essential for orientation and storage awareness (Chapter 3.1).

- **Customize Toolbar Deeply:** Right-click the toolbar > Customize Toolbar... Drag frequently used actions like "New Folder," "Get Info," "Delete," or even specific applications or scripts onto the toolbar for instant access (Chapter 3.1).

- Go to Folder (Shift+⌘+G): From Finder, this shortcut opens a dialog allowing you to type or paste a specific folder path (e.g., ~/Library/Caches, /Applications/Utilities) to navigate there directly, including hidden folders. Use ~ as a shortcut for your Home folder.

- **Quick Actions:** In Finder, right-click a file. The **Quick Actions** submenu provides context-aware actions. For images, you might see "Rotate," "Markup," "Create PDF." You can customize these! Go to **System Settings > Privacy & Security > Extensions > Finder** to enable/disable available Quick Actions (provided by macOS or third-party apps). You can even create your own using the Automator app.

- **Column View Navigation:** When using Column view (⌘+3), use the **Left/Right Arrow keys** to navigate between columns (folders). Use

Up/Down Arrow keys to select items within a column. It's a very fast way to drill down through folders using only the keyboard.

- **Show Hidden Files:** In any Finder window, press Shift + Command (⌘) + Period (.). This toggles the visibility of hidden files and folders (names starting with a dot, or system-flagged as hidden). Press the shortcut again to hide them. Use with caution – don't delete hidden files unless you know what they are.

3. Text Editing Magic:

- **Cursor Movement Shortcuts:** These work in almost any text field (Notes, Mail, TextEdit, web forms):
  - Option (⌥) + Left/Right Arrow: Move cursor one word left/right.
  - Command (⌘) + Left/Right Arrow: Move cursor to the beginning/end of the current line.
  - Option (⌥) + Up/Down Arrow: Move cursor to the beginning/end of the current paragraph.
  - Command (⌘) + Up/Down Arrow: Move cursor to the beginning/end of the entire document.
  - (Add Shift to any of the above to *select* text while moving).

- **Deletion Shortcuts:**
  - Delete (Backspace): Deletes character to the left.
  - Fn + Delete: Forward delete (deletes character to the right).
  - Option (⌥) + Delete: Deletes the entire word to the left of the cursor.
  - Command (⌘) + Delete: Deletes the entire current line to the left of the cursor.

- **Special Dashes:**
  - Em Dash (—): Option + Shift + Hyphen (-).
  - En Dash (–): Option + Hyphen (-).

- **Emoji & Symbol Viewer:** Press Control (^) + Command (⌘) + Spacebar (or Fn + E) anywhere you can type text to bring up the Character Viewer. Easily find and insert emoji, symbols, accented characters, etc.

- **Text Replacements:** Set up abbreviations that automatically expand into longer phrases. Go to **System Settings > Keyboard > Text Input > Text Replacements...** Click '+' to add. For example, set "Replace" omw "With" On my way!. Now, typing omw followed by a space will automatically replace it. Great for frequently used phrases, email sign-offs, or addresses.

4. Quick Note Power:

- Configure a **Hot Corner** (System Settings > Desktop & Dock > Hot Corners...) or use the keyboard shortcut (Fn + Q often works) to invoke Quick Note.

- A small floating note window appears instantly for jotting down thoughts without opening the full Notes app.

- **Contextual Adding:** If invoked while in Safari, you can easily add a link to the current webpage to your Quick Note. If you highlight text on a webpage before invoking Quick Note, it can automatically add both the text and the link. Quick Notes are saved automatically in a special "Quick Notes" folder in the main Notes app.

"Secrets" (Less Obvious Features & Settings)

These aren't truly secret, but they are features or settings that are less commonly known or require a specific action to reveal, offering deeper control or insight.

1. Option-Clicking for More Info:

- Holding down the **Option (⌥)** key while clicking certain Menu Bar status icons often reveals additional information or hidden options:

  - **Option-click Wi-Fi Icon:** Shows detailed network information like IP address, router address, MAC address, channel, signal strength (RSSI), noise level, connection speed (Tx Rate), and the "Open Wireless Diagnostics..." option.

  - **Option-click Bluetooth Icon:** Shows MAC address, firmware version, and detailed status/diagnostic information for connected devices.

  - **Option-click Sound Volume Icon:** Allows quick selection of Input devices in addition to Output devices.

  - **Option-click Notification Center (Date/Time):** Toggles Do Not Disturb mode on/off quickly.

  - **Option-click Battery Icon:** Shows battery condition (Normal, Service Recommended).

- **Option-Clicking Menus:** Holding Option while opening some application menus might reveal alternative commands (e.g., in Finder's File menu, "Close Window" ⌘+W might change to "Close All" Option+⌘+W).

2. Special Startup Modes (Apple Silicon Differences):

- Troubleshooting startup issues on M4 Macs uses a different method than older Intel Macs (which used key combinations like Cmd+R, Option, Shift, Cmd+Opt+P+R at boot). On your M4 Air:

  - **Shut down** your Mac completely.

  - **Press and hold the Power button (Touch ID sensor)**. Keep holding it even after the Apple logo appears.

  - Release the button only when you see text saying **"Loading startup options..."**

  - This brings up the **Startup Options** screen. Here you can:

    0. Select your startup disk (usually "Macintosh HD") and click "Continue" to boot normally.

    1. Select the startup disk, then hold **Shift (⇧)** and click **"Continue in Safe Mode"** to boot into Safe Mode (performs checks, loads minimal drivers/extensions).

    2. Click **"Options"** then "Continue" to load **macOS Recovery**. From Recovery, you can access Disk Utility (to run First Aid), Reinstall macOS, restore from Time Machine, use Terminal, set Startup Security Policy, etc.

- **Resetting NVRAM/PRAM/SMC:** These were common troubleshooting steps on Intel Macs. On Apple Silicon Macs like your M4 Air, these resets are generally **not necessary or possible** in the same way. The functions previously handled by SMC (System Management Controller) and NVRAM/PRAM (parameter RAM) are integrated differently. For issues previously addressed by these resets, simply **shutting down** your Mac completely (not just restarting) and starting it up again often achieves the equivalent effect.

3. System Information Utility:

- For an incredibly detailed report on every piece of hardware, software, and network connection on your Mac:

  - Click the Apple menu (□).

  - Press and hold the **Option (⌥)** key. The "About This Mac" item will change to **"System Information..."**.

  - Click "System Information...".

- Alternatively, go to Apple menu □ > About This Mac > More Info... > scroll down and click "System Report...".

- This utility provides exhaustive details – useful when checking specific hardware specs, USB device connections, Thunderbolt details, network configuration, installed applications, fonts, logs, etc. Mostly for advanced users or troubleshooting with support.

4. Activity Monitor - Deeper Look (Use Cautiously):

- Beyond the main tabs, Activity Monitor offers more:

  - View Menu > Inspect Process (⌘+I): Get detailed stats, see open files and ports used by a process, analyze memory usage.

  - **View Menu > Sample Process:** Takes a snapshot of what a process is doing over a few seconds, useful for developers or advanced troubleshooting to diagnose hangs or performance bottlenecks.

  - **View Menu > Columns:** Customize the columns displayed in each tab.

- Again, be very careful about quitting processes you don't understand.

5. Accessibility Features as Power Tools:

- Don't overlook these!

  - **Zoom:** Use Hover Text (Command-hover) to quickly read small text without zooming the whole screen.

  - **Reduce Motion/Transparency:** Can make the interface feel faster or less visually distracting for anyone.

  - **Voice Control:** Explore setting up custom voice commands for automating repetitive tasks.

  - **Live Captions:** Invaluable for understanding audio in noisy places or for content without good subtitles.

  - **Accessibility Shortcut (Triple-press Touch ID):** Set this up for features you might use occasionally (like Zoom or Color Filters) for instant access.

By exploring these tips, tricks, and less-obvious features, you move beyond basic usage and start tailoring your MacBook Air M4 to work exactly the way *you* want it to, boosting your efficiency and enjoyment. Keep experimenting and discovering!